TO HELL WITH POVERTY!

TO HELL WITH POVERTY!

A Class Act

Inside the Gang of Four

JON KING

CONSTABLE

CONSTABLE

First published in Great Britain in 2025 by Constable

1 3 5 7 9 10 8 6 4 2

Copyright © Jon King, 2025

The moral right of the author has been asserted.

All photos from author's personal collection unless otherwise stated.

All rights reserved.
No part of this publication may be reproduced, stored in a retrieval system, or transmitted, in any form, or by any means, without the prior permission in writing of the publisher, nor be otherwise circulated in any form of binding or cover other than that in which it is published and without a similar condition including this condition being imposed on the subsequent purchaser.

A CIP catalogue record for this book
is available from the British Library.

ISBN: 978-1-40872-156-8 (hardback)

Typeset in Electra by Hewer Text UK Ltd, Edinburgh
Printed and bound in Great Britain by Clays Ltd, Elcograf S.p.A.

Papers used by Constable are from well-managed
forests and other responsible sources.

Constable
An imprint of
Little, Brown Book Group
Carmelite House
50 Victoria Embankment
London EC4Y 0DZ

The authorised representative
in the EEA is
Hachette Ireland
8 Castlecourt Centre, Dublin 15,
D15 XTP3, Ireland
(email: info@hbgi.ie)

An Hachette UK Company
www.hachette.co.uk

www.littlebrown.co.uk

For Debbie

More tears are shed over answered prayers than unanswered ones.

St Teresa of Ávila

INTRODUCTION

1979. Britain is fucked: 1.5 million people are out of work, doubling to 3 million by 1982; inflation soars to 12 per cent; the UK's interest rate is at an all-time high of 17 per cent; 40 per cent income tax from low earners, 90 per cent for the better off.

Massive industrial conflict during the 'Winter of Discontent' sees firemen strike and the army called in to cover; refuse collectors stop work and uncollected rubbish is piled high in city centres; gravediggers down shovels, leading Liverpool Council to store the dead in a Speke factory and consider burial at sea to cope with the backlog of corpses; striking lorry drivers hold up essential supplies; salt, sugar and dairy products are rationed in shops, and animals starve on farms; the blockade of Kingston upon Hull is so total it's dubbed 'Stalingrad'; ambulance drivers strike and the army's drafted in to cover them as well, with only half of NHS hospitals now treating emergencies.

Margaret Thatcher's hard-right regime is set on crushing the unions, especially the mineworkers, a struggle that will squander North Sea oil money now gushing in. The government considers declaring a state of emergency; ultra-right elements within MI5 later claim to have plotted a coup d'état, with the one-time Labour leader Harold Wilson believing ex-military chiefs were forming private armies in expectation of 'wholesale domestic liquidation'. A sectarian civil war in Northern Ireland between Loyalists and Irish Republicans sees thousands killed across the UK, with bombings, murders and atrocities on both sides, with innocent Irishmen beaten into confessions for terrorist offences. British Army and counter-insurgency teams wage both open and secret war against the Irish Republican Army, including assassinations and torture that are condemned by international courts.

The threat of war amps up after the Soviet Union rolls out its next-gen Scud mobile tactical nuclear missiles in Eastern Europe, with a thirty-minute flight time from Russia to Britain. NATO responds by deploying, in late 1979, 160 Pershing II nuclear cruise missiles based in the United States Air Force's Airstrip One aka the UK.

In 1980 UK households receive a booklet, *Protect and Survive*, with handy tips about how to survive the impending apocalypse.

Is this the end of days?

It's the right time to write radical music.

REPO MAN

The keys to the Dino sit on a high shelf alongside a lockbox housing a snub-nosed .38 that Bennett Glotzer, my crooked manager, says I should grab if the armed response guys don't get here in time. 'Just hold it two-handed, point at the perp and pull the trigger!' he says. 'Easy-peasy, BANG! but take the safety off first!'

It's not reassuring. I'm a handgun novice shacked up in a sprawling glass-box bungalow whose curtainless windows hold vibration sensors against home invasion that are often false-triggered by the brisk desiccated winds that swirl up from the valley.

'The alarm goes off,' Bennett says, '*don't* call 911. Likely just a glitch. First, look see if there's a smackhead filching the joint; you think it's kosher, speed-dial the security company and say MOTHER JONES, otherwise their Storm Troopers'll be here inside ten, psyched, locked 'n' loaded.'

'*Mother Jones?*' I say.

'Yeh!' he says. 'The *safe words* that'll stand down the security nutjobs with their Winchester pumps and killer Ridgebacks! Don't forget, otherwise you can kiss your Brit ass goodbye, heh, heh!'

He heads off to glom some other sucker and leaves me be.

The house is a short way up Sunset Plaza Drive, a bendy road that uncoils north from Sunset, the famous drag that runs west from downtown through Hollywood with its Strip famous for bars, clubs and entertainment businesses. It's nice here, the cool sidewalks sheltered by purple jacaranda trees which bloom among dense evergreenery hiding architect-designed ranch-style homes with 5-and-up series Beemers and Porsches burbling on multi-garage driveways with polite warning signs staked on the lawns that promise Armed Rapid Response.

The décor's a surprise. I'm expecting Dictator chic, a smorgasbord of glitz, gilded furniture, music-biz trophies and gold discs, and knock-off kunst, but instead there's a lonely La-Z-Boy and a deep sofa on an acre of polished cedar floor in front of a fuck-off TV the size of a shipping container. Phones on three-yard-long coiled cords hang in every room, even in the khazi, allowing Glotzer to juggle handsets while he non-stop yaks, snacks or sends friends to the coast. I hope he washes his hands.

I'm impressed by this austere Scandi class and make complimentary noises about it to Glotzer's Honduran cleaner, Inez, who's polishing glasses at the mammoth kitchen island. 'No!' she says. 'No es su gusto! Todas sus cosas se las llevó un hombre con papeles legales!' (It's not his taste! All his things were taken away by a man with legal papers!) She points out the front window and says, 'Como ese, over there!'

Across the street, a Mexican-American's sat in a beat-up Honda Civic, humming along to a narcocorrido tune and tapping to the beat on the wheel as he reads La Opinión. He waves cheerily at us. 'A el!' Inez says. 'He wants to take boss's Ferrari!'

I phone Bennett and say maybe Mariachi man's a gangbanger? I should call the cops? All that. Glotzer says, 'Don't worry, the schmuck's a pussy, here most days re the car, some repayment glitch, lost paperwork, it's all cool ... but don't take the Dino out until the motherfucker's bailed, capiche?'

The repo man's here to take possession of the gorgeous red GT4 Ferrari – which is either Bennett's or it isn't – that's sulking in the garage, but he can only seize the wheels once it's on the blacktop. I say, 'Why don't repo men work evenings?' and Glotzer says, 'Go figure!'

The Ferrari's mine to use any time after six in the evenings and at weekends, but I pass. Gunning around in a supercar lower than a semi-rig's lower step's not my thing, give me a motorcycle any day, and only a dickhead could enjoy feathering a performance car's pedals at slug speed in city traffic.

On the poolside deck, I nurse a frosty Mojito and look out over LA's lights twinkling in the orange heat haze and wonder if I'm just an extra in someone else's movie. Am I really me?

How did I get here?

A COMMON CHILDHOOD

1955. I am born in Guy's Hospital, London, a second child to my father, an electrician, and my mother, a housewife. Money's tight and the family lives in two rooms with my dad's twice-widowed mother in a slum house in 45 Rolls Road, off the Old Kent Road. It's a two-up, two-down redbrick terrace with no inside toilet or bathroom, running hot water or central heating. In the scullery sits a concrete boiler that heats the water for the once-weekly Sunday bath we take in turns in a zinc tub, which hangs weekdays from a hook on a wall freckled with black mould and spotted with condensation, the patterned wallpaper damp and peeling. Woodlice skeeter about beneath floorboards that groan under our feet, the wet-rotted joists moaning with the load. At night, mice sport in the overhead rafters, their urgent pitter-pattering audible when the lights dim. I have a vivid memory – perhaps implanted – of jumping in surprise at the sight of a mouse sitting on the gas hob, eyeballing me as it snacks on crumbs, unfussed by my presence.

The concrete backyard catches only high midsummer sun, and the caved-in wartime Anderson shelter is now only a spidery haven for feral cats, so I toddle about with the big boys and girls who play out front in the road: chase games like tip, kickabout footie with chalked wall goalposts, marbles, and jump-rope skipping games. It's safe, with hardly any traffic, and the neighbours keep a beady eye out for strangers. It's typical of 1950s Peckham, a poverty-stricken area of south London still scarred by uncleared bombsites whose rubble and rotting wood has greened with fungi and buddleia, Red admiral and Peacock butterflies feasting on the pyramid blooms.

My paternal grandmother, Martha, is scary and ill-tempered so I keep out of her way and hide behind my mother's skirts when she's about. She's had a hard life, working long hours of manual labour, although I don't know what she does to make ends meet. Her first husband died in a claggy Normandy trench having fathered four children, and after the War To End All Wars takes a breath to prepare for the next one, Martha meets and marries my grandfather, William, the son of illiterate Irish travellers who'd fled to Britain after the potato famine. Like many Londoners, the family tree's richly decorated with immigrants. They produce three boys, one of which is my dad, Ronald. Husband number two is murdered by the flu in 1948. 'Felt ill on Monday and died on Thursday,' says Mum.

My father has little contact with his brothers and none that I know of with his half-siblings, an unexplained *froideur*.

Other than church marriages, baptisms and burials, no one in the extended clan goes to church. Religion for us means a chocolate egg at Easter and pine trees, turkey, and a mandarin orange at Christmas, festive goodies which weren't on sale when shepherds washed their socks by night at the Messiah's birth. It's no surprise I'm an atheist, but I'm not evangelical about it.

My maternal grandparents live a few streets away. They struggle to get by as Nan's a school dinner lady and Grandad's a sometime self-employed exhibition carpenter, one-time petty villain and gambler who Lady Luck will not smile on. He's registered blind, his eyes ruined by childhood measles, and wears jam-jar glasses that just about allow him to read the small print in the *Daily Racing Form*, always with a bet on with some backstreet bookie. A handsome man, a Clark Gable in specs, he's the soul of any party who's always got a funny story to tell and can bash out tunes for beers on the Joanna in the local, playing anything by ear. Unfit for military service, he does time in the Second World War for black marketeering, selling carpets and whatnot looted from the wreckage. My mum says she never forgave him for selling her push bike to pay off a gambling debt.

Nan Bertha – the spitting image of Golda Meir – is the last born of eight children in a well-off Islington family. She's raised by her teenage sister, Nell, after her mother Ellen, my great-grandmother, abandoned the family, a terrible trauma no one will explain. Nan's ten-year-old brother Frederick, who'll die aged nineteen on a French battlefield in 1918, nightly wanders the streets of north London searching for his lost mother, but she's gone forever.

No one knows why Great-nan Ellen ran, vanishingly rare in those days. An affair? Domestic abuse? But once gone, her daughter Nell's anointed stand-in matriarch tasked with bringing up her father's seven kids, including my nan, baby Bertha. Nell later gives birth to a child, Gertie, out of wedlock – Mum says she'd probably been knocked up by a doctor's son when she worked in his father's surgery, but with no shotgun wedding. My severe great-grandfather keeps Nell in the household, which contrasts with his cruel treatment of my grandmother, Bertha, who's cut off without a penny after she meets and marries, without his consent, the son of a bookie she meets *drumming* at a party. She got away as soon as she was of age, but, even so, marry a *drummer*? It's a high price to pay. Bertha's thrown to the wolves.

After Bertha's speed-dated marriage, Great-grandfather George won't see or speak to her again nor answer any pleas for financial help or reconciliation. Nan, shunned, has a determinedly downwardly mobile life journey, circling the drain in a vortex of Depression-era deprivation after her exclusion from the familial embrace. The bourgeois comforts of home life in Islington will soon seem like an illusion; the tailored clothes, soft gloves and handmade shoes, clip-clopping in a sweet pony and trap, sweetmeats and fresh fruit will be replaced by scraping by in a bedbug-ridden tenement with an outside shitter and no running water off the Old Kent Road, a mug on the mantelpiece for the rent money. Soon, Nan's got a bun in the oven and, in 1929 and 1931, brings two children into the world, my mum Olive and Uncle John, just in time to enjoy the Great Depression and full-bore Top Trumps misery. There's no work, no money, no prospects; capitalism has failed them, and how. However, Nan and Grandad luck out when the council offers them a flat in the newly built Kent House on the Old Kent Road, part of London's Keynesian slum-clearance programme.

When they move, all they own fits on a six-by-four handcart, my infant mother and brother John dilly-dallying behind like the Mrs Mills song, to be deloused before moving into a swish new pad with running water and communal toilet along the landing shared by only a few other families. Things are looking up.

When the Second World War's declared, the family's rehoused and my ten-year-old mother and younger brother John are evacuated to the countryside to escape death from above, sent on a train with cardboard nametags dangling about their necks and a single suitcase to lodge in a series of homes with hosts wary of slum kids who spoke funny and hadn't seen a cow in a field before. Mum's very unhappy and longs to go home, but thinks she's been forgotten when Nan doesn't reply to her letters for many months. In her sixties, she will find the birth certificate of a baby girl while tidying Nan's papers.

'Who's this?' she asks.

'Your *sister*,' says Nan, who explains she'd been on a bus in the middle of town that was hit in the Blitz, and many were killed. She survived but was badly hurt and lost one of the twins she was carrying, and spent months in a hospital bed recovering, taking the pregnancy to term and delivering a healthy girl. But the nursery unit, where newborns slept apart from their mothers, was destroyed in an air raid and the new baby perished. The birth certificate is all Nan has of her. She thought it best not to say anything.

There's a bombsite next door to my grandparents' house, a ruined shell still upright fifteen years after being holed by a fat German bomb that plopped through the roof during the Blitz but failed to explode, leaving a crisp circular hole from sky to soil, like some Nazi *conceptuele kunst*. I love playing in the rubble and dust, clambering around the edges of derelict rooms, teetering on first-floor floorboards that project like fungal fingers from the brickwork, rummaging among rusting cans, wartime newspapers, rotting wood, shards of crockery, and mouldy sepia photos of long-dead men and women posing in their best duds, imagining I'm the last boy alive.

After the war, my grandparents move to a new council prefab, a modern Uni-Seco shoebox design with a wooden frame and asbestos cement cladding. They like it a lot. Their factory-fabricated little house was thrown up fast and a hundred and fifty thousand are put together only four years after the war's end to meet the housing crisis. They're meant to be temporary homes until proper bricks and mortar dwellings are built, but people will still live in them twenty years after the Nazi surrender, and in the mid-sixties some will curse their luck that they're still waiting to be rehoused and left shivering in cold, corrugated-iron, round-roofed Nissen huts first designed in the First World War as military barracks.

ESCAPE FROM THE BIG WEN

Age sixteen, Mum and Dad meet, fall in love, marry at eighteen, Dad does his National Service in the RAF where he works as a spark, and they set up shop together, moving into my grandmother Martha's south London hovel. They're desperate to escape the filth and ruination of the Big Smoke and dream of getting out and owning their own home.

Mid-fifties London is a smoke-stained shithole, its buildings jet-blackened by centuries of smoke and filth, still dotted with undeveloped bombsites, attacked in wintertime by thick yellow-green clouds of toxic smog that annually kills or ruins the lungs of thousands. The peasoupers are so dense that cinemas close since the projected light can't reach the screen, street names can't be read more than a few yards away, and coughing commuters' cuffs and collars have greasy dark stains from the particulate-clogged air that chokes to breathe. A stinking sewer runs through the city, the fetid Thames, scummed with turds and floating flotsam and jetsam, devoid of life. Bowler-hatted office workers look neither left nor right at the murdered brown river as they scuttle to desks across its sooty bridges, and wouldn't dream of walking beside its poisonous banks. Up West is different, with Piccadilly's thrilling lights, theatres and nightclubs and upscale arcades for the monied few able to whizz off to leafy shires when the air's a killer to breathe. It's the poor who'll wheeze and croak.

It's no place to raise a family. Although Dad's job at the London Electricity Board isn't well paid and it's hard to save, my parents spot a card in a shop window posted by a group of families – a joiner, plasterer, bricklayer, plumber, painter and decorator, et al. – who are looking for a couple to join them in a self-build housing project, a new route working-class people can take to escape the filth and make a home somewhere decent to live.

The collective has bought a greenfield site in a Kent farming village, Kemsing, thirty miles south of London, with housing development approval. Fields of south-facing chalklands on the scarp face of North Downs woodland will be divided up into nine quarter-acre plots for kit-book homes. It's not unusual: one in six British families will move into new homes in the 1950s, hundreds of thousands being built every year to solve the post-war housing shortage. Working families are desperate to flee urban squalor and poisonous air for the new garden cities and villages now encircling the capital, and subsidised train travel and frequent buses make working in town affordable.

For the next two years, Dad spends evenings and weekends going down and up from Peckham to help construct a row of bungalows with the others, a part of the village's fifties and sixties explosion in size to become an exurb dorm for refugees from the Big Smoke. I'm three when work's finished and we move out of town. Our dank back-to-back in Peckham is soon razed to the ground and replaced by new jerry-built high-rise flats that rear into the skies like giant gravestones – architectural insults a universe away from Le Corbusier's *Unité d'habitation* and the *Ville Radieuse* – that will in time be demolished and replaced by aircraft-hangar stores and value supermarkets.

The new house has a double master and two single bedrooms, living room, kitchen and inside bathroom with toilet. Radiators have been fitted, the water potentially heated by a coal-fired stove, but the central heating's never turned on as we can't afford the fuel.

There's no running hot water except on Sunday evenings, when the children take turns in a once-weekly bath; fortunately, I'm second in after my older brother, Chris, the water darkening after each turn to become an ever more gloopy Deadpool. After a bath, we watch telly in the living room, warmed by a two-bar electric fire that's our only heating. Early on the same day, my mother does the weekly clothes wash. It's quite the production, a barrowload of grubby children's togs clogs the bathroom, waiting for a wash in a single-tub machine that doesn't have a rinse or spin cycle, so the bath's filled high with cold water to soak clothes, which are left to marinade for an hour or so until they're hauled out and fed through a big-wheeled, hand-turned iron mangle to squidge out the wet, and then hung out to dry on the garden washing line. When it's raining – it's always raining – damp laundry is pegged on to a string that stretches across the kitchen above the heat of a one-bar fire.

The conifer wood that looms over the village hums with wildlife; goldfinches and blackbirds trill in the garden, grasshoppers and crickets saw in the grass, and Common Blues, Meadow Browns, and Hummingbird hawk-moths binge on fragrant lavender in the summer sun. From the attic window, I can see the verdant rolling valley to the treelined horizon and at night watch house martins and bats sharp-turning through the skies like billiard-ball breaks as they fatten themselves on the myriad insects dancing above the fields.

At night, I drop off to the sound of foxes barking, owls hooting and the doppler sound of distant trains bouncing from hillside to hillside. I shout HALLOOO at the summit of the hill overlooking the village and love hearing the slap echo LOO LOO LOO that bounces over woods and fields. In the belly of the valley runs a clear chalk stream busy with sticklebacks, tadpoles and dragonfly nymphs, which I catch and examine in jam jars, checking their identity in a pocket guide book. At weekends, I'm out the day long exploring the woods, climbing trees, making hideouts, and scraping caves in the chalk side of an abandoned quarry under pine-tree roots clinging to its lip for dear life. I come home at the sun's death or at teatime and keen for sugared bread. Mum doesn't know what I'm up to when I'm out and lets me be, as most mums do in these days. Life couldn't be better. I've lucked out.*

---

* All this is gone. Work begins on the southern loop of the M25 in 1975 and is completed a decade later. The susurration of insects and birds has been replaced by a constant thrum of traffic on tarmac. The clear-watered chalk stream, where I marvelled at spiky little fish, has dried up and the now homeless frogs and newts have been squished to extermination by passing cars. Hikers will never again smile on hearing the song of a skylark ascending or turtle doves turr-turring.

HOME

A baby arrives when I'm four. She cries a lot and reeks of poo, so I'll keep a wary distance until she's older. Another brother and a sister appear at three-year intervals (luckily, I'm still second in the bathwater), but how this happens is a mystery.

Although terrified of debt, my parents buy a new three-piece suite and carpets on the never-never, and the sideboard's top is soon swamped with knick-knacks found in rummage sales; porcelain shepherdesses, a broken-legged glass Bambi, an Eiffel Tower snow shaker memento of an unseen Paris, and ceramic souvenirs of seaside towns to which we haven't been. Wardrobes are rammed with harvested shoes, handbags and odds and sods like an olive fork or fountain pen sets and carriage lamps. A print of an Impressionist-adjacent painting of a rainy Parisian boulevard hangs on the living-room wall, and will still be there, faded and colour bleached, sixty-five years later.

The sideboard drawers burst with kibble, official letters, pins, skeins of wool in random colours, envelopes and bills, and censor-passed picture postcards from First World War trenches – pretty young women, generals, deposed royals, and stiffly posed Tommies and poilus in puttees and dress uniforms. I enjoy the messages home from the front: 'On active service/REDACTED/I am well/not well/please send gloves, etc.'

A well-thumbed paperback of *From Russia with Love* lurks at the back of the bottom drawer, hidden like a private vice, perhaps the only modern novel in the house. I read it secretly age twelve, my first spy thriller, excited by a world where handsome men with money, guns and Savile Row suits live lives of adventure, shooting it out with the KGB, chain smoking, binge drinking, and going to bed with glamorous, dangerous women who wear nothing but neck chokers – the kind of job I want when I grow up. This may be the only book Dad's read. I've never seen him reading anything apart from the London *Evening News* he brings back from work most days.

I share a bedroom in the loft to age eighteen with my older brother, our single beds a yard away from each other like a prototype Travelodge. My teenage wall shows a double-page spread of a Norton Commando motorcycle and a raddled *Oz* magazine front cover that I nicked from school, showing a psychedelic Bob Dylan in Wayfarer shades – my hero. The room's a decent size but has little natural light as the window's quite small. My parents were nervous about engaging with planning, so didn't apply for permission to have a bigger dormer, nor for a proper staircase that would allow a bedroom to be in the loft. From a regs POV, we sleep in a storage area accessed via steep narrow wooden steps cheated into a space above the never-used coal boiler and chimney breast. We'd be fried if there were a fire.

At bedtime, my bro and I sometimes shove an old mattress into the stairwell to baffle the sound – otherwise we'd hear every word Mum and Dad say downstairs – which works well and cuts the draughts. The bedroom's uninsulated and glacial in the winter, the frost forming fractal patterns on the inside of the window glass, which we must scrape off to see out. Steam rises from the blankets as I bed down, scrunched in a foetal position to keep warm, head beneath blankets sparkling with mini-droplets of condensation, icy be-socked feet pressed hard on a hot-water bottle, so Dad makes a bed warmer from a 100-watt bulb wired inside a flying saucer-shaped metal sleeve, which heats up fast to dry the damp and warm the sheets.

Nothing happens in Kemsing. There's a parade of shops at each end of the village, two pubs, and a church with parish hall near an ancient well dedicated to St Edith, a Saxon era saint and worker of miracles, her USP being curing eye complaints and barren women, not necessarily at the same time. Kemsing's railway station isn't near the village – it's not near *anywhere* – which means commuters to London use the nearer station in Otford, the next spring-line village over, a short walk along a strip of the Pilgrims' Way, which rolls from London to Canterbury, where St Thomas à Becket was chopped to bits for unfriending the king.

Putting up nine homes must have been an intense relationship-building and bonding exercise, forging friendships for life, but although my parents have cordial relationships with others in the new builds, they keep themselves to themselves, don't go the pub or church, and aren't involved in the primary school. There's no time for this, as Dad works all hours, often six days a week. They don't drink, smoke, eat out, listen to music or go to the pictures. At

Christmas, my father may puff on a Hamlet cigar and Mum might sip an advocaat snowball, annual luxuries we enjoy seeing them enjoy. Dad's kind, hardworking and family oriented, but has no friends and only sees his two brothers, nephews and nieces if my mother arranges visits; without her efforts, he'd see no one. He never says a word about his half-brothers and sisters, and when I ask what their names are, Mum says, 'Oh, I don't know. All I know is that Dad's half-sister perished aged ten of a childhood disease.'

PRIMARY SCHOOL DAZE

Kemsing County Primary School has modern, airy classrooms with big windows, a central hall where morning assembly, lunch and indoor events are held, and two tarmacked playgrounds, one for under sevens and the other for older children, and a grass playing field that's big enough for cricket or football matches, summer fetes and playtime games. This is a time when governments of both left and right believe that investing in the social fabric is a good thing. Crazy.

I am five. It's my first day at school. Mum drops me at the gate, to my great confusion. I don't have a clue what's going on and wail and protest as I'm corralled into a classroom, while she and other wet-hankied mothers – no father is ever seen at the school gate except in An Emergency – are steered away by a teaching assistant. The headmaster, Mr Smart, is a firm disciplinarian and *smacks* me hard to stop my crying, saying 'That's enough of that!', which does the job, and introduces me to the humdrum violence of adults towards children.

We little ones are sat down in bright classrooms with lithographs on the walls of sun-bronzed farmers on shiny tractors in fields of golden wheat, or heavy-limbed shire horses ploughing fields under azure skies, a land of plenty where everyone knows their place and nothing need ever change. There are no factories, coal mines or cities, and everyone is well-fed and white.

From day two on, I will walk to school and meet up with classmates on the way, and hardly anyone's dropped off by a parent at the school gates, it's not done. The journey's fun as the school's only a mile away, just a half an hour walk there and a dawdling muck-about hour or more back at the end of the day. Back home, I'll gobble a slice of white bread slathered with margarine sprinkled thick with granulated sugar, nice.

We walk in all weathers and always in shorts, *no one* wears long trousers, even in the Great Freeze of 1962/3. One of the coldest winters ever recorded, snow is on the ground for months, drifting up to eight feet deep in Kent, and the Thames is frozen solid upstream with salty ice floes bobbing where it meets the sea. We trudge through waist-deep snow tunnels to school – which is always open – lobbing snowballs all the way, and at playtime roll snow into huge boulders we use to build battlements of ice on the frozen playing field. It's great.

My best friends Jenny Bryant and Kevin Lycett – later a founding member of the Mekons – live in post-war houses at the opposite end of the village. Jenny's mum Maureen is a school dinner lady who always smiles when I come round to play as she sees me so often standing nose-to-wall in a corridor, a standard infant punishment I prefer to being whacked. 'You're SOO naughty,' she says, and is always nice to me, giving me egg and cress sandwiches on fresh crusty bread, which we rarely have at home, with a cup of milky sweet tea, so I adopt her as a second mother and Jenny as an honorary sister. There's a photo of us on the front page of the *Sevenoaks Chronicle*, because we've raised enough money to buy benches or something – I'm not sure for what – for an old people's home. Jenny's very pretty with her dark hair in pigtails and me gap-toothed and smiley with a home-hacked basin fringe haircut and oval NHS specs. Mum says we did very well and props the paper on the sideboard until tea's spilled on it and it's binned.

Kevin lives in a big house, across the road from Jenny, which isn't like mine. There are pictures of flowers and landscapes on the walls and a *Dining Room*, whatever that's for. His father, Frank – who's the spitting image of his namesake Frank Cannon, the porky 1970s' TV detective – has an *executive* car. Kevin's parents worry about the furniture getting stained and have covered the three-piece suite with crunchy, thick, clear plastic covers, which are squeaky and uncomfortable to sit on, you could be electrocuted by the static. Kevin has a wonky air rifle, which we spend hours practising with, shooting at apple trees or inked paper targets and tin cans in the back garden, although neither of us can shoot straight.

1962: I'm seven, things look bad. The grown-ups think nuclear war's just round the corner, inevitable, a done deal, and the news headlines scream that the Soviets have sent atomic missiles to Cuba, wherever that is, the Americans are wigging out, US and Russian bombers are circling in the air, with pilots waiting for the green light to drop H-bombs that will end the world as we know it. It's grim. We're all going to die. My mum's very worked up about it and goes on Ban the Bomb marches which politicians ignore, and writes letters to the prime minister that are tossed in a bin.

Mr Smart, our headmaster, is keen we survive or at least get to Armageddon Plus One Day so we can slowly starve to death or die of radiation poisoning. He decides the school must have a civil defence exercise called 'Duck and Cover'. In this, a teacher tells us that if a wooing siren sounds,[*] it means rockets are flying to attack us, so we should lie down and cover our eyes, because there'll be a very bright light. It's simple, an end-of-days Sleeping Lions, which sounds like

---

[*] There would have been four minutes' warning before being nuked. In the countryside, 11,000 nuclear warning sirens sat on shelves or sheds ready to be cranked by hand by someone important, like a *Post Office mistress* or a *pub landlord*. Warning sirens were abandoned in the 1990s because the government said double-glazed windows made them hard to hear! Only in Britain!

fun. She blows a whistle and we dive down to sprawl on the floor under the desks, where we muck about, make fart and animal noises, and chuck inky paper pellets at each other until the teacher loses patience and calls the session off. I don't know what difference this would make to our survival and my main worry is, will there be a post-apocalypse *Beano*?

I'm reminded of this exercise when thumbing through the UK government's 1980 *Protect and Survive* pamphlet – issued when nuclear war's just round the corner, we're all going to die, etc., etc. – full of handy household hints about what to do when the H-bombs rain down on every city in Britain. The top tip is to prepare a *fallout room* with clothing-filled bin liners piled on a table to huddle under, and to cover your eyes. If you're caught outside when Armageddon strikes, lie down in a ditch. Happily, I'll be vaped immediately as, these days, I live in a city centre, and finding a ditch will be a bugger.

Apart from being thumped by the headmaster, I like school and am introduced to music I don't hear at home. I learn to play simple tunes on a recorder and a melodica, although it's hard to say which sounds worse. At a Christmas concert, we play Beethoven's Seventh, arranged for massed melodicas, which must have been a torment for the audience. Larking about during the show, I knock the back wall of the set over and am sent to the corridor in shame. The performance will have scarred parents for ever.

JELLY AND TELLY

I love school dinners: meat and two veg with puddings – apple pie and custard! Rhubarb crumble! – served hot, made from scratch in the school kitchens. The food's different to what we get at home, where a typical meal might be boiled mince and onions with mash and processed peas – we usually only have tinned vegetables and don't have a freezer – apart from Sunday dinners of roast chicken with demolished cabbage and potatoes.

We don't eat *dinner* in the evenings, we have *tea*, and don't have *lunch*, because that's *dinner*.* There's rarely fresh fruit or vegetables or crusty bread as they're too expensive, and Mum says we'd just eat it all if it was there and then it would be gone, which it true, so we do without.

Dad often makes tea for us all in the evening when he gets back from work, which doesn't seem right, as Mum's a *Housewife* and at home all day with nothing else to do. She doesn't agree, as she takes on cleaning jobs, or piece work like putting on zips or addressing envelopes. We eat in silence at the kitchen table – the rule is *No Talking At Mealtimes* – with the radio on in the background, plummy-voiced people droning on about how the country's going to the dogs, the young have lost respect for authority, the world will end in a

---

* Posh people have *lunch* in the middle of the day and *supper* or *dinner* in the evening. Northerners, I found when I went to Leeds, also have *supper*.

whimper not a bang (to paraphrase T. S. Eliot's poem, 'The Hollow Men'), etc., etc. My brother and I have to wash up a skip-load of plates and cutlery and pans, or argue about having to wash up until we give up and get on with it.

In the living room is a black and white telly that's turned on before we eat because the valves need to warm up. The shoebox-sized screen has a flat magnifying lens positioned in front of the rounded glass to make the blurred picture look bigger, the image often fragging into snowstorms or zigzag lines until Dad wallops the side of the box to make it behave, or fiddles with the dipole aerial that's perched on the box to get the picture back. It's a delicate operation.

I lie on the floor as close as possible to the TV as I can't otherwise see what's going on, and I'm taken to an optician who tests me and says I'm *myopic* – short-sighted – and shows me lots of printed cards covered in coloured dots, asking if I can see a number in the chaos, which I often can't, it must be a trick.

He says, 'I'm afraid your son's *colour blind*, so he won't be able to be a bus driver, electrician, or an RAF pilot.'

This doesn't seem too bad. I'm only eight and thinking more about being a millionaire or a spy or in a pop group like the Beatles when I grow up.

I'm given a pair of free gold-framed NHS specs and am amazed to see things that are far away. But some things are better blurred, like men in tight woollen swimming trunks. At least I can see what's on the telly now.

My first day at school wearing the gigs a boy shouts 'Four Eyes! Four Eyes!' at me, a disablist insult that provokes me into fist-popping him hard on the nose, resulting in an impressive nosebleed, which I'm very pleased about. I'm made to stand for half an hour in a corridor up against the wall again as punishment. Luckily, fighting's not a bad enough offence to be hit by the head. No one shouts 'Four Eyes!' at me again.

HIGH NOON

I'm capo of one of two gangs at school, which battle to control the upper playground. It's all very mimsy – our crews act like they do in *Just William*, but with glottal stops. One day, throwing mud balls at each other in break time – it's good fun – someone in my mob is hit on the head with a stone instead of mud and has to go to sickbay for stitches. This leads to a showdown between me and the boss of our rivals, who I'll call Terry.

We meet in the woods after school. He and I face off, our gangs behind us, ready to ruck, mouthing insults, clenched fisted, knobbly kneed in shorts. I don't know what to do next. But Terry does, he runs at me and wallops me in the face. BOFF!

'I wasn't ready, it's not fair!' I say.

He laughs and swaggers off with his outfit, leaving me and the boys to accept defeat. But I've got an impressive black eye that I'm pleased with, which Mum makes an annoying fuss about.

I don't grass him up and we become sort-of friends and the playground battles become history. He'll become a skinhead in his teens with an appetite for hard-core aggro, always in trouble. Our brawl was just a starter for ten.

VINGT ET UN

Age eight, during a Christmas visit with nothing on the box, Grandad teaches me and my brother how to play Pontoon, him cool in green eye-shade and silver shirtsleeve garters, chain-smoking unfiltered Senior Service and sipping gin and orange as we go, cautioning me not to trust the dealer: he may have a card up his sleeve or deal from the bottom. 'Like *this*,' he says, dealing an ace. Grandad can memorise the pack, knows what card comes next and what cards I've got without peeking, a gambling skill that doesn't help the family finances. It's good advice for life I should share with my own offspring if I have any. It's the only extended time I ever spend with him.

If we visit him and Nan on a Saturday, Grandad pays us children no mind. He'll have the *Racing Post* close to his face, researching horsey form, always with a bet on at some spieler's; or will be sitting squint eyed and mute in an armchair a few feet from the box watching the wrestling, never missing a Mick McManus smackdown; or carefully scrawling crosses on the pools sheet when the euphonious Saturday football results are read out – Arsenal ... 3 Tottenham Hotspur ... *Nil*. When finished, he says, 'Bollocks to this!' and bins the paper, never winning a bean. As we make our goodbyes, he'll sometimes palm me a half crown – a fortune! – if Nan's out of sight. Proper quality time.

VINGT ET UN

The woods above Kemsing are full of treasure. One day, me and a mate are chuffed to find a dumped car engine in the woods that might be worth a few bob. It's too heavy to carry, so we lever it with branches into my little sister's pram and push it home, the heavy metal leaking gunky brown oil, which dribbles on to the cloth lining and irreparably stains it. The wheels are banjaxed under the load, it's a dog's dinner, the pram's wrecked; Mum kicks off about it, my weekly Mars bar's cancelled as a punishment, it's *so* unreasonable. Upside: I flog the engine to a garage for ten shillings and can buy twenty chocolate bars if I want.

Another time we find an *unopened pack of ten No. 6 cigarettes*, the crisp cellophane wrapper sparkling with promise, like finding Aladdin's lamp. As we're both ten now, it's time we started on the tabs, and we suck and puff and cough as we chain smoke our way through the snouts, five apiece. I feel awful, nauseous, the world's spinning, and I projectile puke BLEURGH! over my friend. It's disgusting. Next time, I think, best give it five minutes between fags.

The family's not flush and during the holidays we kids do piecework jobs on local farms with Mum, like potato or strawberry picking, stuffing our faces with fruit as we go, our shirts crimson stained with juice. But pin money like this isn't enough; it's tough, we're in debt, the mortgage is crippling, tight belts need tightening, and the future's frightening. Mum goes to jumble sales at weekends where she rummages through the tat to find us clothes. She can't resist snagging junk as she goes, which she hoards at home, the rooms piled with scabby children's shoes, parched leather handbags, unwanted toys, and battered encyclopaedias from the thirties, which show exotic peoples from lands coloured pink on the maps. They're the only place where real women's breasts can be seen, but this is OK as they're not Europeans.

One day, with the washing hanging above the electric fire in the kitchen because of the perpetual rain, a nylon shirt falls onto the red-hot bar and bursts into flames, igniting the clothes hanging above which Mum rips down and throws out the window. Flaming fabric and gobbets of molten plastic fall on to her forearms all the while, scarring her forever, but she bravely saves our home from destruction.

I don't sleep well – I'll never sleep well – and Mum and Dad say I often sleepwalk and sit between them in the front room, blank eyed and incommunicado, in a dream time I can't recall. I sometimes wet the bed to wake up soaked in pee, ashamed and humiliated, and will carry the drenched sheets downstairs where I'll sit in darkness, holding the sodden cotton to the bright-barred fire to dry them, an ammoniac stink rising into the air. My night piddles end when we get a cat who adopts me as her favourite and sleeps with me on my bed, her purring presence charming me into nightlong dryness.

One day, I feel movement under the blanket to find she's given birth to four sticky kittens and is licking the mewling blobs clean; I'd no idea she was up the duff, knowing nothing about reproduction. I love my cat and her babies. They're given away when they're old enough and my cat almost immediately disappears and never returns. She must have been heartbroken to lose them, I think, as I am to lose her. I hope she wasn't run over.

TEN POUND POMS

Our money troubles worsen, and my parents decide to quit while they're behind, signing up to emigrate to Australia on its Assisted Passage Migration Scheme, with a one-way ticket to Oz for just ten pounds, compliments of the Aussie government as part of its 'Populate or Perish' and 'White Australia' policies. They weren't alone in wanting to do this: a million Brits emigrated under this scheme in the 1950s, and a UK Gallup poll showed that over 40 per cent of the population were actively considering leaving our shitty cold wet depressing class-bound UK for sunshine and hope and barbies and social mobility on the far side of the world. The poll wasn't phrased like that.

Dad's been guaranteed a job in Oz and will get help with housing and settling in, experienced electricians being in great demand. He's been promised an escape from the drudgery of an exhausted country mired in war debt with failing industries and colonial struggles throughout a crumbling empire. But Mum changes her mind a few weeks from sailing – she's worried she'll never see Nan again – and it's all off. It's a big disappointment. I'd looked forward to seeing a wallaby or a wombat and was well up on Ocker culture, having heard Australian-themed songs like Charlie Drake's racist 'My Boomerang Won't Come Back' and Rolf Harris's 'Tie Me Kangaroo Down, Sport'. They play good cricket there, too, a game the Aussies always win. We don't go. Australia isn't talked about again.

Things improve when Dad lands a new job with better pay, and can afford to buy a second-hand Ford Prefect. It's a five-seater and a squeeze for seven on our summer holiday drive to Hastings, but it's wonderful, and I love washing and polishing it with my dad at the weekend.

LOST WITHOUT MUSIC

My parents never listen to music other than Sunday lunchtimes when BBC Radio's *Two-Way Family Favourites* is on, a request programme designed to connect families in Britain with British Forces posted overseas. It's a dreary hangover from the war – *everything* is a dreary hangover from the war – that plays music so dull it would stun a chicken: Max Bygraves, Frankie Vaughan, Alma Cogan, Ronnie Harris . . . life-stifling music like 'Side Saddle' by Russ Conway or 'She Taught Me How to Yodel', a big hit for Frank Ifield – a *yodelling* song, who buys this shit? This is 1965, the Beatles have just released *Help!* for crissake! If I was doing National Service, crushing democracy in Aden or Cyprus, I'd machinegun the wireless!

I'm desperate to hear noisy, sexy and dangerous pop and rock 'n' roll but it's a rare find on the daytime BBC Light Programme – there's no commercial radio – and for every Supremes number, you'll hear 'I'm Henry VIII, I Am' by the toothy Herman's Hermits, 'You Were Made for Me' by pervy Freddie and the Dreamers or, worse, Ronnie Hilton's 'A Windmill in Old Amsterdam', about a little mouse with clogs on. It's a nightmare. I may be ten and not know much about music, but I know what I don't like. We don't have a proper record player at home, only a wind-up gramophone and a stack of shellac 78s bought as a job lot from a junk shop, mostly novelty songs like

'(How Much Is) That Doggie in the Window' or 'Teddy Bears' Picnic'. There aren't any Delta blues classics.

I find musical escape when I learn how to make a crystal radio at the Cub Scouts – I'm a Sixer, two stripes on my arm, with my own troop – and can tune into Alan Freeman's *Pick of the Pops* music show and hear fantastic songs like 'Twenty Flight Rock', 'Good Golly, Miss Molly' or 'Please Please Me'.

I'm gifted a transistor set for Christmas and am excited to sometimes pick up Radio City – 'The happiest swinging station in the world' – a commercial pirate radio station that gets round the law by broadcasting outside the UK's territorial waters from an abandoned Second World War anti-aircraft fort on the Shivering Sands in the Thames Estuary, constructs on massive concrete legs which looks like the alien invaders from *The War of the Worlds*. The station plays pop, along with jingles and ads, on shows hosted by young shouty DJs who sound like they've had too much to drink. If I was older, I'd guess their *joie de vivre* was down to being off their tits on jazz Woodbines, but I haven't heard about hashish at this point. It's great, but the signal's iffy, wafting about like a fart in a lift.

I've got good recall of tunes and words, and a half-decent voice. I enter a kids' talent contest at the ABC cinema on the Old Kent Road, onstage in my shorts between the Saturday-morning double-bill films, acapella singing 'All My Loving' – and win £1 second prize! (A pound more than I'll make from the sales of the Gang of Four's debut *Damaged Goods* EP.)

In the summertime, we have a two-week family holiday somewhere like Hastings, Sheerness, or Camber Sands, quality family time that kicks off with all seven of us sardined into a compact five-seater Ford piled with things we'd only need in a zombie apocalypse. Our feet perch on bags crammed into the footwell, we're sitting on each other's laps, whingeing and breaking wind. 'What a pen and ink!' Dad says. Just minutes after setting off we'll emergency stop so

I can puke, my nausea triggered by the stale stench of hot leather seats. If Dad doesn't brake fast enough, I'll barf out the window, leaving a trailing V of vomit across the car's back end, its stink malingering in the crammed cabin.

Journey's end, we decamp into a chalet or thin-skinned caravan lit by gas lamps which hiss as they fizz out a jaundiced light too weak to read by. The Smurf-scale beds are fun when you're small but not when you're tall and lying top to toe with a bro who's got stinky feet. On the way I pray we'll be close to a toilet block as it's a pain running in the rain, desperate to give birth to a blind mullet.

At the centre of the caravan park will be an entertainment block with bars, one-armed bandits, pinball machines, Fortune Teller machines and grab games, a chaos of pings, bells, and alarms, a sanctuary where we huddle to stay warm and dry during the endless gloom of an English summer. In the daytime, Bingo for Grannies and kids' clubs for toddlers, or a stretch by the sea ideally huddled by a windbreaking beach groyne. At evening time there'll be a cabaret with comics, vents and singers doing a turn, intro'd by a bright-blazered MC with a broken-veined nose who looks like the wagon fell on him. It's all part of the package, the audience laps everything up, we all do, laughing, clapping and singing along as the men sink pints of light and bitter, a snowball or a Babycham in a coupe glass for the ladies, a Coke with a straw for the kids.

It's my first experience of showbiz. I hover about the event room watching the talent rehearse or tech checks when I can get away on my own; this looks *fun*. At least it's away from the caravan, which can be a torment. Holidays drive me potty, we're never more than a word away from a blow up about nothing, the rain thrumming on the roof of a gaslit shoebox as sometimes day-long guerilla rows unfurl, conflicts which may only dribble out after a sullen drive home. At thirteen I've had ENOUGH! I can't stand it, life's bad enough already with my voice breaking and pubes sprouting. It's so CLAUSTROPHOBIC. So I say to

Mum and Dad I've got to go and ask for the cash to get a train back to Kemsing. I'm alone for the duration, it's heaven. This will be the last holiday I ever take with the family.

I do well at school, love Art and English – I'm in the 'A' stream and top of the class. I draw all the time, battlescapes of ancient Greeks with Myrmidons in plumed helmets and battle armour hacking each other to pieces, inspired by the stories I gobble up of Odysseus' adventures after the Trojan War and Ray Harryhausen's brilliant stop-frame movies; and panoramas of US Civil War troops at Gettysburg sending each other to heaven. At home, I arrange massed ranks of plastic Airfix oo scale figures on the bedroom floor, rolling marbles at them to knock them over, making sure the Union always wins, trouncing the evil reb slavers who've committed treason against the Star-Spangled Banner, as is only right.

I read all the time, anything – Dad's paper, cereal packets, books from the school library, science fiction, history, the Greek myths – and scour any comics I can lay my hands on. Me and my bro have graduated to the *Victor* and the *Hornet*, D. C. Thomson publications with strips about the Second World War, plucky cockney Tommies machinegunning evil Huns and treacherous Nips, Our Finest Hour, racist language in every story just like we hear in the war films that fill the cinemas, *The Dam Busters*, *The Longest Day*, *The Guns of Navarone*, Britons at their best with backs to the wall, winning against the odds, etc.

Somehow I hear about 'Teenagers', no longer spotty adolescents in brown cardis and trews like mini-me mums and dads but dancing the night long hopped up on blues and hooked on the bands on *Ready Steady Go!*, hot boys in tonic suits and girls in Mary Quant miniskirts, mods and rockers fighting it out on Brighton beaches, the Beatles v the Stones ... Technicolor troublemakers giving two fingers to authority and austerity. The seaside brawls look great; I wish I was there throwing punches in studded black leathers and driving along the beachfront on a BSA Gold Star ... but I'm only ten.

My final year at primary school, boys and girls are herded into the assembly hall and sat down at desks to sit the eleven-plus exam that determines who goes to a grammar, technical or secondary modern school. It's not a *test* we're told, just a way to make sure everyone goes to the *right kind* of secondary school. It's a class-skewed exercise that says little about how bright kids are and can scar them for life, because going to a secondary modern means you're a *failure* and a *thicko* – or at least that's what boys and girls who 'fail' often think of themselves.

My brother, bright and capable, 'failed' last year and was consigned to the local secondary modern school aptly named Wilderness. My younger brother and sister don't *pass* either and get a shitty education, whereas my youngest sister passes and has a first-class one, going to the posh Direct Grant girls' grammar school, Walthamstow Hall, in Sevenoaks. The educational apartheid has legs up to the age of sixteen; even the state exams are different: secondary modern school pupils sit CSE exams, the Certificate of Secondary Education, but not GCEs, the General Certificate of Education, which kids do at grammar and Public i.e. *private* schools. This means that – *for the rest of their lives* – kids have low-status qualifications – thanks to an education system designed by and for the privileged – which will prepare working-class boys and girls only for manual labour, typing and housewifery. The exams will be merged into the GCSE in 1986.*

Although the test's skewed toward middle-class kids, a small percentage of bookish kids from lower income backgrounds get through if they're good at solving problems and puzzles. The most

---

* Always keen to emphasise its privileged point of educational differentiation, my old school, now entirely fee paying, doesn't do GCSEs but teaches the International Baccalaureate, its USP.

common reason for failure, according to the '11 Plus Guide', is 'having too small a vocabulary', i.e. not being middle class, or saying 'tea' not 'dinner'.

Here's an eleven-plus example:

Select and write down one of the answers below which makes the best answer to the following:

A woman who had fallen into the water was dragged out in a drowning condition by a man, but she did not thank him because:

a) She never felt thankful for small things.
b) She did not know the man well enough.
c) She was feeling better.
d) She was still unconscious.

[Source: *The Eleven-Plus Book: Genuine Exam Questions From Yesteryear*, published by Michael O'Mara Books]

Kevin and I 'pass' the test, both winning council-funded places at Sevenoaks School, the posh boys-only public (i.e. private) school in the nearby town. Mum's relieved because I won't have a long bus journey to school, as I'm frequently travel sick, which is why Sevenoaks was her top choice.

Being at a top school carries a heavy financial burden, even for kids like me who won a free place. My parents have to buy, from designated retailers only, a charcoal-grey suit, five white shirts, house tie, straw boater, black leather shoes, grey socks, charcoal-grey raincoat, hooped and plain rugby strips, rugger boots, cricket whites and boots, athletics strip, running shoes, etc. I grow fast and the kit needs replacing every year. I don't know how my parents afford it as there are no clothing grants for low-income families. I'm sure other working-class families will back out at this point.

The school has it all: we're taught six days a week on a 100-acre campus ringing the beautiful Knole Park, one of the last medieval deer parks in Britain. The school was founded six hundred years ago as a free grammar school with almshouses for the poor. Irony is not dead. I think most days how the privileged few who have it all are given more at the expense of the rest.

> Whoever has will be given more, and they will have an abundance. Whoever does not have, even what they have will be taken from them. (Matthew 25:29)

PSYCHO TEACHERS, QU'EST-CE QUE C'EST?

A photo shows me standing in front of our house, looking nervy in new uniform and straw boater – called a 'biff' – before I set off to school on my first day. I'm eleven years old, four-foot-ten tall, in my first pair of long trousers and stupid hat that makes me very self-conscious especially when the cute twelve-year-old girl who lives at the end of the road finds it funny to knock my hat off while we wait for the bus to town. Older boys cluster on the top deck of the double decker and smoke all the way home, which I want to do when I'm older as well.

I may be the only working-class kid in my year, and must surely speak like my dad, whose cockney accent is laced with rhyming slang and Yiddish words; for example, he'll say, if we've made a mess 'What a Two and Eight!' or 'Keep schtum!' for staying mum. I assume the world talks like this until my first minutes at Sevenoaks, the middle-class kids in my form thinking I'm an oik as soon as I open my mouth, especially when I say 'five and twenty', the archaic London/Kentish way of saying 'twenty-five'. I've stopped saying this by *lunchtime* and inside a week my old accent is toast, replaced by a dropped aitch but still lah-di-dah *Received Pronunciation* aka *BBC English*. Dad asks why I've started talking like a nob. I think I've become the poshest person he knows. I wish I wasn't.

A prep-school bully sticks a lump of chewing gum on my chair in class for me to sit on, what a jolly jape, so ruining the seat of the expensive new charcoal-grey trousers my parents went without to pay for. I'm ashamed of the gunky mess uncleanably stuck to my arse, it looks horrible, and I swear revenge. *No one's* going to fuck with me! The next day I grab him hard by the balls and squeeze until he says the commoner's playground surrender word *Fainites*, not accepting his pathetic prep school Latin *Pax* – and am put into detention for brawling, an hour after classes on Friday evening, copying out longhand something from a boring textbook. All things considered, things are going well.

My parents don't go to the school's parents' evening, Dad's not back from work in time, Mum can't drive, and it's a different world to what they're used to. I don't mind, I'm a cuckoo in a gilded nest with boys who take foreign holidays, own trendy off-duty clothes, know which knives and forks to use, talk about *subjects* at *dinner*, eat in *restaurants*, get fat weekly allowances to buy books and record players, and have musical instruments at home. I'm given a shilling pocket money a week, five pence in modern money – probably worth twenty times more in 2024 values, or fifty pence – so it would take seven weeks to save up to buy a single.

But since we don't have a record player at home, it's academic, no worries!

We ~~first years~~ 'new bugs' are not in the First Form, or in Year Seven, as in non-fee-paying schools, we're in the Third Form. Second year/Year Eight boys are in the Lower Fourth, then Upper Fourth, Fifth Year, Lower and Upper Sixth. It's all part of the parallel vocabulary that differentiates the ruling classes from the yobs, or me from my brothers.

The challenge is I'm no longer the smartest boy in the room but in an eleven-plus Direct Grant lump working hard to catch up on subjects to which I've never been exposed. For instance, French and Latin! *FRENCH? LATIN?!* Who needs it? I haven't been abroad and don't have a passport, haven't heard French spoken, and think people in France dress in berets and striped shirts and talk like Peter Sellers in *The Pink Panther*, or like Maurice Chevalier in the short-eyes anthem 'Thank Heaven for Little Girls'. Latin's worse, the Romans quit Britain 1,600 years ago and literally no one other than child-molesting Catholic priests and lawyers speaks Latin; it's a dead language, so what's the point? These mad languages insist food, doors and windows even are male or female or neither! What's that all about? We learn by group chanting the declension of verbs 'Amo, amas, amat, amamus, amatis, amant . . .' It's all part of the character armour of the ruling classes, but, despite myself, I enjoy Latin, later wishing I'd stuck at it beyond basic level. It would have made learning Spanish much easier.

~~Homework~~ Prep isn't something anyone can help me with, which has its upsides as no one knows what I'm doing or if I'm doing well or not, least of all me. My school reports say *could do better*, especially in Latin, which I could once I've caught up with the prep school boys' blessed *a cunabula ad sepulcrum*. I work hard but for most of my first year I'm drowning not waving. I catch up by the ~~second year~~ Lower Fourth.

Dad doesn't ask about schoolwork but knows education's a way out from hard times and hopes I won't have to work with my hands. He's clever but had a poor schooling, leaving school at thirteen to become an apprenticed electrician, so he'll read a wiring diagram but not a book. Aged eighteen, he did two years National Service in the RAF, servicing fighter planes, lucky to be demobbed before the Korean War and not a virgin soldier sent to battle freedom fighters as the British Empire disintegrated in bloody colonial struggles.

All Dad says is, School all right?

Me: Yeh.

That's it.

Weekdays there's *prep*, which takes a couple of hours to do. If handed in late, the punishment's two 'solaces', 250 words handwritten on special blue writing paper from an educational text, i.e. *The*

Letters of Marcus Tullius Cicero. As elsewhere, solace's meaning is inverted from 'an easing of grief, loneliness, discomfort' to 'punishment'.

As there's nowhere to work at home and there's a distracting constant murmuration of telly or radio, I stay on at the end of the school day to work in the library where it's quiet, warm and well lit, getting home sevenish. If I've failed/forgotten/can't be arsed to do an assignment, or all three, I copy a *swot's* work first thing in the morning, in exchange for a shoplifted Mars bar, the palaeo version of cutting and pasting from Wikipedia.

We're punished for late work, poor work, no work, attitude, lateness, hair and uniform infractions – *Polished black leather shoes only! No ankle boots! No coloured socks! Hair must not touch shirt collar!* – in an intensely competitive culture where violence is rife and bullying's humdrum, especially among the boarders who make up around half of the pupils. Some of the boys were sent away as young as seven, unwanted by absentee parents who don't care to see them for most of the year. Sobbing themselves to sleep at night in grey-blanketed Stalag dormitories, they're fodder for night-time sadists taking out their own abandonment on the softies.

A boy in my year with big ears – nicknamed Dumbo, obvs – is constantly tormented about his lugs, and is found naked on a boarding-house lawn, croquet hoops pegged over his wrists and ankles. He's taken out of school, a nervous wreck. Heads don't roll and the authorities don't give a shit as weaklings deserve their fate.

The teachers are, mostly, at the top of their academic game with fine CVs but there aren't any female teachers; the sight of a female ankle or worse would stimulate nocturnal emissions. Many are eccentric and/or cruel men who have been psychologically damaged in the last war and have carte blanche to use violence and corporal punishment as they see fit, because it's character building. They do, and it isn't.

One, a disciple of Wilhelm Reich, has grown his hair down to his shoulders to collect cosmic rays from Jupiter or Uranus or wherever, and sharpen his consciousness and liven up his kundalini in a DIY pyramid structure. What he does with his kundalini off school premises doesn't bear thinking about.

Another with shellshock, now called PTSD, is nervy and twitchy and jumps at sudden noises. He can't control his pupils, who torment him as if auditioning for *Lord of the Flies*. My class is put in detention as a group punishment when a boy sets alight a magnesium ribbon that fills the classroom with dense white smoke, while another boy – Andy Gill – in the year below me, perches a bloody lamb's heart on the pull-around blackboard for it to plop horribly before the horrified teacher. I forever regret this cruelty.

Other teachers are more reassuringly violent, like the geography teacher who, seeing me nod off at a desk in a broiling classroom, creeps up behind me and grabs my head in his shovel mitt to bash my forehead BANG! into the desk, which wakes me up. He's a sure shot with a weighty wooden chalkboard eraser – probably a grenadier in the army – which he chucks hard at boys' heads if they're off task, or asleep, or a challenging target. On balance, being hit with the eraser's better than having your head bashed into a desk.

Our chemistry teacher, Willi Bleyberg, is an East German émigré weirdo obsessed with enforcing rules, an amateur Stasi who prowls the backstreets and bushes of Sevenoaks like some tobacco cottager, in and outside school hours, to catch boys smoking. It's odd that he gives a toss about fags, given that he's a champion smoker puffing through ten Consulate Menthols in double chemistry.

Bleyberg drops in on local pubs to catch boys in the bar, and hovers around the cinema door to nobble pupils going in without written permission or being out of uniform. It's tragic as no one gets lucky in a boater. Even day boys like me are supposed to be in full greys anytime we go out, wherever we live. I don't pay any attention to it as no teachers live in Kemsing.

Bleyberg disappears leading a school trip in Yugoslavia and is declared legally dead after being missing for seven years. But he re-emerges after the fall of the Berlin Wall, phoning his adult son in the UK from Moscow, to say he's not dead but alive and terminally ill. A decorated KGB colonel, he'd been a sleeper agent at Sevenoaks, like a character in a John le Carré novel.

My English Literature teacher, Jonty Driver, is an emotionally scarred white South African who'd been involved in the apartheid resistance movement, blowing up electricity pylons, etc., a harsh critic of his comrades who'd broken under torture. He takes against me for no reason I can see, always marking down my homework and says I won't do well at the subject I love. The only thing he approves of is when he tells us to write a poem about Auschwitz, which I think is offensive and hand in a blank sheet of paper. He says in a report that 'I have seen little of Jonathan this term and even less of his work'. This pisses me off – it's not true, I never skipped a class nor failed to hand in work – so I make a formal, respectful, complaint to the head of English about my treatment, and am amazed that he agrees and moves me to his group.

There are paedos on staff – a group of eight ex-pupils will later claim they were abused by a group of five teachers – but we're especially wary of Gerd Sommerhoff, the head of the school's technical department. A grandson of Robert and Clara Schumann, he was interned during the war as an enemy alien, had presented science programmes for the BBC, and is now a well-regarded national figure in science. But he's also a sexual predator who abuses boys under his authority.

Sommerhoff seriously interferes with a boy, 'X', who decides to take revenge by murdering or harming the teacher. X rigs a DIY bazooka using a short metal scaffolding tube holding a fat firework-display rocket that he fires into Sommerhoff's study, where it explodes but doesn't injure or kill the teacher. *Attempted Murder or GBH v Revenge for Sexual Abuse* is a disciplinary conundrum that the school decides is best resolved by beating the boy, six of the best being better than bringing in the bobbies.

The genius of the punishment is to ask my housemaster, Tibby Mason – a kindly man and pacifist who abhors violence, having suffered greatly as a prisoner of the Japanese – to beat X. Tibby wouldn't hurt a greenfly, let alone an abused child. The caning format is for offenders to lean over a desk, trousers round the ankles, to be thwacked hard on the arse and upper leg with a thick and whippy bamboo cane, which can cause purple bruising and draw blood. It's very painful. After being thrashed, offenders must turn, take the punisher's hand and – trying not to blub, it's woosy – say, 'Thank you, sir!'

Instead of whacking the boy hard, Tibby gently taps him half a dozen times, barely touching him, shakes hands with the relieved X, and says, 'Good shot!'

Sommerhoff will transfer to another school for fresh meat, his reputation intact until death, when it comes out in the press.*

Psychos aside, most teachers are talented men who do what they can to bring out the best in us. Hothouse teaching six days a week suits me, and my housemaster seems genuinely interested in how I'm doing. I've won the educational lottery.

The school has a well-equipped music hub, but I'm not involved as

---

* It was only in 2013 that a case involving another boy, A, and the then deceased Sommerhoff was settled out of court by the school, following publicity around Jimmy Savile's crimes and a visit in his Roller to Sevenoaks and our school. Other child-molesting teachers we knew of are authoritatively referenced online. The story about Boy X and the bazooka was told at Tibby Mason's funeral service, which I gratefully attended. He helped me a lot.

I don't have lessons nor an instrument at home. Can't-Pay-Don't-Play! is the motto. Delightful trips are on offer – exchanges with Pontoise school in France, Easter holiday ski trips, etc. – but they're for rich kids as they cost a packet and there aren't any subsidies. It would be nice to go, they look fun, but I don't resent missing out, my parents have to scrimp just to pay for a new uniform and ridiculous straw hat every year as I'm growing fast, a foot taller by the age of thirteen.

CIGARETTES

French New Wave star Anna Karina. *(Photo: © AGIP/Bridgeman Images)*

Everyone smokes. Our teachers in classes, people on buses and the Underground and trains and pubs and restaurants and cafés, doctors puff in their surgeries, movie stars, TV personalities and pop stars, all light up on chat shows, etc., etc. While everyone's aware of the link with lung, tongue, jaw and throat cancers, heart disease and so on, the probability of death and disease isn't enough of a thing to stop doing it against the aspirational sexiness of a gasper.

I love grabbing an illicit fag anytime I can: breaktime in the school bogs or during lunchtime in bushes or on the bus's top deck to and from school. Uniformed boys aged eleven up form a queue at the sweet shop across the road from the school to buy individual cheap fags from the kindly old shopkeeper couple.

Top-end cigarettes are on display in beautiful packaging with erotically rustling gold or silver foil inside, to be undressed and reveal gorgeous branded cancer sticks. My fantasy top five fags are:

- Balkan Sobranie: SMERSH-friendly Russian tobacco gaspers in black paper and gold foil filter sleeve
- Passing Clouds: oval Turkish snouts in pastel shades nestling in a flip-top box like sweeties
- Lucky Strike ('It's toasted!'): unlucky cancer sticks with tar-laden smoke in a pack that shouts 'Amerika!'
- Gitanes: Gallic stink fests as seen in *Nouvelle Vague* movies, essential to bed Anna Karina
- Peter Stuyvesant: the fag for jetsetters and gold-braided airline pilots rogering heiresses and stewardesses in Zermatt or Beirut

Sadly, I can only afford economy cigs like No. 6 or Sovereign, which I chain smoke on the top deck of the 421 bus back to Kemsing, feeling like the man, arriving home stinking of smoke and with fingers yellow with tar. I lie to Mum and tell her I haven't been smoking, it always smells of fags on the bus. It does, but it doesn't explain my ochre fingers.

SPORT

TUTOR'S REPORT

Summer Term, 1967   Name   J. M. King
                       Form   3α

A good term.
He did quite well in the Athletics, but doesn't
seem to be a great cricketer!

                                    JB.s.

A sadist oversees junior sports. We play rugby Tuesday, Thursday and Saturday afternoons in the winter, and cricket or athletics in the warmer months. Football's not permitted: it's a game for gentlemen played by hooligans whereas rugby is the opposite.

In the cold months, we're not allowed to wear vests or underpants under our strip as it's thought effete and disincentivises moving about. We play rugby in rain, ice and snow, which doesn't bother me. I enjoy the game. I'm a fast-running wing three-quarter, the last in line to receive the ball who has to either sprint past the psycho lummoxes in defence or be flattened like a naan. If the ground's frozen so hard we'd break limbs, we're sent on cross-country runs around Knole house, a vast Jacobean pile first built around the time the school was founded whose scale – 365 rooms and twelve staircases – has been called a 'monument to private greed', true of all aristocrats' and oligarchs' cribs. We squelch along miles of muddy misery, sploshing along dirt tracks to a pointless end point, followed by a sprint to a freezing shower block open to the wind. Our goal is to strip off our filthy kit, shower inside a minute, change into uniform, and scarper before the perve sports teacher arrives. If we're slow, it's goodnight Saigon, because Short Eyes will make us drop our strides to stand shivering before him, kecks round ankles, as he close-checks for grubby knees. A micron of mud means stripping off and showering again while he watches us shiver, as white as axolotls, our testes shrunk to the size of cashew nuts.

Summer means cricket and athletics, where 800 metres is my distance. As I'm fast, I run for the school, but I'm not good or motivated enough to win anything.

My true love is cricket but I'm a lousy batsman and can't bowl, so I'm banished to field at deep square leg or long off to wait for a skied shot to catch. Which never happens. I'm not good enough to get in the A, B or C team – if there were one – as Sevenoaks is a cricketing powerhouse turning out prodigies like Chris Tavaré, in my year, who'll open the batting for England, or Paul Downton in the year below, who'll become England's wicketkeeper, and many top pro county players.

Being rubbish at the game doesn't make me love it less, and it's a passion I'll share with Mark White and Andy Corrigan from the Mekons, when we have a flat together in Leeds. The only thing that will silence the music of David Bowie in our front room will be the BBC's *Test Match Special* commentary on international cricket matches, we three clustered on a scabby sofa transported by the meandering chit-chat over a five-day game, a global sport yanks can't grasp. Within the architecture of cricketing small talk, nothing's too inconsequential to explore, and the smallest thing holds interest, like a pigeon on the grass, a cake sent in by a listener, or two-hundred-year-old statistics plucked from *Wisden*. It's the essence of Englishness and a primary influence on the lyrics written by Mark White aka Mark Mekon, punk rock's John Betjeman.

SEX

I know a lot more about sex – or rather the basic topography of naked women – since a boy at school brought in a copy of *Health and Efficiency*, the top-shelf house magazine of the naturist movement, full of pix of hearty young men and women with their kit off playing ping-pong or netball in a sunny outdoors – clearly not England, they'd catch their death. Tits and nips galore but bush and tackle are airbrushed away, with perhaps a smidgen of lady garden that evaded the censor if you peer hard enough. We study the mag carefully to absorb any useful information; it's the first time I've seen a breast other than in an encyclopaedia or art, the women in old oil paintings are always flashing their racks for some reason or other. A classmate tells me he bashes the bishop while looking through the bra section of his big sister's Littlewoods catalogue, which seems desperate but forgivable. We sometimes cluster, giggling, with noses pressed to the glass of the high-street camera shop, window shopping an array of boxed 16 mm films from Sweden that show sun-kissed blondes in the buff on the sleeves, until the shopkeeper tells us to bugger off. Since no one I know has a film projector, the contents remain a frustrating mystery.

One day, our Biology teacher chalks up a picture of rabbits on the blackboard and says, coughing in embarrassment: '*This*' – drawing ♀ under a line-drawn bunny – 'is a *Female* and *this*' – chalking up ♂

– 'is a *Male*. The *sire* mounts the *doe* – penetration occurs, semen is emitted, egg fertilisation occurs, followed by pregnancy and the birth of *kittens*. This is called *sexual reproduction* and is the purpose of sexual congress. This also applies to humans and other higher animals. Questions?'

No hands go up; we've no idea what he's banging on about. *Penetration? Rabbits have kittens? Do mums and dads do this? It's revolting!* I decide sex isn't for me and will stick to wanking.

PEANUTS!

I'm desperate, don't have a record player, the music I hear at school and on pirate radio thrills me – I've got to get one. My pocket money only runs to a Mars bar and a handful of Fruit Salad sweets, four for a penny. I can't save from this.

I hassle the neighbours to wash their cars and take on an early morning paper round pre-school – this is a time when people read *newspapers** that are delivered to their homes, like *bottled milk* is – and save like mad. I enter a cartoon competition sponsored by Mars's Marathon peanut 'n' chocolate bar – later renamed *Snickers* – and WIN SECOND PRIZE for a funny drawing whose subject is a peanut, obvs! I forget what I drew, there's no way to make a copy, but who cares, I won!

The prize money is enough to buy a NEW MONO RECORD PLAYER with a spindle to stack and auto-play 45s and LPs, and a loud, warm-toned, speaker!

I'm blessed!

I rush to the record store and buy 'Hey Joe' by Jimi Hendrix, my first ever 45.

I will love this song forever.

---

* These are sheets of paper that are folded together and have printed words and photographs on them, with stories about things that happened *yesterday*.

I MEET JOHN LENNON

January 1967. I'm eleven, still a 'new bug', the scum of the earth, who the older boys have carte blanche to abuse. A monstrous new arts and dining block is being built, which means that while construction work's underway, school dinners are served at the local Odeon cinema, about half a mile from the school in the middle of town.

This is bad for the small boys as the big ones just barge in front of us and push us back down a queue that snakes from the cinema's first-floor main foyer, where grub's doled out, to a street-level emergency exit, where we file in. This winter often us finds us huddled on the pavement, sodden in the rain and snow, waiting for the fifth and sixth formers to eat up. Unless we're lucky, we're served last or sometimes not all, having run out of time and needing to get back to classes, as lateness isn't tolerated.

Prefects – eighteen-year-old collaborationists who would have prospered in Vichy France – supervise the food line, which means we're doomed as they ignore any and all bullying, seeing our daily sufferings as both character building or a chance to dole out the same misery the older boys endured themselves before their voices broke and hair grew in surprising places.

These class enemies enforce the school's rules, however trivial, and are authorised to dish out punishments, including detentions and violence. Prefects are stationed like traffic cops between the school and the cinema to nab us if we're running – strictly *verboten* – and send us back to base, thus missing the meal. Another may stand near the high street's zebra crossing to make sure we tip our ridiculous straw hats to say thank you to drivers who stop and let us cross; we don't, we're sent back to base, thus missing the meal, etc. It's like newbie Snakes and Ladders except without ladders. None of this happens at my brothers' Secondary Modern school as the education of working-class boys doesn't mandate prefects; it seems much more civilised. The British Empire was built on indoctrinating young men with the virtues of hierarchical physical and mental abuse and explains why ex-public school boys are reported to do so well in prison.

However, today, a kind teacher who disapproves of our lunchtime misery has let us out ten minutes before the End of Class Bell rings, so we can get to the cinema first and be fed. Me and two mates race downtown – no prefects yet prowling the pavements – but as we approach the crossing I physically run into *JOHN LENNON* of the *BEATLES*! In Sevenoaks, the most boring town in England?! On its dozy high street! He's with an entourage . . . is George also there . . . is that Paul, my favourite Beatle? It's gobsmacking, but I'm conflicted – do I hang about, blag an autograph from the most famous man in the world, say how much I like *Rubber Soul*? . . . Or miss *lunch*? NO contest. Hunger wins, we three sprint away the last 100 yards to the Odeon, to be first in line for lamb stew with potatoes and cabbage, rhubarb crumble and custard to follow.

Filling our boots, we talk it over, it's AMAZING! I've met – run into! – *JOHN LENNON*! In *Sevenoaks*, the dullest town in the cosmos!

Back at school, everyone's in a tizz, because the Beatles have come here (Sevenoaks!) to shoot a promo movie in Knole Park, which our school grounds back onto.

The long-haired scousers are filming around a dead oak tree with a deconstructed paint-splattered piano, strings and whatnot hanging from the bare branches. The film, a stoned Spike Milliganesque romp, is being shot for the new Beatles' double A-side single, 'Penny Lane' and 'Strawberry Fields Forever', their most brilliant non-album tracks.

A hyped crowd of school-uniformed boys and girls and rubberneckers is held back by bemused local coppers; it's the most exciting thing to happen here – the *only* thing that's happened here – since 1450's Battle of Solefields during Jack Cade's rebellion. Most boys at the school abandon classes to watch, even the Quisling Prefects and a few hip younger teachers. Amazingly, no one's punished. All is well, and all will be well.

Postscript

Only minutes before I bash into John, he'd bought a Victorian music hall flyer from the antiques shop at No. 44 High Street. This later provided lyrics to 'Being for the Benefit of Mr Kite!' on *Sgt Pepper's Lonely Hearts Club Band.*

'Penny Lane' is my favourite McCartney song, a masterpiece of storytelling and observation, the sprung rhythm breezily bouncing us along Liverpool's famous street, propelled by Ringo's signature lazy snare.

John's track's not bad either.

LEADER OF THE PACK

Me on my Yamaha 650.
(Photo: Debbie Langdon-Davies)

I think about bikes all the time, except when I'm fantasising about getting off with girls approximately every forty seconds. Wanting two wheels takes my mind off the sins of the flesh and I've aspired to be a rocker since primary school when I saw horror-show headlines about mods and rockers battling it out on Brighton beach. These hooligans were morally deficient, had no respect, why we lost the empire, etc., bring back National Service, meaning they ticked all the right boxes from my POV and were having big fun I was missing out on simply because I was a child. The mod look's not for me – those drab parkas, Fred Perrys, tonic suits, and scooters. Nah. Greaser style *rules*: 501s, tees, studded leathers, heavy boots; a motorbike would make life sing, topped by a wild kohl-eyed girlfriend with tousled hair and short skirt on the pillion. Right now, the only way to escape this dreary dorm village is to walk miles or cycle as there's a hopeless bus service I can't afford to use anyway. I dream of gunning a fat bike at speed round bendy country lanes, leaning low as I corner, as free as an elk, 'Born to Be Wild' in my head, a Kentish Peter Fonda . . .

At local village hall dos, I'm hypnotised when the rocker boys and girls take the floor in their oily line dances, clacking and thumping as they turn in sync on the metal heels of their bike boots, the unforgiving fluorescent lights bouncing off their studded jackets as they spin, thumbs in waistbands, elbows out, tossing their lank locks in time with the music, up and down and side to side to Norman Greenbaum's 'Spirit in the Sky', the killer greaser floor filler and time for the rest of us to hug the walls and watch . . . aspirational stuff.

Money, that's what I want, because bikes don't come for free, and I've got to start saving. Kevin and I find farm work in the summer break, he and I cycling four miles at sunup to Wrotham, a village east along the Pilgrims' Way that snuggles in rich farmland, the Garden of England, where there are thousands of acres of fruit trees.

A purple-nosed farmer allots us a giant damson tree whose branches are burdened by clusters of dusty indigo plums ripe for market. We're paid by the box on piecework rates and labour on ladders picking the high fruit to a thrumming soundtrack of wasps and hornets gorging on the rotting and overripe plums that have fallen or been squelched underfoot.

We're unsupervised but work hard, trying to make as much money as we can, picking non-stop apart from short sandwich breaks, except on a Friday when we pop into a farmhands' pub for a livener, our first time in a boozer. We ask for cider, please, and the landlord says, eyeing us over his specs, 'You men eighteen?'

'Yes,' we squeak, while the publican winks and pulls our pints.

In the countryside, all working stiffs count as men, even if a first shave's a year off, and pubs are the best places for teenage boys to learn how to behave in public. A kid fucks about in a country boozer and he's out on his ear.

At summer's end, I've saved sixty quid, which I blow by spring on vinyl.* Heavily influenced by the senior art-room boys, I buy the Rolling Stones' *Let It Bleed*, *Tommy* by the Who, *Led Zeppelin II*, MC5's *Kick Out the Jams*, Free's imaginatively titled *Free*, Dylan's *Blonde on Blonde* and the Beatles' *Abbey Road*.† When I land something new I play it over and over and over in my room, driving Mum and Dad mad downstairs, and write down the words in a notebook, until I know them by heart. I know it's barking to note down the words to any Zep song as they're twaddle – no white blues fanboy cliché is missed – especially the bollocks words on 'Whole Lotta Love', but I forgive any tosh over a Jimmy Page monster riff and John Bonham's godlike skin-bashing. And Robert Plant's got a *voice*. The Stones and Free and Cream inspire me to go to the source, listen to Chicago and then Delta blues, a gift I'll never return. I thrill to hear tracks by Muddy Waters, Big

---

* LPs cost 37 / 6d each. There are twelve pennies to a shilling in pre-decimal currency and twenty shillings in a pound which is called a quid, so there are 144 pennies, 248 ha-pennies and 566 farthings. I can't be arsed to work out what 37/ 6d would be worth in today's terms, but it's a lot. Life's too short.

† I'd have been blown away to know that in fifteen years' time I'd be recording in Abbey Road Studio's legendary Studio 2, where the Beatles made their masterpieces, on our second album *Solid Gold*, as I don't have any music skills at all. I'm still astounded.

Mama Thornton, Howlin' Wolf and the source of sources, Robert Johnson, without whom rock 'n' roll wouldn't be possible, the man who sold his soul to the devil, and went like we'd all like to go, murdered between gigs in a juke joint with poisoned whisky from the jealous husband of the woman you've been shagging . . .

I buy a second-hand copy of 'Down Home Girl' by Alvin Robinson after hearing the Stones' 1964 cover, knocked out by the brilliance of the lyric 'every time I kiss you girl, it tastes like pork and beans', a galaxy apart from Tin Pan Alley chart botherers like 'Sweets for My Sweet'. If I ever write a song, I think, it'll have to be like this, about real life, how people talk . . . but I'm not minded to write anything for myself. I'm wallowing in their genius, and if I'm not memorising the lyrics to rock and pop songs, I'm learning by heart poems by the metaphysical poets, especially John Donne, writers who use words like salmon lures to haul you in. Oftentimes, meaning hides in the noise and won't break cover, like Little Richard's unimprovable 'A-wop-bop-a-loo-bop-a-lop-bam-boom'.

Buying records has knocked my finances off-beam, so I take on any work I can in school holidays, my mind stuck on saving for a bike. I'm six inches taller and can handle myself now, so Dad finds me work on a vast council construction project where blocks of flats are being thrown up fast to deal with the perpetual social housing crisis, hundreds of building trades on a site rife with theft and corruption. Dad says plain clothes cops are about tasked with catching the tea-leafs who rip out and sell newly installed cabinets, plumbing and electrical fittings, but who'll look the other way if you bung them a score. I'm only fifteen but straight off see that whoever has the construction contract is incompetent, being skinned, crooked, or all three. It's a shitshow.* I'm told to take a

---

* Characters like the corrupt ex-leader of Newcastle council T. Dan Smith or the architect and developer John Poulson – 'an incalculably evil man', said the judge at his trial for fraud in 1974 – dropped hundreds of thousands

couple of small doors to four carpenters tasked with fitting them to kitchen units in a newbuild flat. I find them lolling about, reading the paper, radio on, smoking and joking, and one says, as I deliver the units, 'That's enough for now, son, don't bust a gut.' They don't give a toss, they're paid cash in hand by a bloke paid cash in hand by a bloke paid cash in hand, no names, no pack drill. I go to a café until lunch and deliver four more in the afternoon. It's a doddle, and educational, but I'm paid at the day's end. In cash.

In the run up to my sixteenth birthday, a local greaser, John – everyone's called John or Dave – says he'll flog me a CB175 for forty quid which I might be able to get together with a small loan from Dad. I'm desperate, a fidget-arse, marooned in this boring village. My father – once owning a Matchless 350 himself – is smart enough to know I don't need a fuckoff bike, I just need to get around. On my sixteenth birthday, he takes me to the garage and hands me the keys to a Honda Cub 50cc, the best present I have EVER had! This will be the most fun motorcycle I own. I LOVE it!

Inside a month, Kevin has a Honda 50, as well, and Jenny and Janet, my girlfriends who are friends, not *girlfriends*, get Puch Maxi mopeds – up to 30 mph on the flat! – and my actual girlfriend, K, buys a Honda Monkey bike. We swarm like midges from village to village, the air full of high-revving engine whines while we whizz about. A year on, Mekon-to-be Mark White will buy a Lambretta scooter he's always dropping, and Guitar-God-to-be Gill will get a moped. NOTHING's as much fun as 50cc wheels for a teenager, except the things that are.

Six weeks later I pass my bike driving test and borrow a local rocker's Triumph 5TA 500cc, the ugliest bike ever, nicknamed 'The

---

of pounds in bribes in the sixties to bent officials for planning permissions for jerry-built brutalist monuments like the Leeds International Pool, falling apart as soon as it was built.

Bathtub' as its curved rear mudguard is shaped like a Second World War German helmet. I prefer my cute little Cub. *You Meet The Nicest People On A Honda!** This is the life!†

---

* The greatest motorcycle sales strapline ever!
† The Honda Cub is the most successful motor vehicle in history with over 100 million sold. Takeo Fujisawa, its designer, insisted it had to be rideable one handed so the other could carry a tray of soba noodles, the best design specification of all time. I will later own/borrow: Honda CB250, Honda FI 750, AJS 350, Royal Enfield 350, Triumph 500, Ariel Square 4 1000, BSA Golden Flash 650, Triumph Tiger Cub, Triumph Thunderbird 900, Yamaha 650 twin, BMW R80RT and Ducati GT1000 Sport Classic. The Honda Cub is the BEST.

I LEARN TO SNOG

I'm fifteen, in Jenny's bedroom, listening to *Electric Ladyland* with her for the nth time, when she turns the music off and says, 'You kiss anyone yet?'

I wish! I say, 'No, not even held someone's hand.'

'Oh dear,' she says. She's maturer than me, up to all sorts with older boys, and says, 'Hmm, I better show you. But no hands!'

It's an offer I can't refuse! She holds my face with hands on both cheeks and locks on. THE FUCK! She stuck her TONGUE in my mouth and is wiggling it about! What's *that* all about?! I thought snogging was done like they do on TV, lips shut tight, moving from side to side like mopping the floor in an ad for Flash. I'm getting the hang of it, it's pretty good, when she disengages after about twenty seconds.

'There!' she says, patting my head like I'm an old Labrador. 'That's it!'

She swaps Hendrix for Dr Strangely Strange's awful 'Strangely Strange But Oddly Normal', a song guaranteed to nix naughty thoughts in even the most onanistic teenager, a wise call.

We go back to being besties and nothing like this happens again.

But my eyes have been opened!

SOUS LES PAVÉS, LA PLAGE!

It's 1968. Everything's gone tits up. War in Vietnam, revolution in France, race riots and cities on fire across the US, an amped-up threat of nuclear annihilation, proxy and colonial wars in Angola and Mozambique, the assassinations of Martin Luther King and Bobby Kennedy, military coups in Panama, Peru and Iraq, the Soviet invasion of Czechoslovakia... what's not to not like? The Motor City's *burning*!

Things are worse in Kemsing. We've *finally* got a telephone but my parents have fitted a cylindrical lock into the dial, so I can't call anyone without asking for it to be unlocked! It's FASCIST

OPPRESSION! When I complain, Mum says if you *could* phone out you *would*, which might cost an arm and a leg, so you can *take* calls but can't *make* any. Mum thaws and says she'll let me use the phone if I tell her why I want to make a call but only if it's *important*. I'm buggered, as talking shite with friends doesn't qualify, but I concoct the need to discuss homework with a school mate, which I'd otherwise never do. However, Mother stands in the kitchen only yards away to eavesdrop – even turning down *The Archers* for clarity – and ensure I'm not frittering away the family's fortune on bloated phone bills by chatting. This is ripe, as in short order Mother's perma-glued to the handset holding hour-long calls where she says, 'Hmm. Yes? NOO! I don't *believe* it!' etc., etc. It's SO annoying.

Apocalyptic world events, Bob Dylan, unfair education system – *and the phone lock!* – make me realise I'm a socialist. Things should be shared more fairly, it's not right that the rich live parasitical lives on the backs of the working classes, etc. My new political consciousness isn't well thought through, it's a *feeling* rather than a coherent set of ideas, but I instinctively identify with people fighting the power. I'm obsessed with the revolutionary events in Paris where left-wing students allied with striking factory workers took to the streets and almost brought down the government, President De Gaulle even fleeing to West Germany for a bit, with pitched battles between demonstrators and tooled-up French riot cops with paving stones, petrol bombs and tear gas canisters hurtling through the air. It's very exciting; I wish I was older so I could join in. It's much easier to be sure than right.

At school, sixth-form art-room boys, fresh from skiving off school to be battered by cops in the Grosvenor Square demo against the Vietnam War, chatter about a new anarcho-art group called the Situationists who are making radical art among the barricades with posters and graffiti with lines that are both funny and deep: 'Demand the Impossible!'; 'Under the cobblestones, the beach!'; 'Boredom is always counter-revolutionary'; and write things like 'Down with a world in which the guarantee we won't die of starvation has been bought with the guarantee we'll die of boredom.'

I don't know what Raoul Vaneigem's on about, nor anything about Marxism or anarchism, but love the scrawled alternative texts rewiring ads and comic strips, and the sexy contempt for the reactionary old guard who will only allow things to change so that nothing will.

More thrilling than Gallic rebellion and the Tet offensive is the discovery of a newsagent in Sevenoaks, midway between the bus station and school, that sells US Marvel comics! A fat wad of well-fingered titles is squeezed in a display, which the shopkeeper doesn't think much of. 'Yank rubbish!' he says, telling me they're used as ballast on ships from the States and bought as job lots, so it'll be a fluke if there are consecutive numbers. I buy #68, #70 and #72 Fantastic Four comics, and issue #155 of Thor – 'Now Ends the Universe!', the Gesamtkunstwerk of Jack Kirkby (Grant Morrison calls him 'the William Blake of comics'), which must rival the Sistine Chapel, I think, not that I've been to Rome. And there are dog-eared copies of Steve Ditko's The Amazing Spider-Man and Doctor Strange! Two of the greatest artists of the age! This blows what's left of my Marathon prize money. I need to find another way to source vinyl *and* buy more Marvel comics which I do by joining my mother on her weekly pilgrimages to jumble sales. These are usually held in musty church halls where trestle tables are laden with discarded old clothes, schmutter, bags, knickknacks and crockery; a smell of mothballs, dry cleaning, and armpit sweat hanging in the air.

At one of these, I find a discarded cream demob suit, like one of Lee Brilleaux's booze-stained outfits. There are always tables loaded with books and records, chucked out during a downsizing or an empty nester clearing out a departed child's bedroom, and this is where I find vinyl treasure, snagging ratty-sleeved 45s like 'Satisfaction', 'Day Tripper' and 'Good Golly, Miss Molly', only thruppence each, six for a shilling (worth about forty pence today) – scratched and sticky from overplay and good times, classics sheltering in heaps of granny pap like Harry Secombe's 'If I Ruled the World' or Acker Bilk's 'Stranger On The Shore'. I bag anything cool, occasionally even finding blues 7-inchers. My record collection grows. This is good.

I hunt for books too, rifling through cracked-spined tomes and damp-spotted encyclopaedias from a time when the world was one-third pink, and Happily Ever After romance paperbacks ripe for pulping. Among the landfill I find battered hardbacks of *Anna Karenina*, *David Copperfield* and *Great Expectations* that I will reread every decade in the future, understanding them differently each time. Pip's story, a boy plucked from a commoner's life and made a gentleman by an unknown benefactor, in the process losing and finding his moral compass, is a *bildungsroman* with great resonance to me. From now on, if there's a jumble, I'm there digging through the titles, heaven for a cent.

1968's not that bad after all.

A 1971 ART-ROOM PLAYLIST

1. *Blue* — Joni Mitchell
2. *Thank Christ for the Bomb* — Groundhogs
3. *New York Tendaberry* — Laura Nyro
4. *The Band* — The Band
5. 45 singles — James Brown
6. *The Motown Story* — Various Artists
7. *What's Going On?* — Marvin Gaye
8. *Fun House* — The Stooges
9. *In Search of Space* — Hawkwind
10. *Electric Ladyland* — Jim Hendrix

THE ART DEPARTMENT

A bright white room has all-age pupils perched on benches with pens, pencils and paper, while boys clutching brushes worry canvases with oils before still-life set-ups, and some sit thumbing through design, architecture and art books and magazines, or *The Last Whole Earth Catalog*. A seductive scent of linseed oil, turpentine and silk-screen cleaning fluid drifts in the air; and in the background music can be heard, oozing from a mono record deck with a half-dozen LPs stacked shivering on the stalk, ready to drop and play, the skippy needle arm weighted by a penny sellotaped to its head. It's not schmaltz nor mumsy pap but stuff I've not heard before: Dylan, Chicago and Delta blues, psychedelia, garage rock ... Music and art everywhere. *Je suis arrivée!*

 The older boys – this may be the only place where under sixteens mix with or see sixth-formers at work – play music constantly that's unheard on radio. I hear *Highway 61 Revisited* and *Blonde on Blonde* for the first time and my life is forever changed. Bob's stoned, toned, ironic voice is shocking, exciting and life affirming, as he mashes words from the Bible and the Beats, sticking it to The Man or The Woman, ushering me into an alternative world where anything's possible, where the squares and the suits and the bores have no place and get what they deserve. I know which side I'm on. I want to be a part of it.

The Art Department's headed by Bob White, a serious artist and charismatic teacher who talks to us as if we're more than sponges and encourages us to *look* and *think* critically, and to ask *why*, inspiring us all to be the best we can be.

A couple of years on, a giant new arts and dining block is built, and the Art Department moves into a spacious new HQ. Bob has blagged funding for pottery kilns, photographic darkrooms, a 16-mm film studio, silkscreen printing, painting, drawing and art and design areas. It's extraordinary. I'm a lucky soul and can't help feeling how wrong it is that I have so much and my siblings so little. Our class-ridden education system stinks. It's bizarre that the school has *charitable* status.

JACKIE'S DEAD

The front-page photo in the local paper shows a wrecked car on a tow truck, its roof crunched down to door level, the front end mashed into the engine block. Jackie, fifteen, had been in the front seat and was killed instantly. Her older brother, eighteen, who'd been in the back, hung on for a couple of days in ICU until he flatlined as well. They died on a three-lane blacktop with a two-way central overtaking section, a mad arrangement that was a fast track to heaven. A car travelling in the opposite direction had lost control and crashed head on into Jackie's car, totalling both vehicles. Everyone died.

Jackie was my first girlfriend, who I met at a church hall folk club when we were fifteen. She was a funny little thing, cute in a short skirt and suede jacket with long fringed sleeves, a look I liked a lot. I'd sweated about asking her out, finally phoning but she said she was washing her hair, no can do, so I gave up, knowing this is girl code for get lost. A week later, a mutual friend passes on a message from her asking why I hadn't called again, she'd really been washing her hair, though why this was such a big deal is beyond me.

We *go out* with each other for a few months, innocently fool around, chat and joke, and when I visit, we sit in her family kitchen listening to music while her mum – who's very nice to me, she thinks I'm all right – forever busies about, keeping an eye out for hanky-panky. We snog in the back row of the flicks but no *petting*, no way. Once a week,

I walk three miles to and from her house, picking up my mate Tim on the way, not having any money for the bus and a knackered push-bike. A few months on we swap: Jackie goes out with Tim and I go out with his ex. Same routine: the four of us fool around and chat and joke while we sit in Jackie's family kitchen listening to music, her mum forever busying about, keeping an eye out for hanky panky. Me and my new squeeze snog in the back row of the flicks but no *petting*, no way, until we lose interest and drift apart, and don't see each other again.

I'm very upset to hear about the crash, it's my first handshake with death. Jackie was so sweet, my first date, and I don't know what to do other than immediately go to see her mum and dad to say how sorry I am, how hard it must be for you, she was a lovely girl, funny and nice and kind. I weep in the kitchen at the table we used to sit at when we fooled around and joked and chatted. Her mum asks if I'll come to the memorial service at their Catholic church, which will be a major event as they're an extended Irish family, and everyone at Jackie's school has been given the morning off to weep and hug each other before the coffin's in the smoky frankincense haze and guttering candlelight.

My school headmaster isn't happy about this and rules that no boy, i.e. me, can attend the church ceremony. Perhaps he thinks mourning's effeminate or it's *de trop* to show emotion, but he mandates this is an event only for close family – it isn't – and as it's in school hours anyone, i.e. *me*, who bunks off lessons will be disciplined.

The day before the funeral my housemaster, 'Tibby' Mason, takes me to one side and says, 'You know the headmaster has said no one from school should attend this memorial service?'

'Yes, sir.'

'And you understand that if you go, and are out of school without permission, you'll be punished?'

'Yes, sir.'

'You're clear that you'll be put in detention if you do? Do you intend to go?'

'Yes, sir.'

Detention's a doddle! I won't get beaten. Not bad!

At the service, Jackie's mum finds me a place near her and squeezes my hand as I sniffle my condolences. It's her who needs comforting more than me, I think.

Back at school, Tibby asks me if I went to the funeral service.

'Yes, sir.'

He nods and shakes my hand. 'Well played,' he says.

Postscript

A reunion: five years from now, my close friend Steve Wood, twenty-one, is also killed in a car crash, having driven in the wrong lane of one-way roadworks to hit an oncoming car head on. Steve's parents, in another extended Irish family, are close friends of Jackie's family, whom I haven't seen since the funeral. A memorial service is held in the same Catholic church as for Jackie, packed with friends and family among the smells and bells. I'm head downed in a pew when there's a nudge at my side. Jackie's mother sits beside me, her face a mask of sorrow, and says, 'We must stop meeting like this.'

VELVET UNDERGROUND

1971. I'm sixteen. My friend Toby's playing an LP he's filched from his dad, a journalist who reviews music and film for *The Sunday Times*. His father thinks the record's godawful, no tunes, just a noise. The sleeve, by Andy Warhol, has a peel-off banana skin under which is a photo of a banana. Super cool. It's called *The Velvet Underground and Nico*, a double-album sampler of the band's first three albums.

I'm blown away when the needle drops. Dissonance, angst, dark words from a chthonic reality. I love American music and have gorged on *Blonde on Blonde, The Band, Electric Ladyland,* Motown and James Brown, but this is totally fresh, awesome.

'Sister Ray' is a relentless seventeen-minute racket that grunges on in an amped-up vamp to a tsunami of noise under Lou Reed's deadpan narrative about a druggy demimonde that blossomed under the threat of nuclear Armageddon, far-right repression and social collapse. I play it loud, thrilled by John Cale's conservatoire genius and his aggressive one–two with Reed, two prize fighters after a musical TKO. It's as good as music gets, but no surprise it fails to chart in the UK and its high spot on the Billboard chart is 195. I'll be mindful of this track, seven years on, when writing 'Anthrax'.

Lou Reed's tenement tales are a junkie's *Seven Brides for Seven Brothers*, a love letter to Chinese rocks, with a disengaged chanteuse force marching through these hymns to street life. Nico's voice is as flat as a kipper's dick, missing every note, her off-key drone on 'Sunday Morning' a hymn to anomie. It's beautiful, inspiring the teenage me two thousand miles and years away with its outsider ambition, truth, and not-giving-a-fuckery. I long term borrow/steal the vinyl from my mate, listen to it time and again, writing out the lyrics, as I do with every record I love, into notebooks filled with messages from an elsewhere.

1972, *Live At Max's Kansas City* drops, a sparkling recording from a thrilling milieu a kid from a dull English town can only dream about. By the time I go to the US at eighteen, in 1973, the Velvet Underground are toast and I never see them play.

Decades later, I'm introduced to Lou and am tongue-tied in his presence, with nothing interesting to say, and will another time bump into Nico in London, who's crashing at our manager's place, a beautiful ruin destroyed by smack. Further down the line, I'll perform with John Cale and his band at Wrocław's Music Theatre Capitol in one of John's tribute shows to Nico, and will sing 'Mütterlein' and 'Fearfully in Danger' – in *German*, which I learn phonetically, not speaking the language.

Ich habe genug.

No one who loves outsider music could fail to fall for the Velvets, their work a proof that integrity blossoms in failure. Their music still inspires me.

MOTHER'S PRIDE

(Photo: Clive Limpkin/Stringer/Getty Images)

June 1971, school holidays, waiting for the results of GCE O-level exams. A minimum five or more good passes means I can stay on in the sixth form as the school doesn't tolerate failure. This is when the slackers, underachievers, and losers are winnowed out to ensure optimal rankings in the public i.e. *private* school league table. I'm not expected to do well and predicted to pass only a few, not enough to get into the sixth form. This annoys me as I think this is more to do with snobbery than performance, but it may be the end of my academic gold ticket. I'm thought not to try hard enough on course work (maybe true) and be off with the fairies much of the time (true). While I can't shake off the sense of being an imposter, I've acquired by osmosis the smug assumption that tomorrow belongs to me, a belief the ruling classes hold that their blessings are earned and not the undeserved outcome of some cosmic genetic, geographic, or social raffle. Despite the gloomy warnings from teachers, I'm sure I'll be OK as I'm good at exams, cramming suits me as I have strong recall of what I've recently read or heard and can often regurgitate them word for word

There's no point in worrying, so I decide to hitchhike to Amsterdam to see the Rembrandts and modern art at the Rijksmuseum and the Stedelijk, and go to a coffee shop, not necessarily in that order. But I'll need some cash to do this and I'm not asking my parents to front me, they're hard up as it is.

Asking around, a friend's father with management juice at the Mother's Pride Bakery in west London, close to London (later Heathrow) Airport, swings employment for me and his son working nights, Sunday to Friday, loading delivery vans with mass-market bread baked onsite.* We clock on at 8 p.m. and off around 6 a.m.

We're the only white guys here, the others all young men recently come to the UK from Pakistan, a friendly bunch but with skinny language skills. The foreman's basic English is good enough to tell us what to do. It's not complicated. A conveyor belt feeds new-baked loaves from the ovens on to a carousel to be picked up by hand and plonked into relevant branded plastic sleeves. The blokes who do this don't wear gloves or hairnets, or ever seem to wash their hands,

---

* The factory follows the Chorleywood process, a method of making industrial quantities of cheap bread with a long shelf life using hard fats and chemicals to make the loaves that are soft and pappy. I grew up eating this junk. Around a third of the ultra-processed bread bought in the UK – 680,000 tonnes – is thrown away every year.

which means the bread could be bug central and I vow never to eat white sliced bread again. Me and my mate load the wrapped loaves on to wheeled racks and roll them over to parked delivery vans in the loading bay; each van has a pick list and we load them up accordingly. Simple.

Thursday night, the foreman says, 'Work fast, OK? Special Tea at two, OK?'

'What's Special Tea?' we ask.

'Work fast, two a.m., OK!' he says. 'All finish work by two, OK.'

Everyone runs around like mice on meth to get the work done double quick so by 2 a.m., we're all sitting in the tearoom, shielding our eyes from the retina-scouring fluorescent lighting at scabby benches piled with Punjabi papers. The foreman, stood next to a steaming samovar, announces, 'Tea up! Poppy!'

Opium tea! A first for me and an unheard of work perk, a top-notch pick-me-down early in the morning with nothing but rosy-fingered dawn to look forward to.

As we slurp from our mugs, the foreman says, 'Find van, lie down, OK! *Nimble* good pillow OK!'

I bed down in the back of a delivery van between the bread racks as the poppy tea thrills my endorphins, head resting on a plump *Nimble* loaf, sound advice from the foreman. *Nimble* is a *super-aerated* slimmer's loaf, air is its USP, marketed to help weight reduction: 'Only forty calories a slice!', an image of a tape measure around the circular loaf. Of course, slimmers could just inhale more deeply – it's probably just as nutritious, I think, dreaming away, my brain full of the earworm classic by Honeybus, 'I Can't Let Maggie Go', the music to a TV commercial that shows a sexy mini-skirted babe chomping a slice while dangling from a branded Nimble hot-air balloon in the Alps. When the pillow loaf's as flat as a chapatti, I swap it for a new one – 'Real bread but lighter!' – and squish three more before I'm back in the grey world of work at 4 a.m., like the rest of the blitzed shelf-stackers and bakers. We all slope off early to avoid the van drivers who'll complain of flattened loaves, a supply-chain SNAFU that management can't get to the bottom of. Work's better than I expected!

After a month's work, I hitchhike to Amsterdam where I have a fine time. I pass my GCEs with good grades and am accepted into the school's sixth form in September 1971.

Postscript

This would have been the perfect London-wide drug distribution set-up, only a road away from Thiefrow Airport, then notorious for crime, drug imports, and luggage theft. Its insecure wire-mesh perimeter fences and lax security will have made it easy to move gear from runway to pavement. But who knows? Things were simpler then. The bread factory was demolished and a McDonald's stands on its site.

THE ART-ROOM BOYS

At seventeen, I meet Mark White, later Mekons singer and lyricist, and Andy Gill, Gang of Four guitarist-to-be, both in the year below me at school, and taking Art A level. Until the sixth form, no one would *dream* of hanging out with a boy in the lower years, it would rupture all social norms, and this is the first time boys call each other by their Christian names. Andy is fifty–fifty called *Gill*. I already knew my old friend Kevin's first name so no changes there, while Paul Greengrass who's also in my Art A-level year group isn't Paul but *Greengrass*. He'll become famous as the director of the *Bourne* movies, *United 93*, *Captain Phillips*, etc. Adam Curtis floats in and out although I'm not sure why. He's very clever, and will become famous for his brilliant BBC documentaries like *Pandora's Box** and *The Century of the Self*. We're a competitive bunch, forever sniffing out new things to put our snouts in.

Mark White is Bob's son, good at painting and drawing, determined to become an artist. We talk about art and politics a lot and bond fast, so I suggest he joins Kevin and me at the Crown pub on Saturday nights. He's under the legal drinking age, but so are we and say Alex the landlord doesn't give a monkey's, but Mark says his father won't let him go. I think this is harsh, so I talk to Bob, who

---

* Gill and I will write the title music to this BAFTA-award-winning series.

encourages mature conversation, and say, 'I know you're his father and that, but maybe you're being *over-restrictive* for Mark, he needs to *spread his wings*, he's *sixteen* now,' etc., etc. Bob mulls it over and says, 'OK, but *you've* got to look after him when you're out together.'

Me? Fuck's sake, not my intention at all! But I agree to act *in loco parentis* – a challenge as I'm not a caring person – and decide the best way for Mark to *find himself* is to let him do whatever he likes. The right way to manage teenagers, I think.

He drives to the pub on his beat-up Lambretta, and I give excellent advice: Don't Drive Fast Drunk, which doesn't make a memorable acronym. He forgets this and will drop the scooter a lot, as I do my Honda 50, regularly sliding into roadside ditches and hedges, but nothing serious.

At first, I wonder why Andy's doing Art at all, as he's no good at drawing or painting, but see he's a gifted silkscreen printer and loves anything involving processes or systematic work. He makes fine images of Plains Indians derived from Edward Curtis's mournful photographs and is righteously angry about the murderous European immigrants' settler colonisation extermination of the indigenous peoples of America. He treasures *Bury My Heart At Wounded Knee*, one of the very few non-course work books I'll ever see him read.

He and I are very different, yin and yang, whatever he is I'm not and vice versa; I'm impulsive and he's orderly, I read all the time and him not at all. But despite this we're a good team and become best friends, making each other laugh and sharing the same tastes in music.

He invites me to his house where he lives with his mum, Sylvia, a divorced teacher, to hear the Band's magnum opus *Music from the Big Pink*. The house is a post-war semi-detached in a glum suburb of stodgy Sevenoaks, with its manicured privet hedges, well-waxed company cars, and the occasional patch of elephant grass on the front lawn, a sure sign, I'm told, of suburban swingers advertising their left-field appetites. I don't think Mrs Gill would ever lob her car keys in a bowl for transgressive nookie, she'd be too busy hoovering, bleaching and washing dishes. She carries on like Hattie Jacques in *Carry On Nurse*, always *doing* something, and goes ballistic when Andy doodles in pencil on the tabletop, which he must do just to annoy her.

Gill explains the marital split and says, 'Parents split up when Dad had an affair or something, I dunno.'

I once meet Gill's father, Stanley, who's a lecturer in something or other, and find it hard to believe he was a love rat: not a looker, anally retentive, drinks a lot and loves fishing, not necessarily in that order; not much of a *catch*. Andy shows me a story about angling that his dad wrote, a fishy tussle climaxing in a money shot of the author cradling a silver, moist and palpating creature in his arms that's gasping for life. I say, 'Hmm, it's a bit pervy, isn't it?' and Andy says, 'Yeah, too right!'

Andy says, 'It's a *nightmare* when a girl comes round, even just a friend and not a *girlfriend*. Mum insists my bedroom door's wide open, forever nipping up the stairs so no *petting's* taking place or shouting An-DREEEW! from the hallway to put me off or telling me to take the bins out or whatever.'

I say, 'Can't you just get off with someone somewhere else?' but Gill says, 'Where? It's always wet out and I don't have a car.'

Sad but true, a backseat's a must for teenage how's-your-father.

'Your mum's probably sexually frustrated,' I say. 'That's why she's always fussing about. Her sex-drive's expressed in tennis and tidying up.

Gill says the idea of her *at it* puts him off his nosh. 'It's not nice, leave it out.'

Mrs Gill says Andy was a sickly child who nearly died from a severe asthma attack, which he suffers badly from, which explains why he's whippet thin with spindly legs, leading to his school nickname of

'Stickman'. He doesn't do sports, and we joke he should have 'Off games' written permanently on his forehead. Instead, he joins the school army cadet corps for a while and is such a crack shot on a .310 Cadet rifle that a military talent spotter talks to him about joining up and becoming a sniper. The army's a fine career, but Andy passes on the offer. He'd have been very good, but I'm glad he'll focus instead on bar billiards, fussball and pool that we both like to play.

Too young to drive a car, Gill has a moped that's legal to drive solo at sixteen without passing the test. It's in poor shape and the headlamp's blown, so rather than buy a bulb he tapes a torch to the handlebar, which throws an illegal weedy light. Since he doesn't want to pay the road tax – he's tight with money, last to buy a round – he hand-paints a copy of a tax disc, as delicate as an Elizabethan miniature, and sellotapes it to the bike. It's not bad, but when he's pulled over by a traffic cop who's spotted the illegal flashlight, the policeman sees the pathetic forgery, bursts out laughing, and says, 'Just fuck off home! I'll nick you if I see you again.' Gill gives in and pays for tax and a lightbulb.

We write a few comic songs together, the first we'll do, Andy strumming on acoustic guitar and me singing and writing the words. We play them at a church hall dance as the Bourgeois Brothers, our first time on stage. We enjoy the attention and hope girls will admire our panache. They don't. But it's a start.

MOVING ON

Back row: Paul Greengrass, Pete Cannon.
Front row: Kevin Lycett, me.

I want to go to Art College and make a life as an artist as I love drawing and painting. Bob White encourages me to do the best I can, questions my jejune ideas, tells me to take artistic risks, never sit back. Alongside practical work, I'm constantly reading art history, seminal texts like Berger's *Ways of Seeing*, Gombrich's *The Story of Art* or Vasari's *Lives of the Artists*. Whenever I can, I go to the National Gallery or the Tate or the Courtauld, although mostly in the holidays as I'm at school six days a week. Bob notices my interest in art history and suggests I think about taking a Fine Art degree at a university rather than art college and says the same to Kevin. He points us to new combined practical and academic courses on offer. I hadn't thought of this as an option, and it excites me. Two courses stand out: Newcastle University's Fine Art Department headed by the famous British Pop artist Richard Hamilton, or Leeds University, headed by Professor Lawrence Gowing, a globally eminent academic, establishment figure, and accomplished painter within the Euston Road Group of artists. My A level grades are good so I apply to both, taking a year out between school and university – assuming I'll be offered a place – to get a portfolio together, earn some cash and hitchhike to Spain.

In the autumn, at the start of a new school year, Bob swings Kevin and me three months for free at our school that would normally cost fee-payers thousands. We're either, I think, considered by the school to be Oxbridge candidates being prepped for the entry exams, or as classroom teaching assistants. While we're still in principle supposed to wear a grey suit and tie, I don't, and arrive at school each day wearing instead a navy-blue wool donkey jacket with leather shoulder yoke – super cool, I think – over a white T-shirt, 501s and monkey boots. Kevin and I supervise occasional entry-level classes for eleven- and twelve-year-olds in exchange for free materials and the use of silkscreens and the photographic dark rooms. This allows us to get a portfolio together in three months and avoid the year-long pre-diploma course usually needed to take a Fine Art degree.

Dad wonders why I'm back at school after A levels; shouldn't I find a job? He's concerned I might go to an *art college*, full of scruffy layabouts who are always making trouble and won't ever get a proper job with *prospects*. This is of course true, but prospects are overrated in my book, and being a scruffy layabout is right up my *strasse. C'est moi!*

I explain I'm thinking about going to a university, which he likes the idea of and sounds like a step up the social ladder. I'm in a Boomer cohort that will see social mobility of scale for the first time in our fossilised society, and I'll be the first person in my family to go through further education – only 14 per cent of school leavers take a degree at this time, and a disproportionate percentage of these are from public, er, *private* schools. I won't have to get my hands dirty, although I've always got paint or ink under my fingernails, which doesn't count.

Tuition's free and a government grant will cover my living costs. In this topsy-turvy world designed by the rich, the taxes paid by the majority of lower income people who don't go to university pay for the education of the minority of well-off middle- and upper–middle-class kids who do.

Dad has no interest in art or culture and never sets foot in a gallery, but says OK, and since he doesn't earn big bucks I'll get the maximum student grant of £495 – £6,465 in 2024 values!

Kevin and I need to show work that covers the territory of a one-year art foundation course in an art college, covering drawing, painting, understanding of methods and materials, silkscreen printing, etc., and *life drawing*, but this can't be done at school. Prudish parents objected when it was mooted, I assume because they thought teenage boys could be morally corrupted by looking at naked human beings, so life classes are *verboten*. They should sit in on one, a pencil or brush in hand staring at crinkly geezers with love handles and turkey-neck ballbags or droopy-breasted women with creases and stretch marks. While it may be true that some eighteen-year-old boys may not have seen a female in the buff, poor bastards, a life class is a reality check on what time will do to us all. Sadly, the models look more like Ena Sharples or Charlie Drake than Julie Christie or Paul Newman. It could put you off leg-over for life, or at least after forty, when getting your end away ends anyway.

Kevin and I devise a DIY plan: once a week he, Jenny, Gill and I take turns to pose nude for the others to draw in my bedroom. It's a good system that's entirely chaste and Bob's impressed by our commitment. Our portfolios are complete!

UNIVERSITY

Studying Fine Art in Newcastle is my first choice because:

A: The city has fantastic architecture, a large student population, and Geordie boys and girls contemptuous of ice and rain and up for the craic who strip off their shirts or sport skirts as thin as string.
B: It's far from home in the gorgeous northeast of England where glooming castles lurk on every hillside overlooking windswept romantic beaches, peopled by locals with a mellifluous accent.
C: The Fine Art Department's headed by Richard Hamilton, the great British Pop artist and Marcel Duchamp aficionado who'd reconstructed Duchamp's *Large Glass* to make a perfect replica of a key work by an artist I'm obsessed with. Duchamp is the scallywag who'd exhibited an upside-down urinal in 1915, named it *Fountain*, and signed it R. Mutt, thus making it *art*, to huge public disgust and criticism that echoes through time. A masterstroke. He'd also renamed the *Mona Lisa* by scrawling 'L.H.O.O.Q.' on a cheap print, and appropriating it as his own. L.H.O.O.Q. spoken in French sounds like '*Elle a chaud au cul*', which translates as 'She has a hot arse', a gag that hovers between clever and silly. It informed conceptual art

from then on and prefigured the 1960s Situationists. My kind of thing.

When I'm interviewed there, the tutors say they love my work and my attitude and offer me a place on the spot. I send a telegram* to my girlfriend Debbie to share the good news.

Leeds University makes an unconditional offer of a place without an interview, but suggests I come up for a *chemistry* meeting. I'm minded not to go, as Newcastle has fired me up, but Bob says it would bad form not to show up as Sir Lawrence Gowing himself will meet me. It's quite a compliment, he's a remarkable man, a brilliant academic, a fine painter, and the world's leading authority on Vermeer and Cézanne, two of the greatest ever artists to use a paint brush. So, I go to Leeds, where the department secretary informs me that the great man has a profound speech impediment which may require patience but *never* sympathy.† Well prepared, I'm ushered into his office where a lanky, bespectacled man greets me and wafts me to a wingback chair before a book-burdened desk.

He says, 'SO, you must be [BEAT] b-beh beh [BEAT] be JONATHAN!' and a huge dollop of flob shoots on to the table, PLOP!, which he smears away with a leather-elbowed sleeve, insouciant, the spit shining like a snail's trail across the leather top. 'Weh, would you like a SHERRY?' he says, handing me a delicious *Oloroso tradición*.

---

* Readers under fifty can find out what this is on Wikipedia.
† Lawrence had an appetite for medieval woodcut porn, effusive about the dirty pictures once shared across Europe of a naked Aristotle harnessed and ridden by a nun – the first mass media content to be read one-handed which cheap printing had made possible. Off campus, Gowing persuaded fit female students to strip off and roll around on canvases covered in paint, à la Yves Klein, in the name of *Kunst*, but I don't think inappropriate touching or happy endings were involved. He apparently just liked to watch, but this is hearsay. He wouldn't get away with this now and shouldn't have then. Different times.

'Of course!' I say.

We talk art, the state of the nation, an hour rushes by, he's utterly charming, I love him already! I say no to Newcastle and choose Leeds. Kevin has a similar experience, minus the dribble, and decides to come to Leeds as well, and he and I will room together in our first year.

LEEDS

Mid-70s Leeds slum. *(Photo: Leeds Libraries)*

Stick out a thumb at the M1 slip road in north London, and you'll fast find a ride to Leeds at the motorway's end. You'll arrive sooner than a smoke-filled and oxygen-starved coach from Victoria station full of hyper infants and over-sharing depressives who'll insist on telling you how life's rich tapestry is no more than a stained toilet mat. Hitching also carries the risk of misery memoirs from lonely drivers who may spill stories of infidelity, chronic illness, and career doldrums, but hearing this stuff is a small price to pay for having no price to pay.

After four hours, you'll arrive in an *echt* northern city struggling with decline, unemployment and dereliction, and you may see as you drive by the grim blocks of flats where Mekon Mark White once lived, which he alleges was where *A Clockwork Orange* was shot. It wasn't.

A ring road is under construction that will sever the architecturally award-winning university campus from the city centre, and thousands of back-to-back terraced homes unfit to live in have been demolished, creating acres of wasteland, with many more queuing up for oblivion. Abandoned warehouses cluster around the noisome Leeds and Liverpool Canal, pregnant with shopping trollies and rusty pushbikes in its polluted waters still dotted with pillboxes and concrete blockhouses from the Second World War. The Leeds police are bent and incompetent, this has been a home for fascist extremism since the thirties, and the city hosts a notorious football hooligan crew which follows the Damned United, the dirtiest team in England.

But it's also a fun town with a massive student population in its top-ranked university, polytechnic, music college and medical school, and the best place to see rock and pop concerts in Britain. Touring national drama, dance, and opera companies can be seen at the famous Leeds City Varieties, home of The Good Old Days. And although the shitty, soot-blackened two-up, two-down houses are damp, dirty, and due for destruction, they're dirt cheap to rent.

Leeds ticks all the boxes, it's the place for me.

WHERE IS AMERICA?

(Photo: Tim Hartley)

Having accepted the offer from Leeds, I'm mulling over what to do before going up to university on my year off when I'm sent a letter from the friend I shared a tragic mid-teen girlfriend with, who I haven't seen since her death.

Tim writes he's working in Buffalo, New York, USA, so he can be near a serious girlfriend whose family relocated to Oklahoma City from the UK, as her dad's a player in the oil biz. However, he only realised that New York state and Oklahoma are 1,200 miles apart when he got there, so he's only seen her once, like moving to London because your significant other lives in North Africa – what a dimwit! He can't move to Okie territory because his US work permit is linked to a crappy trainee sales rep job for a frozen seafood franchise that supplies restaurants in upstate New York, and wonders would I like to come over and stay for a bit?

Going to Buffalo, New York, sounds wonderful as I've always wanted to see Manhattan's skyscrapers and Central Park and go to MoMA and the Frick and eat pizza slices and all the rest. I write to say I'll come as soon as I've earned enough to buy a ticket. I'm the only person in my family with a passport and will be the first to ride on an airplane, a thrilling prospect, and the first to go to NEW YORK! I plan to drop by the Arensberg collection in Philadelphia – surely just down the road – and see the greatest body of Duchamp's work in the world! What's not to like?

I land a job at Otford Paper Sacks – it's a factory in the village of *Otford* which makes *paper sacks* – where I'm a charge-hand who checks the stitching on sacks sewn by the *girls* – all women, whatever their age, are called girls – who sit lined up in rows like supermarket checkouts at huge industrial sewing machines, stitching the ends of dustbin-sized brown paper sacks as they're fed from a conveyor. I riffle through bundles of fifty sacks as quality control to make sure the stitching's not on the piss. That's it. I'm a competent riffler, time flies fast, and in a couple of months I'll earn enough to fund a US adventure.

The foreman, Ted, is a twat who shouts a lot and waves his arms about. He'll have a coronary if he carries on like this, I think, and, Jesus, how can you get aerated about *paper sacks*? We start work at 7 a.m., when we push a cardboard card into a clock machine which punches a hole in it with the exact time so wages can be calculated: if we're more than five minutes late, fifteen minutes' pay is docked.

One day, after weeks of apocalyptic rain, the river in the nearby field breaks its banks and the valley runs deep with flood water that laps at the factory gates. Although the access road's a foot under and cars and buses can't get through, I manage to slosh in on my plucky little Honda but punch in six minutes late, slowed down by the deluge.

I'm sitting in the tearoom, reading about the Arsenal in the *Mirror*, when Ted storms in and says, 'The FUCK you DOING?' His BPM's up to 180, he'll bust a blood vessel at this rate.

'Reading,' I say. 'I'm not paid till quarter past so I'm staying put till then.'

Ted says, 'Get the FUCK in the FACTORY! You're the only cunt here!'

'No,' I say, 'unless I'm paid, I'm not moving until *exactly* fifteen minutes past.'

This I do, mooching about on my Jack Jones in the deserted factory, no riffling to be done until the *girls* drift in hours later. Ted's, I think, a little embarrassed by his harsh words, and perhaps realised I'd heroically fought to get in where others pussied out. At day's end, he says, 'Want any overtime?' The juicy largesse of time-and-a-half OT is in his gift.

I say sure, and Ted tells me to watch a conveyor belt as the sacks come in. So I sit and watch newly made sacks belch from a machine on to a conveyor belt on which they run until they spill off at its end into a pile in front of me. A hour on, it's quite a heap, towering over me.

'WHAT,' Ted says, 'the FUCK you DOING?'

'Watching the conveyor,' I say, 'like you said.'

'You CUNT! You're the only cunt here! You're meant to pick up the sacks and put them on a pallet!'

'You should have said! And I'm not the *only* cunt here!'

I expect to be fired the next day. But I'm not and a week later Ted offers me a full-time job as his number two. I'm a man after his own heart and have won his respect using the C word. But I say, 'Fuck off, I'm off to America!'

All I know about US geography is that New York's on the right-hand side and Los Angeles is on the left, and nothing at all about what's in-between. I had no idea that New York *City* – which I think is just sky-scraping Manhattan – is in New York *State*, somewhere as big as Britain. I didn't once look at a map, thinking Buffalo, New York, was like Peckham, London, a borough in the Big Apple.

Uh, it's not. Buffalo is 380 miles away from Manhattan, as far as Edinburgh is from London. I land at JFK and am spewed out into its heat and humidity and hustle and noise and I don't know what to do. I'm shocked seeing handguns for the first time, the low-hanging fruit swinging under the fat guts of sweaty Gotham cops chewing gum while they watch the world go by. It's a world away from Dixon of Dock Green, who'll give you a thick ear with a cheery smile; these killers would shoot me in the gut just to watch me die.

I collar a porter and ask, 'Where can I catch the bus to Buffalo?' and he says, 'Whoo-wee! Man, you not from here, are you?' and shakes his head. I'm obviously an idiot. 'You ain't nowhere you want to be, anyhow.'

He points me to an information desk where I'm told to get on a flight to Buffalo airport, many miles away, a ticket that chews up a third of my money.

Tim picks me up and says nothing. Two dimwits in one car.

He rents a two-bed maisonette in a scuzzy part of Buffalo – 'It's nasty but cheap,' he says, 'and the good news is the mafia are all over the district and launder money through the local supermarket, so it's never held up, super safe, why everyone shops there. It's the upside of organised crime, don't knock it.'

The shop isn't stuck up while I'm here, unlike everywhere else from gas stations to diners to mom-and-pop stores. The local TV news is a miserable litany of violent crimes, so maybe having Wise Guy owners isn't so bad. Although it is.

We have a wild time driving slowly around in his deep-burbling 4.6 litre V8 Chevy Impala, landing in bars where we drink pitcher after pitcher of ersatz beer that's taste free and barely alcoholic. His friends love my exotic accent, thinking I'm posh and must know the queen and everyone in London, asking me to say 'Water' over and over, my southern English long 'A' impossible for them to imitate. I dial through radio stations while we drive, wall-to-wall music from dozens of stations cut with unctuously voiced ads for cars and food and pest control. I love it all. We've only had commercial radio in the UK for six months which is so restrained and petit bourgeois in comparison.

At Tim's gaff, I struggle to sustain attention on the plots of my favourite shows *Star Trek* and *Kung Fu* because shitty commercials break up the episodes every nanosecond, with slogans like 'You Don't Have to Die to Collect' (life insurance) and 'My bologna has a first name, it's O-S-C-A-R' (hotdogs). I think this is how things will be, everywhere, soon and I will be right.

I'm in the Chevy with a pair of Tim's local buddies and working the radio dial when I'm excited to hear the Supremes' 'Stop! In the Name of Love', and turn it up to the max.

'Get that n----- shit off!' says one of the boys, punching the radio presets to retune to an album-oriented radio station playing Maria Muldaur's 'Midnight at the Oasis' – music that's played in hell – segued into a redneck country track.

I'm shocked: what's with these arseholes? It's the first time I've heard the N-word spoken, I've never heard racist shit like this at home or school or met anyone who talks like this and only seen the word in *Huckleberry Finn*. I can't believe Tim's chummy with these scumbags. They're slagging off the people who invented every type of music that thrills and delights me and the world outside, bebop, the blues, jazz, rock 'n' roll, *everything* that white music's built on, teetering on the shoulders of giants like Robert Johnson, Bessie Smith James Brown, Billie Holiday, Little Richard, and Miles etc., etc.! Preferring *Maria Muldaur* over *Motown* is *insane*. What was the US Civil War all about anyway if not to be free to enjoy 'Get Up (I Feel Like Being a) Sex Machine'? Are they slaver confederates in disguise? After dropping them off, I tell Tim I never want to see these creepy racists again.

I want to see all I can while I'm here and go to Niagara Falls, only forty-five minutes away, like all tourists do. Since the best side of the falls is in Canada – the US falls are a weedy dribble compared to the massive and majestic flood of water in Canada – I drive up after seeing them to Toronto, a cool city in a much less violent land which has spawned Leonard Cohen, Joni Mitchell, the Band, and Neil Young, musicians who perfectly understand and reflect back to America its dreams and imagined past(s): no wonder some Yanks patronise the Canucks, they must be jealous.

My days are spent at Buffalo's fine Albright-Knox modern art gallery, while Tim's schlepping seafood. But having run out of things to do here I talk Tim into motoring down to Washington, DC.

The drive's crazy. Following October 1973's total ban by OPEC on oil sales to any country supporting Israel in the Fourth Arab–Israeli War, the price of petrol has doubled in a year, with gas stations running out of fuel or rationing it and traffic cops everywhere pulling over cars busting the fuel-saving 55 mph speed limit just introduced by the federal government. Like most locals, Tim ignores the speed cap and guns the Impala at a hundred miles an hour down to the capital, lucking out by filling up a thirsty road boat that does only eighteen miles per gallon, and somehow not getting ticketed.*

Family friends of his parents put us up in DC, a wealthy white couple living outside the Beltway that circles Washington. White and Black people live apart, it's a doughnut city with an empty heart, the majority African American population housed in neglected residential districts outside the administrative and museum centre, with its luxury hotels, the White House, and tourist must-sees. While the core's humming in daylight with legions of white government drones hurrying about, it falls quiet in the evenings as the salariat flees to Caucasian exurbs, the silence busted by the sound of cop car sirens as police race to an atrocity in the darkness. I don't warm to this widowed place, but there are world-class museums and galleries and I can walk its centre checking off the white-stone monuments.

Tim has to return to Buffalo to boost crab legs and lobster tails, so we make our goodbyes when he drops me on a slip road to the highway, the last time I'll see him, we lose all touch. I hitch a ride north to Philadelphia where a friend of a friend of a friend puts me up.

My host is disturbing, a National Guardsman to the right of Genghis Khan who shows me an armoury, racks of well-oiled long guns, shotguns, and pistols; shelves of body armour and metal ammunition crates. He says you gotta be *prepared* for the next one, but is the next one a new 'Nam – the old Vietnam's still grinding on, a couple years more illegal bombing of Cambodia to go before the

---

* We did things differently in the UK. The roads are so shitty, and there are so few motorways, that a 55 mph speed limit would seem like a petrolhead's dream. Late in 1973, drivers in the UK are issued with petrol ration books with tear-off coupons entitling drivers to buy fuel. I was only able to buy a half gallon of petrol a week, the allowance for a motorcycle up to 250 cc. On a Honda 50, that would take you halfway round the world.

Yanks pull out – or is it teargassing college students and yippie demonstrators? Despite being a hard-right gun-nut, he's super generous, giving me a bed, feeding and watering me, a complete stranger. I stay two nights with him, in the days making pilgrimages to the Philadelphia Museum of Art's collection of Duchamp's work. My host insists on picking up the tab for all food and drink, which is handy as I've almost run out of cash and have only enough for a couple of nights in a cheap Village flop and the airport bus to JFK, with a flight home in three days' time.

He takes me to a I-95 feeder road where I cop a ride north to the Big Apple and am dropped, brilliantly, in Greenwich Village. I go to the 14th Street YMCA for a room, but the receptionist looks me up and down, shakes his head, and wags his index finger, saying 'Nooo, I don't think this place is for *you* ...' I find a room at the famous Chelsea Hotel, burning all the bucks I have left bar the airport shuttle bus fare and a dollar for a pizza triangle, my favourite street food. Starving's a small price to pay to be where almost everyone who's been a player in the creative arts has stayed: Hendrix, Nico, Warhol, Stanley Kubrick, Jefferson Airplane. This is where Dylan wrote 'Sad Eyed Lady of the Lowlands' and where Leonard Cohen was blown by Janis Joplin and bragged about it in 'Chelsea Hotel No. 2'. Four years from now, Nancy Spungen will be murdered here by Sid Vicious.

I'm not going to be a wuss and beg Mum and Dad for a cash transfer to a Western Union, it would be pathetic, and the call itself would cost a bagful of quarters I don't have. So, for the next two days all I eat is a slice of pizza and sachets of complimentary creamer that's supplied with in-room instant coffee. I don't care, Manhattan's wonderful to walk and see the sights from street level: the perma-honking gridlocked traffic, yellow cabs, steaming subway vents, fat cops whistling at jaywalkers, the Metropolitan Museum, galleries if they're free to enter, Central Park, Times Square's hustlers, hookers and hobos, the skyscrapers and everything.

My last day, I bus early to JFK for an afternoon plane to London, but the flight's cancelled, an airline stooge saying there's been a hijack or something. I'm not bothered as I'm given a voucher for food that I scoff like a starveling and am overnight roomed in a terminal hotel where I bliss out in crisp cotton sheets with an all-you-can-eat breakfast thrown in, FOC.

Flying home, I say to myself: *Je reviens.*

BRICKS

Me and Andy Gill.

Back in Britain, Gill and I decide to hitch through France to stay at my girlfriend Debbie's family house in Catalonia, where she'll be most of the summer. It will be a last long break before going up to Leeds in October 1974 to start my Fine Art degree course.

I need money to do this and get a job as a labourer in a Brickworks in the next village over, Seal. Invisible from the road, it's a nineteen-acre industrial complex surrounded by arable fields and bungalow houses with an access road logjammed in the mornings with flatbed brick trucks queuing for a load. A gloomy factory sits in the centre whose production machinery is powered by a pre-WWI engine with a great iron wheel that drives flappy overhead conveyor belts that shuttle sand and clay to the brick press. Mock-Tudor management offices with pretty pots of red geraniums are nearby, and a distance away lie deep steep-sided quarries. There, a huge excavator on a railway track scrapes away tons of sticky clay that pours on to a half-a-mile-long conveyor belt to the factory, where it's mixed with sand and moulded into a brick shape. The nearby fields are filled with a million or more blocks of bricks stacked in corridors up to fourteen-feet high, waiting for a home.

My first day, I clock in at 6 a.m. and present myself to the foreman, George.

'Well,' he says, 'you the student then?'

I say, 'Yeah, what do you want me to do?'

'Well, there's nothing to do, so hide up till break. Off you fuck then!'

It's a big site, mud everywhere, decaying outbuildings, rusting machinery abandoned in long grass verges, diggers and forklifts and conveyor belts and sand hoppers all over, so I soon find somewhere out of the way to skulk in and shelter from the mizzle.

At the noon break I sit at a bench in the smoky tearoom and munch on a cheese sandwich while the men smoke scrawny rollups or suck on stinky pipes of Ogden's Flake – made famous by the Small Faces – and complain about their bones and their waterworks and their wives and their dogs.

One is crunching through a raw onion and says he never gets a cough or a cold – no surprise as his halitosis would zap any microbe and no one dares sit close enough for a virus to infect him – and says to me, apropos of nothing, 'How's chunky?'

Obviously it's a knock-knock kind of joke, so I say, 'Who's chunky?'

'The man with pineapple bollocks!' he says and explodes in laughter.

No one else cracks a smile; they've heard it before, and it's not funny anyway. Old men are really annoying.

Onion man was a farmworker for decades until he was made redundant and turfed out of the tied cottage he'd lived in all that time. He says he had to shoot his two collie dogs; they went bonkers with no sheep to boss.

I change the subject and say the countryside here's beautiful and he says, 'Fuck off! No better than this fuckin' filthy factory. You try living off the soil you can't never own, bowing and scraping before money-grubbing landed cunts throwing working men in the gutter and flogging off their homes as weekend fuckpads for Londoners!'

Whoa! I was just admiring the view! But I catch his drift.

A half an hour later we clock back on – *punchcards* ensure strict timekeeping – and I ask the foreman what he'd like me to do in the afternoon.

'Well,' he says, 'as I said, there's *nothing* to do, so hide up till we clock off. Off you fuck!'

Day two's the same. It's excruciating, there's *nothing* to do.

'Don't bring in no book,' says George, 'because if management catches you *reading*, it'll prove there's nothing to do, which is true enough, but you're only here because there's a union agreement that says there must be *cover* in the holiday period for the full-time employed men with nothing to do. This agreement falls, jobs will go, so fuck right off and hide up till the shift ends!'

I sit on a crate in a shed away from the works and watch the rain fall. The seconds drag by like hours, the hours are like days, the dog day drags on and on and on. I can't stand it, I'll have to pack it in, though I'm desperate for cash. On day three, I beg George to give me a job, *anything*, I'm so bored. He thinks for a bit and hands me a broom, saying. 'Sweep up, then.'

This is good, it'll kill time. The grimy factory could do with a brush-up; dirt and grime caking every surface, the air flecked with dust, which dances in the darkness while a constant rain of sharp sand sprinkles down from an overhead conveyor belt, like a gloomy Piranesi print.

I'm doing well with the broom, I think, when George comes over, well pissed off, and says, 'The fuck you doing?'

'Uh, sweeping up, like you said.'

He looks at me with the stink eye and says, very slowly, 'We. Don't. Get. Paid. Enough. To. Work. Hard. Sofuckingslowthefuckdown!'

I go into slo-mo mode and when we clock off I've tidied an area about the size of a walk-in fridge in a building the size of St Paul's Cathedral, like a work of conceptual art.

Next day, I plead for more to do, I'm going mad. George sighs and says, 'OK, you can see the sand come in.'

This is a prestige job, much coveted, which involves watching a lorry dump sand into a hopper having pressed a big red button that starts a motor, which makes the skip shake so sand drops evenly on to a conveyor belt to be trundled away to the factory and mixed with clay to make bricks. When the hopper's empty, I press the button again. This is a great gig that suits my skillset. I can legitimately sit in the sun *and* read the *Sun* while the sand dribbles down, and don't have to hide in a mouldy hut out of sight of management. Sadly, sand's only delivered once a day, and everyone wants to watch it.

Next day, fortune smiles on me. I'm asked to cover for someone who hasn't come in and actually *does* something, rather than replacing someone with nothing to do. This means moving thousands of bricks by hand.

Massive mausoleums of bricks, the size of a basketball court and as high as a pyramid, stand near the quarries. Each stack is made up of a yard-deep layer of charcoal over which has been laid, by hand, layer upon layer of wet newborn bricks stamped into form in the factory, their indented frogs crisp and sharp and even. A hundred thousand or more bricks are carefully arranged until the heap is capped off. The charcoal's then set on fire and burns slowly through the base of the stack, the flame taking up to a year to run through and months to fizzle out, baking the bricks as hard as ... bricks. After twelve months, the stacks have cooled enough for the bricks to be taken out and sorted. The outer bricks, exposed to the elements, are crumbly and weak and only good for hardcore. A yard into the stack, a stratum of standard bricks is revealed, evenly coloured red, good for building, and closer to the core are seams of gorgeous multi-coloured 'firsts', burned red, blue, orange and gold, the highest grade beloved by hip architects and heritage home owners. The central core, where the heat was intense, can be too hot to touch after two years and reveals glassy, flintlike lumps as hard as granite, cooked coal-black and Prussian blue, which have been deformed by the inferno and will be laid in suburban garden walls.

My job is to fill a wheeled trolley with wet bricks belched from the factory's stamping press and push the load along steel tracks to a stack under construction, and then unload them so a new mountain of clay can be built and cooked on a high heat. I sometimes lay them out, too, which is very satisfying – I can see why Carl Andre likes them – or I might have to dig out and sort fresh-roasted bricks from the side of a stack stepped like a ziggurat, placing still-warm bricks one by one on to a wheeled pallet, which I push away to wherever. Every single brick is handled at least four times before baking, and a couple more times after, before being sold or stored.

This is a labour-intensive production method that has hardly changed since Roman times, but which won't see out the century, the firm going bust in 1991.*

* The abandoned brickyard will become a privately owned 'Site of Special Scientific Interest' with a geology packed with fossils, especially ammonites.

Feeling positive at the end of week one, the days going by quickly now, I meet up with Gill in the Crown pub, our weekend meeting place. Alex, the landlord, has a relaxed view of licensing laws and serves booze to anyone out of nappies, despite the law saying eighteen is the drinking age. We don't have to show ID – no one in Britain carries ID – and the bar's heaving with acned teenagers playing table football, flirting and getting hammered, not necessarily in that order.

Gill says, 'Work good?'

'Yeah, you?'

'Got sacked, a bugger.'

Andy's had just one week working at West Kent Cold Storage, a light industrial unit where they freeze and package vegetables for retailers.

'Why's that?' I ask and Gill says, 'Nabbed gobbing in the peas.'

'What?'

'You spit a good blob of flob, it flash-freezes midair into a ball of ice and mixes with the veg. It's great! But got seen doing it and was sacked on the spot.'

'But why do it?' I ask.

'Because *everyone* does it, duh.'

G-R-O-S-S!

Gill needs another paying gig so we can pay our way to Catalonia, and luckily straightaway gets a job in a petrol station as cover for a holidaying pumpista.

Back at the brickyard, I'm put on loading lorries, standing in for a full-timer who'd rather skulk in a shed all day and do nothing while I'm here. I stand on the back of a flatbed with a bloke at ground level who hurls bricks up to me, five at a time, gripped tight together as they fly through the air for me to catch, CLACK!, and lay them out on the truck's floor, two to three thousand bricks per load, twenty thousand or so bricks every day. Since each brick weighs about 4 lbs, I'm catching about 8 to 12,000 lbs every day, and become accidentally ripped. The hours fly by.

One lorry driver is nicknamed Mad Bob; he's twitchy and jittery and nervy, impossible to make small talk with, you can see he's in psychic pain, off with the fairies. After loading his lorry, George tells me when Bob was my age, eighteen, he was in a British Army Royal Artillery unit that liberated the Nazi Bergen-Belsen camp where Jews, Soviet POWs, commies and enemies of the state were tortured, murdered, worked and 'exterminated through labour', *Vernichtung durch Arbeit*. Bob was shattered by the sight of skeletal survivors begging to be fed among thousands of corpses scattered like leaves and piled like twigs. It was the worst thing ever. How could anyone do that to another human being? He never recovered from his nervous breakdown. George says Bob's proper mental, but we have to make allowances for him. I will, too.* My generation's a lucky one.

I load lorries from dawn to noon, with bits and bobs in the afternoons, like shovelling lime from a storage pit knee-deep in the stuff, only a thin cotton mask over mouth and nose as I shovel the powder into sacks, the air thick clouded with lime dust making me as white as an Arctic fox. At the end of an hour doing this I'm given a half pint of milk to wash the lime down my throat. When I ask George if I can take photographs, he says, 'Fuck off. You want us to get shut down?'

By month's end, I've saved forty pounds, all I can take out of the country, as the UK's a financial basket case and the government's currency control bans British citizens taking more abroad. A stamp in the back of my passport shows I've complied.

---

* When liberated, Bergen-Belsen held sixty thousand skeletal prisoners, many on the verge of death from starvation; thirteen thousand corpses lay rotting on the ground.

I check in with Gill who tells me he's been fired from his new job at a petrol station, he'd been stealing money, but they didn't call in the Old Bill, thank fuck, just told him to clear off. I ask if he's saved anything at all, and he says, 'No worries, I nicked enough.'

In a week's time, we set off for Catalonia.

Y VIVA ESPAÑA!

Although Spain's south – I'd checked on a map – we head north to Belgium, not en route at all, to crash at a friend's father's pied-à-terre in Antwerp. We stay there a few days until we've eaten all the stored food, chugged all the Trappist beer, and drunk all the wine, like *The Tiger Who Came to Tea*, but not teetotal like the stripy cat is. When the cupboards are bare, we get a train into France – borders are hard to get a car ride through as drivers worry about hitchers trying to smuggle gear through passport control and customs – and start hitching proper.

Our first hour, no one stops. It's puzzling, it should be easy to pick up a ride, since we both have cropped hair and look like we're doing military service. Old people always stop for conscripts in France as their sons all do time in the armed forces. I notice that drivers slow, look as us quizzically and then speed away, clearly not liking what they see. I turn to see Gill faking weightlifting, arms quivering and shaking high over his head as he struggles under the immense imaginary barbell weights.

'The fuck you doing?' I say.

'Pretending to weightlift,' he says, 'to get attention.'

'Cut it out! People must think you're a nutter. No wonder no one's pulling over.'

He stops and we get a ride in minutes. We're taken via the lovely *route nationale* roads, passing through forests and fields and chocolate-box strip villages that hug the road, never a soul to be seen, enjoying the foreignness of the blue-shuttered houses and fading posters boosting Total, Gauloise and Champagne Billecart. France has the best roads in the world, I think, and a kind mother gives us a ride and buys us a menu-lunch at a Les Routiers truck stop, the best places to eat. Her son's doing his *mili*, she says, and she and I chat as we go, my school French finding a purpose.

At end of our first day, midway down the country, we sleep in a roadside copse, beneath a tree in sleeping bags under a plastic sheet flown over a branch, falling asleep to the trilling drone of cicadas. This is *proper* France. Day two, we're picked up by a hippy couple in a floral-stickered 2CV who take us through dense Dordogne broadleaf forest and farmland until further south we drive through roads framed by queues of plane trees which strobe the light as we pass, a dreamy scent of resin in the air announcing our arrival in a warmer climate, where red-roofed houses are hustled by dome-headed Mediterranean pine trees and Occitan is spoken. The couple share their lunch of crusty bread and cheese with us and drop us near Toulouse where we pick up a ride east to Narbonne and another south to the border town of Perpignan. We buy train tickets to Girona, stopping on the Spanish side of the border to hop tracks onto their broad-gauge trains, watched by gimlet-eyed *Guardia Civiles* sipping brandy and coffee *carajillos*. We arrive at midnight, too late to catch a bus to the coast, so hunker down to sleep on a railway station bench when two *tricornio*-hatted paramilitaries with sub-machine guns grab us. '*Ve! Ve!*' – Go! Go! – they shout, hustling us from the station to the street. We're not welcome here and Franco's fascist goons can't be reasoned with, even if I could speak Spanish.

We've enough pesetas for a taxi to the coast, and endless summer begins.

CROMER TERRACE

Kevin Lycett, Iannis Kourakis and Shelley in the
Cromer Terrace studio.

The first year in Leeds, Kevin and I share a campus room in Cromer Terrace, a cobbled street with triple-storeyed redbrick terraced houses, a short stroll to the university's core and Student Union.

In our communal kitchen we meet two other students who room in the house: a Chinese guy, Hàorán, a post-grad chemist, who's very dour and eats a whole chicken and a bucket of rice every day, and a bleary-eyed stoner, Mike, taking a degree in pharmacy or medicine or whatever, who's moved in with a stash of distilled hash oil that he lines up neatly in 35-mm canisters on the mantelpiece. '*Winning's* all about efficiency,' Mike says, dipping a match in the thick brown gunk and striping a sticky wide line of THC down a Woodbine, 'and *this* saves time skinning up.' He flames up straightaway and hands me the smoke to toke. Whoa! This is *nuclear* shit, it's hard to breathe, the fragrant fumes morphing the house into one big bricks 'n' mortar bong. No wonder he's so fried!

Mike's big idea is that breakfast steals valuable minutes – although I'm not sure what he does in his room, other than wank – so anything that can minimise this theft of time's a winner.

'Look at this!' he says, opening a cupboard drawer lined with greaseproof paper that's filled six inches deep with a couple of gallons of mass batch-cooked porridge oats congealed into a seal-grey slab. 'All you need do now is slice off a chunk, mornings, and Bob's your uncle! Breakfast *est arrivée*! In seconds!'

I pass on the slimy oat doorstop he offers me that looks like a squared-off turd and leave him to memorise Cheech & Chong routines, with 'Dave's Not Here!' being all his baked brain can manage.

A week on, the oat slab in the drawer is fuzzed with a fine fungus and spotted with black mould, probably toxic to all life other than cockroaches.

Mike disappears mid-term and isn't seen again.

ANCIENT ROME

Week one in my first year, there's a social in the Fine Art Department, a fancy-dress party the theme of which is 'Ancient Rome', where we're asked to wear togas, etc. I'm not keen, and won't ever do this again, but I grit my teeth and make an outfit from a sheet. I look pretty good, I think, shows off my fine calves.

Everyone drinks too much cheap wine, and after a while Lawrence Gowing sidles up to me, looks me up and down from head to toe and says, lubriciously, 'You know, even in a skirt, you're so *resolutely* heterosexual.'

GILL LANDS IN LEEDS

Andy Gill.

Andy, a year younger than me, has been given a place in the new intake of Leeds's Fine Art Department, along with Tom Greenhalgh and Mark White, soon both to become Mekons. I've moved out of the room I shared with Kevin, now shacked up with a girlfriend, and living in a shared house in Kelso Road, a residential street not far from the campus. The room next to mine fell free so I bagged it for Gill, who moves in.

Everything has changed on the Fine Art course as Lawrence Gowing has gone, perhaps to persuade girls at the Slade, which he'll now head, to strip off and roll around naked on canvases, like he did here. No wonder Francis Bacon likes him so much. Someone will stand in for Gowing while they look for a replacement.

Gill doesn't mind. He's happy to get away from the South but hasn't looked after himself before. Rebelling against his house-proud mother's perpetual bleaching, wiping, cleaning, polishing, scrubbing and vacuuming, he embraces a seedy modus vivendi that would outrage Mrs Gill, his room an art installation of squalor even Tracey Emin would be freaked by. Litre-sized orange-juice bottles brim-full with urine hug the bedroom walls, the liquid's palette spanning pale yellow, as delicate as vintage Manzanilla, to a disturbing ochre, because Gill can't be arsed to walk the ten yards down the corridor to piss in the communal khazi.

It's impossible to cross the room, as he beds down in a sleeping bag on a mattress in its centre, a triangle of grey wood ash spilling across the carpet on to his bedding from a fireplace where he burns fence posts stolen from a council yard, fresh posts leaning at the side of the mantelpiece. The room reeks with the powerful fishy smell of a dried Chinese croaker he'd stolen during an impulsive breaking-and-entering raid on a flat for food, but which is never eaten as it's so smelly. The stench and lack of a chair are why we hang out in my room next door, which Gill's mum would prefer even though it's overrun with mice, because at least I use the bog and don't store pee in fruit-juice bottles.

Before nights out, Gill and I often sing songs together as we preload sherry from the plastic – made in Leeds, high alcohol plonk – mixed with cider. We do anything by the Band – 'Cripple Creek Ferry', 'Long Black Veil', 'The Weight' – we know all their songs by heart. Or sing Muddy Waters's tunes – 'Mannish Boy', 'Hoochie Coochie Man', 'Rollin' Stone', etc. – Gill bashing along on an acoustic that struggles to stay in tune, as we do.

Post pub, we make up funny songs and tape them on a cassette recorder, but they're not worth listening to – they don't crack a smile sober – and by the year's end, tired of humour, we've started knocking out songs inspired by Dr Feelgood, verses and bridges and choruses, the whole nine yards.

GIG CENTRAL

Leeds is one of the best cities in Britain for gigs. The university's 2,100-capacity Refectory is an A-list venue where in the early seventies acts like the Rolling Stones, the Kinks, Elton John, Rod Stewart, Paul McCartney and Wings, Black Sabbath and many others play. Possibly the all-time greatest live album, the Who's *Live at Leeds*, was recorded in the standing-only hall. Between '74 and '78 I'll see Bob Marley and the Wailers, Roxy Music, Hawkwind, Dr Feelgood, the Kursaal Flyers, Toots and the Maytals, the Runaways, the Damned, the Clash, Bunch of Stiffs, etc., and can sneak in FOC as our friend Hugo is a player on the university Entertainments crew.

In the spring of 1978, Gang of Four will play here on a triple bill with the Buzzcocks and the Slits and a year later we will headline supported by Delta 5. It's unreal.

Months before we start Gang of Four and Mekons, Andy Corrigan, Mark White and I see the legendary bluesmen Sonny Terry and Brownie McGhee at the Refectory. It's a wonderful show. They play a masterclass of guitar and harp classics like 'Easy Rider', 'Long Way from Home', and 'Key to the Highway'. They are key figures in the bottomless well of African American artists white rock musicians draw on for inspiration when they need a jump start or fresh ideas. After the show, we hang around backstage to pay homage to the great men. They're really friendly and love to talk. It's amazing to be in their presence. For no reason, I pussy out and head back to bed, a bit embarrassed to be a fanboy. Big mistake. Next day I bump into Mark fumbling to make strong coffee in the kitchen, his hand jittery with a day-after drunk's palsy, his face as pale as a polar bear's arse, and find he and Corrigan went back with the blues legends to their hotel room and downed a bottle or more of bourbon with them, talking till the small hours about music, life, Mississippi and Chicago blues, everything you'd want conversation about. I'm an idiot and a fool. You only regret the things you don't do.

We don't just see shows at the university's Refectory Hall. Leeds Polytechnic's just across the road bridge from the Fenton, and its Union Hall is where hot breaking acts play. I see gigs here whenever I can, it's more my thing and cheaper too. This is where I see bands like Talking Heads, the Jam, Subway Sect, XTC, Siouxie and the Banshees, the Ramones and Jonathan Richman. We go mob-handed – Kevin, Gill, Mark, Corrigan and I – to the legendary late 1976 Sex Pistols/Clash/Damned/Johnny Thunders and the Heartbreakers gig, which didn't sell out despite only costing a quid. We were all interviewed by hacks desperate to uncover punk-rock filth that might outrage the bourgeoisie.

Corrigan is pictured on the front page of the *Yorkshire Evening Post*, under a photo of Johnny Rotten, the caption reading 'This punk rock fan wore a razor blade earring'.

It's super cool.

CROMER HOUSE

Mark White.

In the centre of Leeds University campus, at No. 5–7 Cromer Terrace, sits Cromer House, a dilapidated Edwardian redbrick sulking behind a high wall on a granite cobbled street. Marooned among university departments and facilities, this once imposing privately owned and managed house is now a sanctuary for students, losers, and scabby cats. It has a walled yard scattered with drifting litter from overfilled bins; a wheel-free Ford Cortina sits propped on breeze blocks with dank oil puddled under the engine block, beside which I park my shiny Honda CB250, a lovely thing even in Yorkshire's perma-rain.

Importantly, Cromer House is only a short hike to the Fenton pub and Leeds city centre, and where I now share a flat with Andy Corrigan and Mark White. Other students – and even someone with a *job* – doss in a dozen other bedsits in the old servants' quarters in the attic and basement. The house is managed by Mrs Firth, a dipsomaniac Irishwoman the size of a Smurf with wild black hair and teeth like Ken Dodd, who rooms on the ground floor where a concierge might live were we in Paris or Barcelona. She has a sharp ear for nonsense, especially the moaning, squeaks and cries of legover, telling me, 'That hoor in the cellar's at it again all the night long! The noise she's makin' would be less if she were gettin' her leg amputated, so it is! The plaster's falling off the walls with the bangin' it is!'

Mrs Firth herself has a fancy man, a lorry driver with a family down south who drops by every other week or so to deliver meat and roger her, not necessarily in that order. I think he probably enjoys a grilled chop before burying the brisket, but I'm glad not to know what they get up to, as she stays schtum and entertains him in silence, which is a relief.

Better him than me.

Her lover gone, she's left with a stack of Tupperware boxes stuffed with gobbets of flesh but she doesn't have a freezer and foists plates of raw liver at me, saying, 'You and your friends are not looking your best, pale as priests, so you are, iron's what you need, just look at yourself.'

It's true. I don't need a mirror to know I've got a jaundiced complexion and dark black eye bags, or that Corrigan looks like a louche undertaker or an auditionee for a Hammer Dracula movie. But Mark is top of the pallid-boy charts, his aspirin-white face and panda eyes irresistible to some girls; it's his USP, along with the striped tank tops he non-ironically wears. But really, bloody hell, liver's the last thing we want to see, even FOC!

Our rooms open on to the landing at the turn of the main stairs on the first floor. We have a bedroom each, a teeny kitchen, and a large living room with a collapsed sofa and mouldy armchair. Tom Greenhalgh and Julz Sale (soon to be of Delta 5) move into a bedsit room next door, so it's band central for a while, especially when Jon Langford, another future Mekon, drops by to hang out and listen to music. Corrigan's Hi-Fi is the best any of us have, a top-end Cambridge amp and fine record deck with huge walnut speakers the size of coffins with a sweet sound, volume, and bottom end that shakes the furniture. It's ideally suited to the rich layers of Bowie's Berlin trilogy we play on loop and Led Zep, and new release punk-rock 45s, like Television's 'Prove It' or Richard Hell's 'Blank Generation'. In the summer, all music's off when BBC Radio's wonderful *Test Match Special* is on; Mark, Corrigan and me cluster around the wireless, its non-stop chat a model for our later *Special Performance* art happening.

We don't have a TV – no one has a television – and briefly set up a 16-mm projector to watch arthouse films rented by the Film Society projected on to the living-room wall. There's no sound so we improvise and take turns to lip sync imagined dialogue to the picture – I do American accents the best – which is only funny until it isn't, which is soon.

There's no central heating, but we're cosy from open fires fuelled by coal filched from a heap left in the basement. The electric's free as we've bypassed the meter, severing the cash chamber's security seal so we can feed a single fifty-pence piece through the slot into the box as often as we like to get more juice.

We're on the losing side in a war with the mice that overrun the kitchenette and chew through our supplies, squirting whiffy trails of wee all the while. Contemptuous of the traps we set, they nibble through the bait without springing the spring, immune to rat poison, treating it as a rodent amuse-bouche before their nightly food-shelf raids. Corrigan sometimes sits beside the stove in the dark, our communal air pistol in hand ready to take them out, while Mark and I in the front room relax to ricocheted PINGS, PEOWS and THUDS, but never a mousy death squeak; Andrew's aim is not true, and the walls are pockmarked with pellet holes.

For a while we pool food money and take turns shopping at Leeds central market late Saturday afternoons when stallholders close up and dump superannuated veg and overripe fruit for chump change. This doesn't go well, Corrigan once returning with a giant bag of wilted celery he got for fifty pence and 5 lbs of cow's stomach lining. We eat tripe with boiled/braised/raw celery every day for a week until the wilted remnants are binned, a Pavlovian experiment that leaves me unable to face the vegetable again for years. The system collapses when Mark and Corrigan go shopping *à deux* to blow the house float in a downtown boozer and impulse-buy Andrew a silver penis earring, which pisses me off. We eat chips that night.

We're a three-man crew, always out and about together, in sync with trips to the Fenton, other pubs and movies, and occasional trips on the bus to places like the wondrous Adel Parish Church – described by Nikolaus Pevsner as 'one of the best and most complete Norman churches in Yorkshire' – the pretty little village of Blubberhouses in the Dales or the Brontë sisters' home in Haworth, sheltering in a trough in the wild Pennine Hills. Yorkshire really is God's own country.

Needing to make our own entertainment and mix things up, we stage a happening, which we call *Special Performance*. Corrigan, Mark, Tom G and I set up an environment that mimics our flat, a big table layered with kibble and beer bottles, an unmade bed, and a projection screen on which runs a film, *Red Route*, a twenty-minute film shot on Super 8 by Kevin and Corrigan. It's a tracking shot with minimal editing down what either is or isn't the longest corridor in

Europe; Corrigan or Kevin as cameraperson lying on a trolley pushed by Kevin or Corrigan. It's good because it occupies time without anything occurring and while it's running we take turns talking about things of no consequence. My piece concerns how traffic can sometimes be busy, but is often not, but Mark's the star of the event, a man who can find poetry in the banal who shares a monologue about how people move from sweet to dry wines. He's a genius at describing a particularly British petit bourgeois view of the world, tempered by disappointment and sexual frustration, a worldview that finds misfortune in every beery, leery glass. Tom downs too many pints and passes out, sliding to the floor, which is a shame as something noteworthy actually happened. Mark says later that 'We tried to put something together which we felt would be hard-hitting, incisive, and powerful. And which had something to do with disillusion and nihilism. But largely it was incredibly long and incredibly dull, and had no great viability at all, and certainly at the end we felt we'd reached a definite dead end and that wasn't the direction we needed to go.' Corrigan says, more pithily: 'It looks like three drunk blokes really.'* The audience will never get that hour back.

We rethink. *Special Performance* is an artistically sterile dead end and a waste of time. We talk more about how we need to find an effective way to talk about our dissatisfaction with the way things are.

As a last alt-art fling, and as art festival money is available, we book a pair of Australian conceptual/physical theatre artists to do something arty. This involves them going onstage hammered – they've toped all day – and one of them biting into a pint glass, not too clever, spitting out a fountain of blood and crystal shards. I'm not sure if it's their usual act, it's a bit strong, and Corrigan has to take the glass cruncher to A & E for stitches to his mouth, show over.

* Quotes taken from Gavin Butt, *No Machos or Pop Stars: When the Leeds Art Experiment Went Punk* (Durham, NC: Duke University Press, 2022).

Kevin has a black-painted ex-General Post Office Ford Anglia which he sells to Corrigan for fifty quid, opening up rich adventure opportunities. On a Sunday night with nothing going on in Leeds, Mark, Corrigan, and I decide to drive to Margate in Kent for fish and chips after the pub, it's only 260 miles away. We load up a slab of lager and drive through the night to arrive next morning in Margate but the town's fast asleep, and the fish and chips shop doesn't open on Mondays, which is a pain.

Changing tack, we drive to Ronnie Scott's in London for late-night jazz, Mark paying for our entry, blowing the cash given him by a young aunt who'd recently died of cancer and stipulated he had to spend it on only on enjoying himself, nothing *useful*.

We have a fantastic evening and drive back to Leeds, coughing and juddering and spluttering up the M1 at around 25 mph, blue exhaust fumes trailing behind us from the knackered engine firing on only three pistons, to arrive in the ruination of Leeds as dawn's rosy fingers light up the sky.

It's been an excellent trip.

The Ford is taken to a breaker's yard.

LEEDS AND THE BOMB

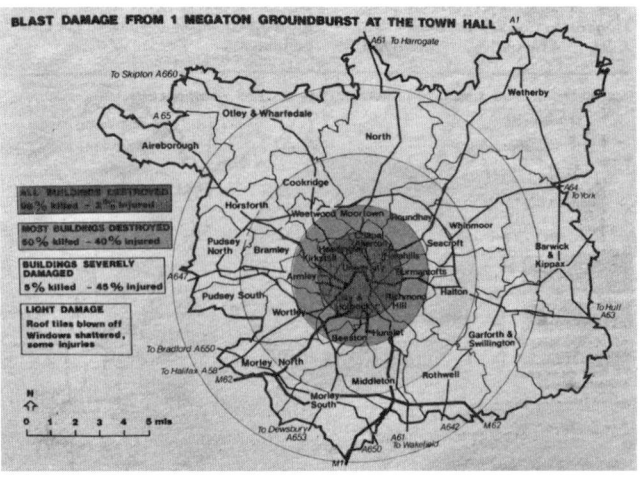

Prospective blast-damage map from Leeds City
Council's booklet, *Leeds and THE BOMB*.

The advice in the government's 1980 *Protect and Survive* booklet is familiar, and not much has changed in Armageddon terms over the last twenty years – in short, we're all going to die. My primary school 'Duck and Cover' training is still *au courant*: hide under a table and cover your eyes. Since we don't have a table in our Cromer House flat to lie under this would be a concern, but no worries, we're so close to the blast centre we'll be vaped instantly.

Leeds City Council are ordered by the warmongering Tory government to issue their own pamphlet, which is called *Leeds and THE BOMB*, bomb being CAPITALISED for some reason. It could have read *Leeds AND the bomb* or, better, *LEEDS and the bomb*, as it's about Leeds. Just a thought.

It's very helpful. I read it with great interest and make plans accordingly, i.e. none. Should a measly one megaton ground-burst bomb centred on the town hall explode, everything within a 1.75-mile radius will be destroyed instantly. This means me! FFS! I know I'm not a primary target, but why the Soviets have got it in for our overworked town councillors is beyond me. They've got enough to do with the potholes and rubbish collection as it is. You couldn't make it up!

The worst place to be – although this is already the worst place to be – is the cursèd earth halfway between Leeds and Bradford city centres, as this is where stunned survivors will choose between croaking from radiation sickness, burns, their wounds etc.; anyone left alive will have a once-in-a-lifetime opportunity to starve to death. A command centre 'War Room Region 2', off the Otley Road in Lawnswood, near the cemetery, is where a hundred apparatchiks and suits will hunker down in a concrete bunker to rule over the minions after the Scud missile shitshow. If all goes swimmingly – after the mass deaths and disease, and total destruction of industry, agriculture, housing, utilities and financial institutions – survivors may enjoy, to quote the City Council, 'something like a medieval society based on a system of barter', so no great change in Beeston.

The big question is, after the bomb drops, will anyone be able to tell the difference between before and after?*

---

* Apologies for repurposed gag, usually made about Liverpool.

TERRYS ALL-TIME

Terrys All-Time.

Midnight in Leeds. Andy Corrigan, Mark White and I are in Terrys All-Time, a twenty-four-hour caff on Woodhouse Lane among a cluster of condemned Victorian buildings scheduled for slum clearance. It's midway between our flat in Cromer House and the Heaven & Hell nightclub downtown, which has a weekly new-wavy night, and a late-drinking licence.

Over the door, a sign shows a clock set at ten to two. I ask what this means, but the old dear sweating over a fry-up says it's just a sign, who cares. Signs are never just signs, I think, even if sometimes a cigar is just a cigar; it could be a message from Terry himself who no one's ever seen and is rumoured to be a cab driver or a crim or a space alien or a Freemason or banged up or in the British Movement, or all of them.

Obviously, our time is cheap. Terrys – no apostrophe – is a dump. Stinking of rancid oil, BO and fags, drunks, punks, and bag men and women are drawn to the poop-coloured leatherette benches and chipped Formica tables, 'Fuck You!' written on one. Copies of the *Sun, Mirror, New Musical Express*, and the *Racing Post* lie heaped in a corner alongside a jukebox, which houses classic sixties pop, northern soul and local bands' 45s.

We love it here. It's the Gang of Four/Mekons' late night go-to joint, where we enjoy the house speciality, fried egg and chips in a bap, announced by the *chef de cuisine*, 'Eggburger going cold!'

This evening, uniformed filth come in for a fry-up and sit next to us, bristling with aggression, their walkie-talkies crackling. We know enough to leg it immediately. Mark writes this up in the Mekons' 'Never Been in a Riot':

> I was in this late-night caff
> I was eying up the till
> when in comes the British Police
> Getting their bacon grill.*

Terrys was demolished years ago.
The Leeds Beckett Wellness Centre now stands on its site.

---

* Lyrics reproduced with the kind permission of Mark White.

MURDER

Seventies Leeds is a violent and murderous city. Between 1975 and 1980 Peter Sutcliffe, the so-called Yorkshire Ripper, slaughters thirteen women and will be found guilty of attempting to murder seven others. There are almost certainly other unknown victims. Women in the city are afraid and try not to travel alone, safe shuttles are arranged to take female students to and from campus halls of residence, and women have defensive weapons close to hand, such as bundles of keys or heavy mag lights; a friend carries an iron in her handbag.

Women everywhere fear rape and male violence. In 1977 the Women's Liberation Movement in Leeds starts the 'Reclaim the Night' movement, a response to West Yorkshire Police telling women they should stay away from public spaces after dark; and night-time marches take place in Chapeltown and Woodhouse Moor, which converge on City Square. Inspired by Leeds WLM, a dozen marches take place on the same night in other cities.

The Leeds police are incompetent misogynists who don't prioritise these serial murders because they believe the Ripper only targets sex workers. It's only when Sutcliffe slaughters sixteen-year-old Jayne MacDonald, a sweet girl who loved dancing and the Bay City Rollers, that the cops are forced to take the killings seriously after a public outcry. Jayne is described by police as a 'respectable young girl' and Jim Hobson, a senior detective, says in an open letter that the Ripper 'has made it clear that he hates prostitutes. Many people do. We, as a police force, will continue to arrest prostitutes. But the Ripper is now killing innocent girls . . . You have made your point. Give yourself up before another *innocent* woman dies.'*

In the event, Sutcliffe will be captured by chance.

---

* The stupidity, incompetence and sexism of Leeds's cops involved in the Sutcliffe murders in the 1970s is brilliantly described in David Peace's novels, *The Red Riding Quartet*.

THE DEAD

30 October 1975:   Wilma McCann, 28, Leeds
20 January 1976:   Emily Jackson, 42, Leeds
11 February 1977:   Irene Richardson, 28, Leeds
23 April 1977:   Patricia Atkinson, 32, Bradford
26 June 1977:   Jayne MacDonald, 16, Leeds
1 October 1977:   Jean Jordan, 20, Manchester
21 January 1978:   Yvonne Pearson, 21, Bradford
31 January 1978:   Helen Rytka, 18, Huddersfield
16 May 1978:   Vera Millward, 40, Manchester
4 April 1979:   Josephine Whitaker, 19, Halifax
2 September 1979:   Barbara Leach, 20, Bradford
20 August 1980:   Marguerite Walls, 47, Leeds
17 November 1980:   Jacqueline Hill, 20, Leeds

This is not a time for songs about nothing.

ANTI-FASCIST ACTION: TRUNCHEONED BY A COPPER

Swastika graffiti on a flight of steps leading up from Servia Hill to Grosvenor Hill, in Woodhouse, Leeds, 1970. *(Photo: Leeds Libraries)*

A late spring day in Chapeltown, warm and sunny under a mackerel sky. Nice. Hugo has a house here, a lively district at the heart of Leeds's Afro-Caribbean community. The sound of deep bass dubs in the wind, Linton Kwesi Johnson saying it like it is, with the sweet smell of ganja meandering by. The cops corralling us on the pavement pay the weed no heed; they're here to separate anti-fascist demonstrators and the hard-right extremists who've come here from across England to hold a meeting in a nearby school hall. They'd originally wanted to march through this mostly Afro-Caribbean district and chant racist filth while waving Union and red-crossed St George flags, but as this posed a serious risk of public disorder, Leeds council banned the parade. The fascists are now holding a private meeting here instead that the authorities can't prohibit. A murder of skinheads with Celtic crosses, 'Blood and Honour' and '88'* tattoos is crammed inside, ready for a ruck.

Outside the hall, a cluster of Rastas, rude boys and lefties mill about, protesting this presence. Mark, Corrigan, Hugo, Kevin, Gill and I are in the melée, along with other local 'Rock Against Racism' activists. It's good humoured, we're chatting and joking with the Old Bill in the warm sun, nothing doing.

It suddenly all kicks off. Hard-right goons pour out of the hall, led by Martin Webster, their neo-Nazi leader, exercising their right to walk to the mid-city railway station. The police say it's OK so long as they don't chant or flaunt their flags and banners, but it's clear this is bullshit and whose side the police is on. In seconds, there's jostling, hustling, fists flying, screaming, shouting, whistles blowing, the demo's on TILT. The cops – who only a minute ago were smiling and chatting with the crowd outside – default to attack dogs of repression, truncheons out, shouting spittle-mouthed 'BACK! BACK!' to defend the plucky British patriots taking the road to the city centre. Soon, the skinheads are running, us after them, the cops lagging behind, whacking us as they go.

The demonstrators are stopped at the City Square before the railway station, police in riot gear lined up on horseback, their Saturday anti-football hooligan format, the huge horses puffing and stamping, forming a wall to shield the Nazis as they saunter to the station, giving us V-signs and screaming verbal abuse. I'm not with Hugo

---

* 88 = Heil Hitler

and the others but among a clump of demonstrators squeezed onto a pavement chanting 'THE NATIONAL FRONT'S A NAZI FRONT! THE NATIONAL FRONT'S A NAZI FRONT!' until a mounted cop loses patience, spurs his horse into a trot and rides at me with truncheon out and WHACK!, smacks me across the forehead, and I drop to the deck. Out for a few moments I'm helped up and stagger away among the shocked Saturday shoppers. A protesting medical student checks me out and says I should be fine but could be concussed, need to take care, take some aspirin, go home, etc. I'm OK other than an egg-sized lump on my forehead and a headache. Others have come off worse.

Back at Cromer House, Mark tells me he was squashed to a wall by a police horse trained in anti-football hooligan control that made dainty Lipizzaner sidesteps to crush back the crowd, but he dodged away before being walloped.

When he and I meet the others at the Fenton, we're received as heroes and bought pints of Tetley's all night. It's been a good day.*

I later hear that when Webster and chums were in the station waiting for a train back to London, they ran into the Leeds United Service Crew football hooligans arriving home fresh from a barney at an away game. Hearing their Southern accents, they attacked Webster and his boot boys, thinking it was a London soccer crew, and he was taken to hospital. This either happened or it didn't, it would be poetic justice to think it did.

---

* This 1978 bust-up is an echo of the Battle of Holbeck Moor in 1936 when a thousand Blackshirts came to Leeds to march through the Leylands Jewish quarter, their leader Oswald Mosley ranting about blood and honour and antisemitic filth. The march had been banned and thousands of people turned up to oppose them leading to a riot where Mosley was hospitalised with minor injuries. He was imprisoned during WW2 as a potential traitor.

THE FILM SOCIETY

Kevin and I first meet Andy Corrigan at the Fine Art Department's social for new intakes. He looks cool with shoulder-length hair, a sheepskin bomber jacket and sulky swag who we bond with when we find a shared passion for film. The three of us join the student Film Society which puts on a double bill of arthouse movies each week, allowing us to watch them for free at the Polytechnic as well – the only way to see films as no one has a TV or can afford to go to the cinema. Movies become central to our lives in Leeds, and Corrigan, me and Kevin, among other fanatic cineastes, get directly involved in scheduling and booking movies for the Film Society, with Corrigan somehow becoming its President. We don't have a manifesto nor direction of travel other than putting on whatever we most want to see but can't in a mainstream Odeon or ABC theatre. We put on Nouvelle Vague and arthouse movies, euro comedies, and Westerns; films like Truffaut's *Les Quatre Cents Coups*, Resnais's *Hiroshima Mon Amour*, Godard's *Numéro Deux*, *Breathless*, *Le Mépris* – good paired with a Western like *Last Train from Gun Hill* – Warhol's relentless *Empire* and *Sleep*, Kurosawa's *Dodes'ka-den*, Ozu's *Tokyo Story*, Oshima's *In the Realm of the Senses*, Paul Morrissey's transgressive *Flesh for Frankenstein* and *Blood for Dracula*, *La Grand Bouffe*, various *Carry Ons* ... I'll watch on average four movies a week during my four years at the university, and this directly feeds into my songwriting.

especially the split-screen and ambiguous narratives of Godard, and what the philosopher Jean-François Lyotard calls the post-modern 'incredulity towards metanarratives' – a story that explains all other stories, like Marxism or Christianity.

MAKING FRIENDS

(Photo: Kathe Deutsche)

There are twenty students in the 1974 Fine Art degree intake; I'm the one in the bottom right-hand corner of the strip. I make friends with Andy Corrigan, Iannis Kourakis, Dido Powell and Kathe Deutsche, as we all love film, funk and fun; they're a talented group who've all done a year's pre-diploma course at art college.

Visiting Corrigan's studio, I'm impressed by his unique art production MO: he pours liquid resin paint straight from the pot on to canvas stretched across the floor, turns the gas fire up to full burn, and dozes off in the heat as it dries, knocked out by the noxious fumes. After a term or so, this proves too demanding, so he cuts out the paint part and focuses on sleeping.

I befriend Mick Wixey, a tall, long-haired northerner in leather jacket and jeans who's studying Mining, who I meet parking up my Honda alongside his oily BSA nicknamed 'The Beast'. Mick's clever and funny and will in two years' time become the Mekons' manager. One evening in a bar he says, 'Watch this, I'm going to pull that bird, she's well fit,' pointing at a woman sitting at a far-off table. He goes to the bar and buys a Babycham served with a coupe glass which he plonks in front of her. He comes back to our table and says, 'Dead cert!' She soon comes over, their chemistry's electric, and she and he became a thing, at least for a night. Babycham! Jeez! Who knew?

HUGO

At a Funk Society dance Gill and I are approached by a guy who looks like a thrift-store Elton John: patterned shirt, budgie smuggler chinos and clip-on braces with a *printed bear footprint* design. A fashion atrocity! He sidles up to Andy and says, 'Nice coat,' nodding at his Gestapo-style leather trench coat. Gill says, 'Yeah, cheers,' unsure if he's being hit on – we're often the only boys on the dance floor as most male students huddle near the bar being hetero-normative – and before he can say get lost we hear 'Double Barrel' by Dave and Ansel Collins, the first awesome recording with the teenage Sly Dunbar on the skins and a reggae classic, and we all hit the dancefloor, led by my friend Dido, the best dancer *ever*.

Elton – not a bad mover – introduces himself. He's called Hugo Burnham, an English and Drama student at the University who loves Trojan Records, James Brown, and the Sensational Alex Harvey Band. He has membership card No. 13 in the David Bowie Fan Club and was beaten up after David's Rainbow gig by skins objecting to his gay-boy face-paint, and Bowie sent him flowers in hospital! He'd booked *Genesis* and the *Pink Fairies* to play at his school and says he can drum like Simon Kirk. He'd been a rugger bugger with the private schoolboys who sneer at the oiks and drop their pants when they're pissed but had twigged he wouldn't get laid hanging with them as women aren't turned on by blokey prats displaying their ring pieces. We fully embrace him when he says he's on the university's Ents team who can get us into gigs free.* The bear-print braces won't help getting any sack action, I think. But the next time we meet he's got a new look: Ben Sherman, Levi's, DMs, cropped hair, a cool suedehead/skin look. I *like* this guy!

---

* Andy will say in an interview that he offered Hugo the drumming gig in Gang of Four because 'he had a van', which isn't true. Hugo was Transit-free when the band began.

NEW YORK CITY AND CBGB

The Bowery between Houston and Stanton,
facing south, 1976. *(Photo: Kate Simon)*

In the third year of four-year Fine Art degree courses, undergraduates have to write a 5,000-word thesis on an art historical subject of their choice. This is a challenge, as I've paid only passing attention to the academic part of my degree, even though it represents 30–50 per cent of the mark, as I spend all my time painting and life drawing.

Professor Lawrence Gowing, who'd tempted me to Leeds two years before, left at the end of my first year to be Principal at the Slade and to curate landmark Cezanne exhibitions in London, Paris and New York. He'd been a fine painter and member of the Euston Road Group of left-wing and communist artists who wanted to create accessible and socially relevant realist art. This kind of art failed in its mission, the gloomy naturalistic pictures of daily life looking not like calls to the barricades but like gloomy naturalistic pictures of daily life. Very restrained and English, and with a soupçon of intellectual slumming, like George Orwell or Martin Amis. Academic study under him at Leeds was a privilege, his brilliant talks on Vermeer and Cezanne were a magnet to people from many other disciplines, and it was often tough to find a decent seat in the packed lecture theatre. His old-school MO was a Monday morning seminar where he'd project a picture on screen and stab a finger at one of us, saying, 'Artist? School? Date?' expecting all three. We had to prepare, be sharp, do the work. I enjoyed this, taking it all in, and score well watching *University Challenge*.

But after facts come opinions, or maybe the other way around. I'm reading a lot of Marxist art criticism – Louis Althusser, Critical Theory, Theodor Adorno, etc., and want to make art that could escape a self-referential content straitjacket, be about real life, and shake things up. We've had a year with a caretaker head of department with a practical specialism in methods and material – how to *do* things – so it's a thrill when our new professor turns out to be Tim Clark, a big dog in New Left art criticism who'd once been a player in the Situationist movement.* I'm taken by his books on nineteenth-century French art,

---

* In 1996 Tony Wilson will ask me to join him and Mark E. Smith on a panel at the UK's first ever symposium on Situationism at the Hacienda, Manchester: 'On the Legacy of Situationist Revolt'. I give a talk on how Second World War Vichy French franc coins communicated reactionary ideology, the Nazi collaborationist government having changed the French state promise 'Liberty, Equality, Fraternity' to 'Work, Family, Country', hard-right core beliefs. It goes down so well I'm denounced for 'fetishising the object' – i.e., I'd hung onto these worthless coins for too long – which was excellent. You're nobody on the Left unless you've been denounced.

breakthrough texts that looked at Impressionist artists of that time through a socio-historical lens. He has a fresh perspective on artwork that talked about the mad parade of modern life, a world being turned upside down: paintings of trains and railway stations, of the outdoors where light and colour flips in a moment, families at the beach or seaside, the bourgeoisie at play and on parade or in theatres, bars and at entertainments. It was a seismic shift from romanticised subjects drawn from classical antiquity that bragged of wealth and social order and aligned itself with oppression.

Tim has persuaded a cadre of remarkable people to come on board: the brilliant feminist art historian Griselda Pollock; Fred Orton, leading Marxist social historian of art; and art lecturer Terry Atkinson, who'd been a key man in the Art and Language group (and later will be nominated for the 1984 Turner Prize).* An incredible team making Leeds the most radical Fine Art Department in Britain, with a 180-degree turn from Lawrence's approach.† I'm taken by Griselda's semiotic feminism and Terry's gritty approach to art production, and the notion that learned structural patterns can (over-) determine human thoughts, feelings and actions. I think about this a lot when I later write the words to 'Natural's Not in It'.

Despite this, or perhaps because of this, I decide to write about the non-wordy US pop artist Jasper Johns, famous for painterly images of the Stars and Stripes, targets and paint pots, although not in that order, or in the same picture. Like many other American sixties Pop

---

Later, in conversation with the Fall's Mark E. Smith and Tony Wilson, after hearing a punter's minutes-long monologue about psychogeography disguised as a question, Mark replies, answer of the day, 'I've no fucking idea what you're talking about, you cunt!' He's always good value.

* In the late seventies Red Krayola will open for us on a UK tour, the band featuring Mayo Thompson, another member of seventies Art and Language crew.

† Gill, Tom Greenhalgh and Jon Langford of the Mekons would get full benefit of this group, all in the year below me with three years to go.

artists he loves pretty paint – lots of sweetie-box colours – and wallows in mass-market imagery with a social emptiness and cultural triumphalism that characterises the US in his time. I don't care much about his work – I find it decorative and bland – but think I might be able to blag a research grant that would cover the airfare to Gotham, saying I'd need to see Johns' pictures up close and personal. What I really want to do in New York is to mooch about, see my favourite bands, and see art that thrills me, like Picasso's *Guernica* or Pollock's drip pictures. The pitch works and the money comes through.

Result! I buy a ticket to New York, then a crime-ridden, corrupt and decaying city saved from bankruptcy at the last minute in 1975, when it was clear that the city's default would threaten stock and bond markets, and the dollar. A US newspaper had run a cartoon of a tramp lying in rubbish below the Brooklyn Bridge, captioned: 'We're going down, America, and we're taking you with us.' Thousands of cops and firefighters have been fired, and social and public services slashed.

In 1975, travellers arriving at New York's airports were handed pamphlets with a hooded death's head on the cover, warning them, 'Until things change, stay away from New York City if you possibly can.' The pamphlet was full of ludicrous exaggerations and inventions that could have described a first draft script for John Carpenter's *Escape from New York*. But its warped truth was based on hard facts – murders, car thefts and assaults in the city had doubled over the past decade, rapes and burglaries had tripled, and robberies had increased tenfold. It was pretty lairy, but it's just like Leeds, with its ruinous housing, crime and hard-right violence.

My plan is to go to Max's Kansas City, where the Velvet Underground recorded their classic live album, and see, wherever I can, happening new bands like the Ramones, Television, Blondie, Talking Heads, and the Voidoids. It would be a blast, made better when Andy asks if he can tag along, an excellent idea. We'd hitched to Spain together and always had fun, so it would be a lark for him to join me in the Big Apple.

Gill – in the year below me at Leeds – doesn't have to write a thesis, which means blagging an art travel grant would be tough, but he applies instead to a funding body that gives out small amounts of money for personal development projects. He floats, 'A photographic study of Gothic Cathedrals in Northern France, travelling by motorcycle': the elevator pitch being he'd drive from place to place on a Honda CB250, take pix, and record this life-affirming cultural experience in a journal format. It's a fine spiel, and he is given enough money to cover the airfare to New York. A great deal, apart from him not actually going to France, taking any pictures of its holy architecture, or planning to write a word.

Needing somewhere to stay in Manhattan, a friend of a friend suggests I get in touch with a rock journalist called Mary Harron, who lives in the shitty East Village. I write and ask her if she'd put me up for a few weeks, an impoverished student doing important art research, and Mary generously says yes, there's room at her studio apartment on St Marks Place, 8th Street, in a row of down-at-heel brownstones, their signature New York fire escapes zigzagging from roof to first floor, familiar to anyone who's seen the photo of exactly here on Led Zeppelin's *Physical Graffiti*, or seen almost any movie made in Manhattan.

The East Village is in a bad way, just like Leeds. To the east across First Avenue is Alphabet City – the avenues here, like Avenue A, have letters rather than numbers – where there are blackened shells of burned-out brownstones, set afire for insurance frauds or arsonists' hijinks, or both. Public services have been massacred in spending cuts, and litter flutters across the streets from overflowing trash cans spilling soda cans, plastic, and glass across the sidewalks, its doorways homesteaded by junkies nodding out in the shadows.

Mary knows hardly anything about me, we haven't talked on the phone, neither of us have one, and she isn't expecting me to have a plus one, Andy. But she welcomes him, too, and says we can both stay. She's only got one long room, so we crash on the floor in sleeping bags at the far kitchenette end, separated by a rickety wooden bookshelf from her living area and single bed on the street side. Giant cockroaches scatter as we hunker down, and some annoyingly overnight in my shoes, to be shaken out in the morning, scattering for the darkness.

I can't believe my luck. This is the coolest street in the world; rundown, scuzzy and super cheap (a two-room walk-up going for only $125 a month), peopled by punks, artists and outsiders. My kind of place. As Ada Calhoun writes in *St Marks is Dead: The Many Lives of America's Hippest Street*, St Marks Place is at the epicentre of counter culture, the home of the Five Spot jazz club where Billie Holiday, Thelonious Monk, Ornette Coleman, Charles Mingus, John Coltrane and Miles Davis played; where avant-garde artists and musicians hung out – William S. Burroughs lived at No. 2 and Debbie Harry a block away at No. 113. CBGB is only a short walk away, the locus of the punk-rock universe. Trotsky and W. H. Auden once lived here, and Warhol ran a nightclub on the street.

Daytimes we go to MoMA, the Frick, the Whitney and white cube galleries, and evenings we take in every gig we can. Since Mary writes for New York's *PUNK* magazine, its bible for new music, not only does she know everybody who's anybody in the punk scene, but she's also a *face* who gets comped in with her plus twos to CBGB at 315 Bowery, only seven blocks south.

The coolest club in the world* sits in the heart of the city's Skid Row, an area rich with flop houses, the homeless, and crime. CBGB is small, 350 capacity, with a low raised stage at the far end of a long dark standing room only chamber, its walls a riot of graffiti and band tags on one side as you squeeze past the long drunk-rammed bar.

* Mary Harron will become a name as a movie director, directing *American Psycho*, *I Shot Andy Warhol*, *The Notorious Bettie Page*, *The Moth Diaries* and others. It says on Wikipedia that she dated Tony Blair at Oxford University. We all make mistakes.

Every happening band hangs out and plays here. As Mary's guests, we're waved in for free, seeing the Dead Boys, Richard Hell and the Voidoids, Talking Heads and Suicide. The Ramones rip through a blistering sixteen-song set in under forty-five insane minutes, including 'Beat on the Brat', 'Blitzkrieg Bop', and the classic 'Now I Wanna Sniff Some Glue'. This is a band who's summited the Everest of punk rock.

The local bands are super cool: Stiv Bators, the frontman of the Dead Boys, wiping snot from his nose on salami he'd stapled to his shirt and then chomping it down; Richard Hell, in ripped T-shirts with home-made designs, baked stage chat, and degenerate swagger, an era-defining look shamelessly plagiarised by Malcolm McLaren as playbook for his Sex Pistols boyband. Hell had it all, and his nihilistic 'Blank Generation' single was 100 per cent proof of his fuck-you attitude.

All the musicians we meet assume we're in a band, because almost everyone else is, and ask what our group's name is, so Gill says we're the Mudflaps. It's a gag, but we start thinking about forming a band when we get back to England. Why not? We'd written a raft of sub-Dr Feelgood songs when we roomed next-door in a shared Leeds house, me singing into a manky cassette recorder as Gill strummed on an acoustic, so we'd made a start. All we need is a world-class drummer and bass player, an electric guitar, equipment and good songs.

Gang of Four is on.

Postscript

I didn't write about Jasper Johns, having nothing interesting to say. Instead, my dissertation was about Carl Andre, the minimal sculptor, a descriptor he didn't like, infamous for his 1966 *Equivalent VIII* artwork, an arrangement of 120 bricks, two deep, six across and ten lengthwise, on the floor. He said he didn't want to turn one thing into something else, although of course he did but without craft-based work or messing with materials. His other artworks were made from blocks of wood arranged like *Konzeptkunst* Jenga, and squares of lead, steel or zinc laid on the floor in neat grid patterns. Semiotically, the sign – the lead/steel/zinc/ bricks/blocks of wood, etc. – doubled up as the thing itself, signifying a work of art, although Andre would always say that they stayed what they are, though if that's the case, why put them on show in a gallery? He said his sculpture went out of fashion around the time of Stonehenge.*

When the awards body ask Gill to submit his French Cathedral photo essay, or pay the money back, Andy asks me to help. I say I'll get creative and make something up for him, as I'd driven through France the year before on my bike, and had visited Chartres, so could bulk up my Gothic bullshit with a smidgeon of truth. I write the sad story of a highly productive, intellectually and emotionally rewarding motorcycle pilgrimage that tragically ended in the theft of Andy's Praktica SLR camera, all his 35-mm film cartridges, and his diary. Ergo no pix nor narrative.

I don't think they swallowed this tosh. But he didn't have to give the money back.

---

* Carl Andre became notorious when in 1985, his wife, the artist Ana Mendieta, died during a drunken marital fight after accidentally falling/deliberately jumping/being pushed out of a window. Although acquitted of her killing, many thought Andre had got away with murder. Feminist activists the Guerilla Girls called him 'The O. J. Simpson of the art world', which seems fair.

HAVE A NICE DAY

Mary's cat has tapeworms. She asks me to go to the pet store for worming tablets, where I explain the problem to the owner. He says, in a thick Brooklyn accent – every vowel a double sound – 'You know why cats get worms?' (Pronounced *woyims*.)

'No,' I say, 'I never wanted to find out.'

He says, a thousand words a minute, 'Worms live in cats' guts so when sick kitty lays a turd she's squirting worms and worm eggs alive in her poop so when other moggies come along that love to sniff each other's rings and crap and sex-parts, they poke their cute little fucking noses wherever and the worm-riddled crap rubs off and gets into new puss's insides and hey, that's how it goes – a cool cycle of life for a tapeworm but not so good for tiddles – so what you got to do is give pussy these pills, keep her away from shoving her schnozz in cat shit or some moggy's stinking fucking ass and *voilà*, there you have it! Have a nice day!'

I don't know what he's talking about, and say, 'I'm sorry?'

'I *SAID*. HAVE. A. NICE. DAY. YOU FUCKING DEAF?'

DIAMONDS ARE FOR NEVER

Gill and I are mooching around Times Square among the bustling crowd, grifters and bums to a soundtrack of shouts, cop whistles, and honking horns, SOO *Taxi Driver*, it's a trip. A Black guy comes up to us, immaculately dressed in a thousand-dollar suit, silk tie, glistening shoes; he looks like an ad in *Vogue*, that is, if *Vogue* ran ads with people of colour in them. I'm in torn Levi's and a 'Manny's Schlepper' T-shirt, Gill's in stained chinos, a Pep Boys top and a tatty Harrington. Our new friend looks like an emperor in comparison.

'Can you help?' he asks. 'I must go to ze bank, I have money, and need a white man to come wiz me?'

His French-Caribbean accent is so thick you could brick up a nun with it; Haitian adjacent, like Inspector Clouseau on ludes. Not that I've been to Haiti. But he's not French French.

'No,' we say, 'this is America! You don't need no one, it's a free country! We're no use anyway, we're Brits, foreigners here.'

'*Mes baggages*, my bags, she is *déposés à l'aéroport*, must collect, but need help. I have this,' he says, hand burrowing in a pocket, '*avec moi*. I cannot travel with her.' He produces a velveteen bag and spills sparkling gems into his palm. 'Can you care for these for me?' he says, waving the glass before us. 'Please. I must return to La Guardia, for my *valise*. I trust you, just tell me where you live.'

The gems either are or aren't diamonds – how would I know? – but even if they're not, they *could* be, they look real enough, it's not good.

We're in pre-embourgeoisement Fear City, the most dangerous place in the West – over a thousand murders in New York and counting so far this year – and are stood next to an idiot/crim/grifter in Gucci flashing precious jewels, or fake gems that look enough to be worth impulsive robbery with violence.

My sense of security in New York is based on us looking like penniless losers not worth a respectable mugger's time which explains why we've never been hassled by any of the scumbags down in the East Village because we look like scumbags ourselves. Displaying things worth pinching – basically anything worth more than a Timex watch – is a stone-cold no-no.

'Fuck's sake!' says Gill. 'Put it away, this is mad!'

Our sharp-dressed friend puts away the rocks/maybe rocks/not rocks and pulls out a fat roll of what looks like $100 bills, which are either real or fake.

'I have this *argent*, also. Will you take it?'

'No way,' says Andy. 'Can we get off the street?'

Freaked, we go into a nearby Chock Full o'Nuts coffee shop and sit in a window booth, backs to the wall, a table top between us.

'I'm René,' our man says, his baroque accent morphing from Papa Doc's homeland to pure 110th Street, and lays the road wedge roll and jewellery pouch down before us. 'Take it. I trust you. Give me your address and I collect later, when I have the bags from La Guardia.'

Alarm bells ring. I mean, who'd trust *us*?

'No,' I say, pushing it back. 'Just go to a bank. We're not from here, we can't help.'

'*Non!*' he says, hard voiced, his Haitian accent now *disparu*. 'Take it!' he says, pushing the money and velvet baggie back at us, like a crook's version of *Pong*.

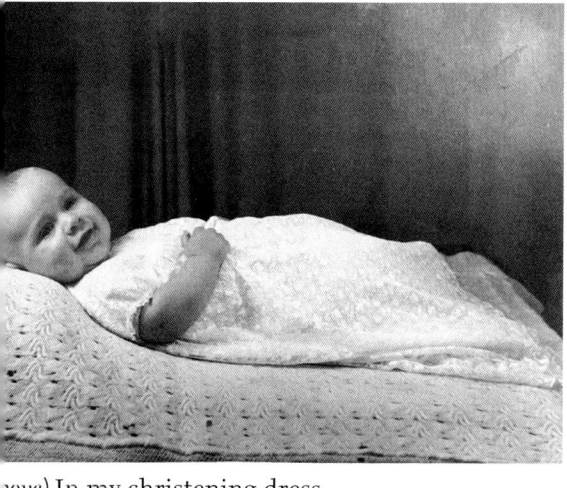

(above) In my christening dress.

(right) Sister Deborah, RIP, me, big brother Chris.

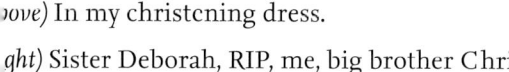

(above) Mid 70s Leeds slum. *(Yorkshire Post)*

(right) A magazine boys once read single-handed.

(Above) On Chevy Impala, Buffalo, NY, 1973.
(Right) Andy in a New York gallery.

(Above) Me in a New York gallery.
(Right) Mid 70s warning to Manhattan visitors.

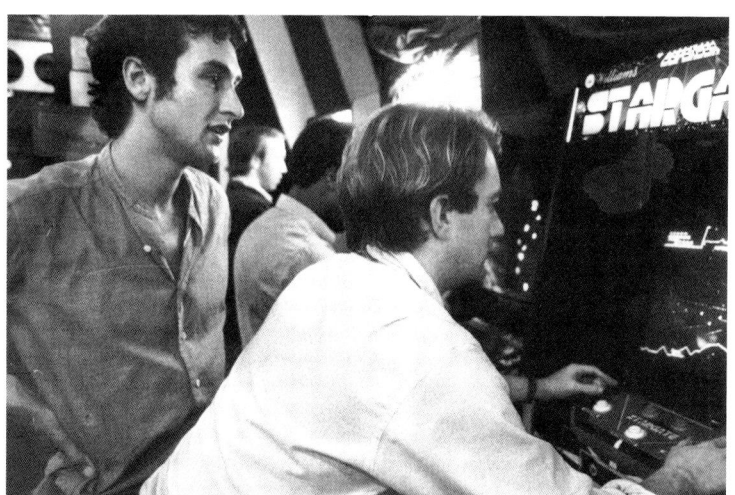

Gill and I at an arcade game.

John Botting, our tour manager, and Andy.

Me in front of The Fenton, Leeds.
(Debbie Langdon-Davies)

(Above) Gang of Four outside condemned rehearsal room. *(Andrew Corrigan)*

(Right) Kibble.

(Below) Me sat before my Cromer Terrace art studio.

Rock Against Racism gig, Cromer.
(Virginia Turbett/Redferns/Getty Images)

Andy drumming on 'It's Her Factory'.

in San Francisco, 1979. *(Larry Schorr)*

(Above) Hard promo pic. *(Fin Costello/Redferns/Getty Images)*

(Left) Gang of Four on Leeds Town Hall steps. *(Andrew Corrigan)*

(Above) On Cheyne Walk house boat while recording *Entertainment!* (© Nicholas Corke)

(Left) Me, Sara, Andy, Hugo. *(EMI promo)*

GANG OF FOUR

protest in a New York store against Reagan's 'Make America Great Again!' election triumph. *(NME)*

(Above) Me, Debbie, and Andy after hitchhiking to Spain.

(Above) Debbie and me on the houseboat. (© *Nicholas Corker*)

(Right) Andy, Debbie, and me clubbing Heaven, 1982.

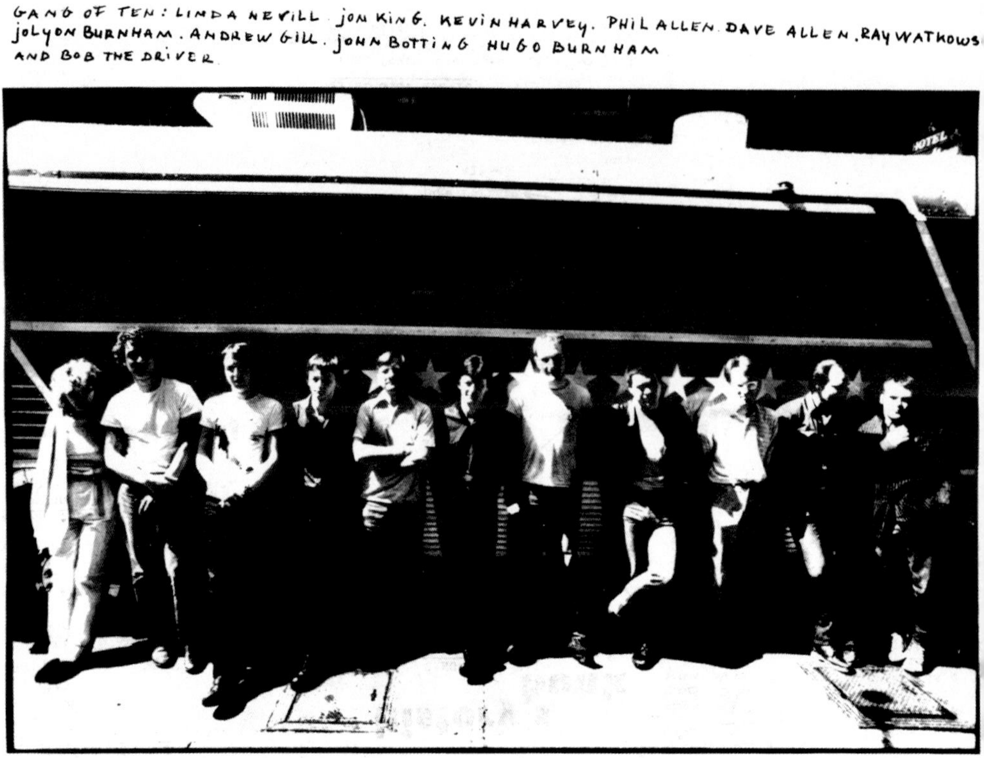

GANG OF TEN: LINDA NEVILL. JON KING. KEVIN HARVEY. PHIL ALLEN. DAVE ALLEN. RAY WATKOWS. JOLYON BURNHAM. ANDREW GILL. JOHN BOTTING. HUGO BURNHAM AND BOB THE DRIVER
HOTEL

Solid Gold tour entourage, 1980.

KNAC In association with
LARRY VALLON PRESENTS
Return of URGH!
Iggy Pop
Gang of Four
TUESDAY, NOV. 11th
SANTA MONICA CIVIC
General Admission $9.50

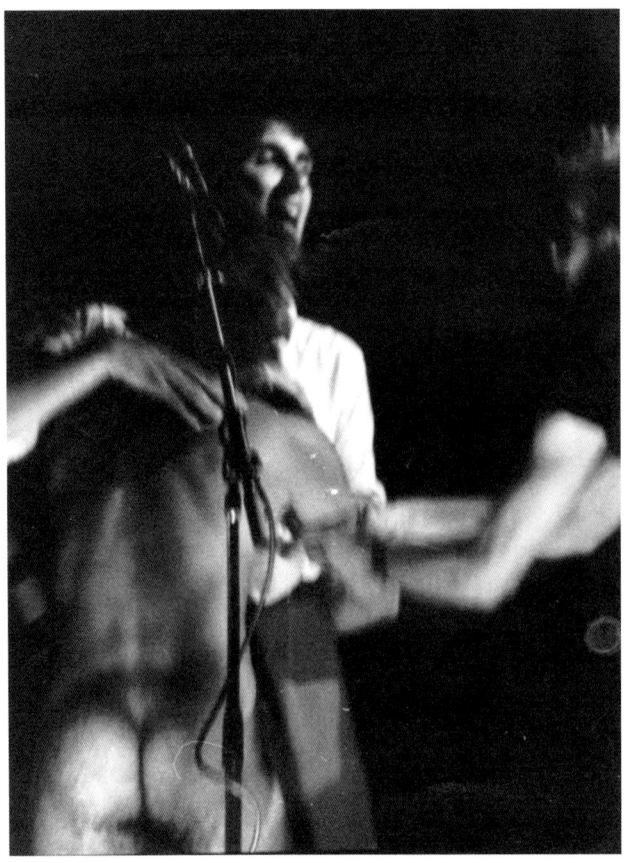

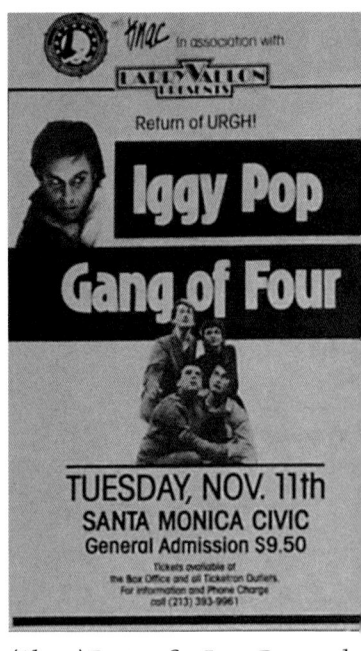

(Above) Poster for Iggy Pop and Gang of Four show.

(Left) A naked Flea grabbing me onstage at Perkins Palace, Pasadena.

Uh-oh. This is either the back end of a robbery, a *Candid Camera*-style gag, or a con; or all three. Either way, it stinks. Gill and I swap looks and leg it, leaving René with his stash.

We talk it over at Mary's. It's a mystery. Gill thinks we should've given a false address, kept the money, bought guitars and booze, hired a Cadillac, and headed off on a road trip to nowhere. My feeling is, we did this, we'd be toast, discovered in a few days decaying in a dumpster. I can't figure the grifter's angle on laying off the diamonds/not diamonds and money/not money to us, even if we're the biggest nitwits he could find. It was smart to scoot.

Maybe he really was from Haiti with his luggage stuck at the airport, the jewels and the cash were real, and he trusted our innocent faces.

Nah.

A NAME

Mark White, Gill and I are in Andy Corrigan's car. Corrigan sees a headline on a newsstand about Mao Zedong's widow, Jiang Qing, and three other party members who persecuted hundreds of thousands during the Chinese Cultural Revolution. It reads:

GANG OF FOUR ON TRIAL

Corrigan says this would make a good name for our band 'because there are four of you'.*

We have a name.

---

* He also says: 'Jiang Qing sounds like Jon King, which is funny.' Meanwhile, in the UK, there's another group tagged 'Gang of Four' in the press, centrist Social Democrats breaking away from the Labour Party. They're less interesting but not murderers. Our Wikipedia entry once read the band name references the Big Four French philosophers, Baudrillard, Lacan, Derrida and Foucault, which would have been great were it true, but it's not.

GOF V 1.0

Andy and I are keen to get a band together like the ones we'd seen at CBGB, so we pitch it to Hugo, who says he's in. We three then ask David 'Wolfman' Woolfson to sit in on bass, a decent jazz-funk player and nice guy who looks like a Furry Freak Brother, but we don't hold this against him. Gill still has cash stashed from his petrol station larceny and buys an Ibanez 2681 electric guitar – the heaviest and ugliest axe in existence – and a cheap Carlsbro transistor combo. The guitar's super sensitive and squeaks and squalls whenever Gill gets near the amp, which has the bright, crisp and clean sound we wanted. Hugo steals a couple of microphones and stands from an Ents lock-up and we've got all we need to play.

A friend, Andy Sharpe, who's squatting in a death-row house among the ruins of an old working-class area that's being knocked down, says we could practise in the abandoned back-to-back next door, and we can hack free electricity from the grid. It's perfect. 'Bossa Nova Estrada' is spraypainted in big letters on the bay wall out front, but no one knows why. Fat rats forage among rubbish that's drifted knee high on the cobbled streets; an acrid scent of wood smoke hangs in the air with grace-notes of petrol and burning plastic from fired piles of floorboards, mattresses and armchairs that smoulder in the constant mizzle. There's a non-stop grumble from bulldozers and lorries and jack hammers and wrecking balls worrying the ruins and taking away the hardcore spoil. There'll soon be no trace left of a working-class community which looked out for their neighbours, left the doors unlocked, and would lend a cup of sugar when neighbours were short.

Our dingy rehearsal room's windows are boarded with planks and protected by a padlocked pappy front door fainting on its hinges. We've stuck skip-scavenged carpets and egg boxes on the walls to dampen the noise, not that it matters, as we can play as loud as we like since there's no one left to annoy apart from Andy next door, who often sits in as we jam. It's as secure as any building listed for demolition can be, i.e. not at all, but no self-respecting burglar would come to this wasteland. It would squander valuable larceny time to leg it here to boost ratty schlock you couldn't lay off in a pub. Much better to pillage your newly rehoused neighbours in the brutalist high-rises and housing estates now decorating Leeds like graveyard teeth, with award-winning off-road pathways in the skies that are ideal for slinging dope and ambushing biddies for their pension.

We put together a set here, fast R & B guitar tunes with dopey lyrics that sound like a cross between the Feelgood's and Richard Hell and the Voidoids; we cover 'Day Tripper' to bulk up the set, playing it as fast as we can, stretching our abilities. When we take five, I sometimes sit on the scabby sofa and knit with my BGF, Andy Sharpe, who's a dab hand at casting off, helping me with my one and only attempt to make a woollen jumper, which looks like a dog's dinner when it's finished. Soon, we've got a bunch of songs ready to play:

1. 'We Condemn the Gang of Four'
2. '(The last Bus is) Ten Past One'
3. 'Waiting for My Elevator'
4. '(Don't) Call Me a Wanker'
5. 'Day Tripper'
6. 'Give Me a Reason'

7. 'What We Want' (NOT the much later funked up 'What We All Want')
8. 'Armalite Rifle'
9. 'John Stonehouse'

However, despite Hugo calling everyone he can, we can't get any support slots as we're an unknown new band that's never gigged and we're without a demo tape. There's no local punk scene to tap into, it's only happening in London, the Pistols played to just forty in Manchester's Lesser Free Trade Hall four months ago and it's not New York, so we'll have to do it ourselves. Hugo sweet talks a local promoter, John Keenan, to help us put on a show in a manky room in the basement of the deserted Leeds Corn Exchange on Briggate, a once magnificent Victorian building without a purpose, derelict and threatened with demolition, its fine limestone facade crumbling and blackened by a century of soot and acid rain.

Fifty or more people cram into the space, more than expected, to watch us accelerate through a deafening forty-minute set, with one bright white light at stage left, lit like a scene from *The Cabinet of Dr Caligari*. The night's a wild success, everyone's buzzing, it's a first in Leeds. But Wolfman's not right: he looks like a Furry Freak Brother and although he's a better musician than we are, he plays too many notes, up and down the frets like a bride's nightie. The simple songs need air – it's naked R & B not Weather Report. With regret we tell him it's not a fit, which he's cool about. I'm not sure he liked our stuff anyway, so we part on good terms.*

---

* David will become one of the UK's leading anger management therapists, which would have been useful in a band like ours.

DAVE

We need a replacement bass player, so Hugo posts a flyer on a newsboard, which reads: 'WANTED – FAST RIVVUM AND BLUES BASS PLAYER' (why 'rivvum' and not 'rhythm' is a mystery). Dave Allen answers. He's looking for a gig having come to Leeds from Kendal, fleeing the dainty tourist-clogged market town in England's Lake District famous for mint cake, cagoules and dreich. He'd had troubled teen years, restless and caged in a petit bourgeois household, his mum and dad running a busy fish and chip shop in an un-cultural hinterland, although he'll never says anything about them to me. Dave had had his fill gigging with low-rent show bands knocking out pop, C & W and jazz covers for foot-tapping mums and dads downing milk stout and bitter in pubs and clubs. He says he wants to make dangerous music that's funky and furious, inspired by the bleeding-edge punk, reggae and dub tracks he hears on John Peel's unique indie music radio slot. We share a love of Lee 'Scratch' Perry, the Meters – Dave nails 'Cissy Strut' – and James Brown. He's in after a short audition, he's got the chops, he's the *nuts*. GOF V.2 plays a single show with the new line-up and then it's the summer break.

Dave's not only a fine bass player, but he's also a hustler with a *payphone* in his shared house, so becomes our de facto rep, constantly on the blower to promoters and pubs and clubs for a slot. It's hard work with just a lo-fi C-60 tape of our material to share and not a word's written about us in a music press reluctant to review gigs north of Watford. Dave doesn't give up and blags support sets every few weeks. When the Buzzcocks are lined up to play at Ilkley College, he hassles the events booker, calling him over and over, for us to open for them until he caves and says just turn up then, but there's no fee. We drive over more in hope than expectation, unload our gear and wait, finding there's already a support act much annoyed to see us loitering about. We're about to bail when Richard Boon, the Buzzcocks' manager, takes pity on us and says, 'OK, you can go on when the doors are opened. Just don't get in anyone's faces.'

We do a short set to just twenty punters but are knocked out to see Richard watching us from the desk.

'Good show!' he says. 'I like what you're doing.'

A week later, Dave receives a telegram:

BUZZCOCKS EUROPEAN TOUR – STOP – WANT GANG OF FOUR TO BE SUPPORT BAND – STOP – CALL ASAP TO CONFIRM – STOP – RICHARD BOON.

It's *incredible*. We say YES! and then play two weeks with the Buzzcocks across Europe, being paid just enough money to cover our costs. Our first proper tour, it's a wonderful experience. The Buzzcocks are very good to us, and we get soundchecks and a dressing room with sandwiches and beers.

On our return to the UK, they give us more support slots, including a show at Leeds University's Refectory with the Buzzcocks, the Slits and John Cooper Clarke, our first show on a high stage. The same line-up plays Manchester's Mayflower club night, and it's a blast. A guy shouts out at the Slits' Ari Up from the mosh pit, 'Show us your cunt!' And Ari says. '*I'll* show you a cunt!' and jumps into the crowd and smacks him in the face, a mass brawl breaking out. She's brilliant, mad as a brush, a one-off. I love the Slits, one of my all-time favourite bands, and we're lucky to share an office with them and the

Pop Group in London as they're managed by Dick O'Dell, who's helping our new manager Rob Warr shop us a deal.*

When we're in Manchester, the Buzzcocks' singer Pete Shelley puts us up at his two-up, two-down terraced house in Gorton. It's in a right state, bare earth in the kitchen, the slums being bulldozed nearby. We sleep on the sofa and floor. Richard, Pete and guitarist Steve Diggle champion us, and we learn how to warm up a cold room, bettering ourselves and our material as we go, steadily replacing formula with more challenging tunes. Richard encourages us and says we're getting somewhere with Anthrax. Pete says, 'The trouble with you lot is there's too many chiefs and not enough Indians,' which is probably true.

When we're not gigging, we leave our equipment up in an empty warehouse where we've set up a rehearsal room. Mark White, Andrew Corrigan, Kevin Lycett, Ros Allen and Jon Langford use our kit if we're not there, and start a band called the Mekons after the *Dan Dare* comic-strip character. They're very different to us, and where we work at being crisp and even, they revel in chaos and make a virtue of their lack of musicianship with discordant rackets overlaid by Mark's poignant vignettes of sexual and social disappointment. It's as much art as music, but thrilling and funny and I love their routine. Although Jon (drums) and Ros (bass) have a music background, they both embrace the amateur aesthetic and the Mekons start gigging, often supporting us or at political benefits and Leeds Rock Against Racism. Their masterpiece, 'Where Were You?', will soon inject them into the national punk indie consciousness.

Our women friends use our kit, too, and another band's born: Delta 5, featuring Bethan Peters, a Leeds Poly 3D design student, the Mekons' Ros, who is a Leeds University Fine Art student, and Julz Sale, who'd come to Leeds for the craic. It's a fierce feminist outfit

---

* It's hard to get a sniff. One of many rejection letters, Stiff's is simply stamped 'IN THE DUMPER'.

with dual bass players, Bethan and Ros, and Julz on vocals up front with two men, Alan Riggs and Kelvin Knight, on drums and guitar. Their distinctive sound has a sinuous groove and fractured guitar overlaid by Julz's angry lyrics. They come up with a keeper song, 'Mind Your Own Business', for their debut single in 1979 that will in 2021 become the global soundtrack to Apple's ad campaign – all hail the long tail. The Mekons get noticed by Bob Last, an Edinburgh businessman who's started an indie label called Fast. He rates their song 'Never Been in a Riot' which he puts out as a 45 in 1978, saying 'the critical thing [about his decision to sign them] was that they really could not play'. Mary Harron later says the Mekons are 'a strange combination of sophisticated theory and technical incompetence', an on-the-nail analysis. We're proud of our mates putting out the first 7-inch from the collective but a *little* jealous, especially when they land a John Peel session on the back of their 'Riot' release, which Peel plays often on his show. When the session's first broadcast we all squeeze into Andy's flat to hear it, it's a big deal, we're excited but at the same time disappointed in our lack of progress. But this changes when the Mekons big us up to Last, who signs to record an EP at Cargo Studios in Rochdale. There, we record three songs for the first time: 'Damaged Goods', 'Anthrax' and 'Armalite Rifle'. Soon, everything will be different.

I QUIT!

There is a tide in the affairs of men. Which, taken at the flood, leads on to fortune.

William Shakespeare, *Julius Caesar* (1599)

I never wanted to be in a full-time band. Ever since I was a teenager my ambition was to become an artist, maybe do a post-grad course at the Royal College of Art or Chelsea, and make a living from making art. Gigging, rehearsals, interviews, schmoozing, all that stuff eats into my painting and drawing time just when I've started getting somewhere with it, winning the university's Passey Prize for art, having a painting on show in Sheffield's Mappin Gallery as regional finalist of the Winsor & Newton young painters' competition, and even selling a picture to my tutor.

While I enjoy the buzz about the band, I don't want to be famous – Gill later says I did well at achieving this objective, miaow! – and prefer being unnoticed offstage, happy to be anonymous in the crowd. It sets me apart from Gill, Dave and Hugo, who LOVE being in a band and ADORE the attention.

Besides that, I'm exhausted by the argumentative band dynamic where we – I'm just as guilty as the others – constantly snipe at each other and row about anything from Hegel to the price of a Mars bar, and are intolerant of each other's failure to *get it*, whatever *it* is. We're all as one in wanting to make something transcendent but while we dream about a shining light on a hill, we can't see through the dense fog of conflict that darkens the way. On the plus side, intolerance of mediocrity is a big reason why the work's getting better as no one can relax and tune out, but the point scoring's often personal and cruel, especially by Andy towards Hugo.

Me, I'm pedantic and a know-all, while Dave's contemptuous of our New Left politics, which he doesn't share, saying we're just intellectual poseurs as we're private school-educated boys from privileged backgrounds, which disqualifies us from holding socialist views *authentically*. I point out, rather pedantically and pompously, that two giants of the left, John Wesley and Karl Marx, were both bourgeois intellectuals, and they did all right in the ideas market. And Dave is himself a grammar schoolboy from a solidly petit bourgeois family even if he has a Lancastrian accent, which he says isn't the point as he doesn't claim to be a socialist, etc., etc. These conversations go on and on until they spiral up their own fundament and I need to lie down in a darkened room. Whatever, while I don't *like* it, I've got to accept in Leeds I'm seen as a posh boy from down south, while no one in London would make this category error. They'd hear Islington when I speak – all those glottal stops in what will later be called an *Estuary* accent.

On top of this, rehearsal/writing sessions are often a drag because Gill regularly shows up very late or not at all – no one's got a phone for reminders or apologies – leaving Dave, Hugo and me to sit around talking shite until he bowls in or not, often just before we'd planned to finish. Andy's so lazy he wouldn't work in an iron lung, last in and first out, never practises or prepares anything, and only touches a guitar in the rehearsal room. Our friendship's souring and I'd rather be Andy's mate than pissed off with him in a band.

So, I say I'm off but want to stay friends, concentrate on art not music, it's not you it's me, etc., etc. The others are sorry to see me go but say they'll carry on, find someone else on vocals, which is fine by me. I return to drawing and painting, and in the life class every day happiest when I'm holding a pencil. I'm loving the change, and hear that Hugo, Andy and Dave are auditioning singers, even Mick Wixey, the Mekons manager, has a try-out, which is weird, but whatever, it's not my gig, might be a great idea, a long-haired biker hooligan up front murdering a mic could be great. He doesn't get the job.

Nor does anyone else. A few weeks on, Gill asks me to rejoin the band as they can't find a decent singer who's not an arsehole, can write music and lyrics, and will work for nothing with poor prospects in a toxic work environment. Or something like that. I'm pleased by extension I'm not an arsehole, although the jury's still out. Andy says come back and we'll make sure the band doesn't take over every waking hour and allow me to paint and draw. He has similar motives as he wants to complete his degree and is absorbed by the art history work he's doing under Tim Clark's tutelage, who he's bonded with much more strongly than I have, as Gill's no good at making art and prefers the academic side of the course; he should really have done a pure Art History degree.

I ask him if Dave and Hugo are copacetic and he says, 'Yeah, they're totally onboard, two hundred per cent,' so I say all right, I'll come back, but *only* if I can do the artwork for the outer sleeves of any new records, you *promise* to turn up on time, we try to change the world and kick out the jams ... I don't want to be in a band just to be in a band. We shake hands on making great art through music, changing the world, and doing it together. I unquit.

Nothing changes.

DAMAGED GOODS

Saturday afternoons we may wander through the bright white aisles of Morrisons supermarket looking for discount food near its sell-by date and hoping to find a new Tennent's *lager lovely* to complete our beer can collection. The store's strapline is 'The change will do you good', with the clever double meaning of 'change' as in money and 'change' as in switching store – someone got paid for this rubbish! This started me writing about a relationship near its sell-by date where a good physical thing had become too much of thing. Andy adds the iconic 'Damaged goods, send them back', which reinforces working the self-commodification motif over a call-and-response bass and choppy guitar duh duh DINK! Duh duh DINK! building the song around it with dynamic drop outs allowing everyone to feature, staying to two chords only. It's a writing milestone, and when we pen 'Anthrax', too, we know we're on to something outside genre. We record them both on our debut Fast Product EP, which becomes an indie hit and reveals us to the world. Without it, we'd have been nowhere.

We didn't get an advance, are never accounted to, and don't get a penny from record sales. Having been ripped off like this, we re-recorded the tracks on our debut album *Entertainment!* to avoid losing even more royalties. I wish I'd floored Fast's label boss. I'm often later asked why we signed to a *major* label if we're so *alternative*. I say at least EMI will pay.

BUSTED IN THE LAKES

November 1978: *Damaged Goods* is selling fast, topping the indie chart. Gang of Four, the Human League and the Mekons share the bill on a sell-out concert to 1,500 in London's Electric Ballroom, showing off the Fast Records roster and the first time London's seen the leftfield new Yorkshire bands. We still haven't had a live review for a year despite playing dozens of shows with the Buzzcocks and others; no one knows anything about us other than the EP tracks. We're no longer Dr Feelgood impersonators but have changed without trace and become ourselves with a radical set and a fierce onstage presence, having learned to work rooms with tough crowds as no-name support to the Buzzcocks and others in the UK and Europe.

The Camden Town new music cognoscenti are knocked out by our be-funked angular guitar politico thing, unlike anything in the capital, and the show wins rave reviews. From now on, promoters will return our manager Rob Warr's calls, and bookings come in fast. We're selling out larger rooms and paid enough to draw some cash for the first time. Four months from now the same line-up will play the 2,200-capacity Lyceum Theatre on the Strand, and a few months after that, we'll headline the same venue on our own. We're on a roll.

The *NME* plans a cover story about us and has embedded the crack team of writer Adrian Thrills and photographer Pennie Smith with the band, driving up with us and my girlfriend Debbie in our splitter van to cover a concert in Kendal, Lancashire, where Dave Allen was raised, which will be a triumphant homecoming.

Heavy snow's falling when we arrive, with the temperature forecast to plummet to sub-zero, freezing unlagged water pipes and white blanketing in an icy chocolate-box vision the lovely limestone housing, castle ruins and countryside. Only nine miles to Lake Windermere, and with easy access to the M6, Kendal's a pretty market town in the heart of the Lake District which caters to everyone's rain-soaked holiday needs; and a base for myriad hordes of bright-cagouled ramblers pilgrimaging to the gorgeous Lakeland fells while nibbling its world famous and diabetes-inducing mint cake as they look forward, perhaps, to warming themselves in a quaint pub beside a blazing wood fire while they savour a delicious *après* hike pint. That would be nice.

But it's not an option. We've been banged up shoeless, clueless and beltless in cold holding cells by the Kendal drugs squad.

The gig at the Brewery Arts Centre was wonderful, a warm crowd proud of their prodigal son's return. Dave's forgiven, for what, I don't know, and stands centre stage to take many moist-eyed bows after too many encores. The after-show over, we split up, Debbie and I staying with a local friend of a friend, and the others bedding down in the house of an old schoolmate of Dave's.

After a chilly photoshoot with Pennie – one shot of Gill and me will form the *NME*'s front cover and launch us into indie fame – we set off back to the Big Smoke, admiring the countryside blanched by snow, and chatting with Adrian, who interviews us as we go. However, our easy access to the M6 south is barred by a police roadblock and we're waved to the shoulder, with a plainclothes car pulling up to the bumper behind us. Fuck's sake!

A uniform comes over, asks where we've been and what we've been doing, there's been a shop break-in, televisions and that stolen. Rob says we're musicians, gigged here last night, heading back to London now, etc., etc.

The cop says, 'Let's look in back.'

'Okey dokey,' says Hugo, opening the rear doors to reveal backline kit, no TVs, nothing to see here.

'Right!' says a plainclothes cop, jumping from the unmarked car. 'All of you, out of the van! Turn out your pockets!'

'Umm,' says Hugo, 'I thought this was about nicked tellies?'

'Don't get *smart*, son,' says the copper. 'Cut the backchat.'

We're searched. No televisions are in our pockets.

'Let's look *again* in the back,' says the uniform, 'and *you* all,' pointing at us, 'hands on heads!'

Hugo watches as the cop digs about in the back while his plainclothes buddy rummages solo upfront, unsupervised. No one's bugged, there's no gear in the Merc; the boys smoked the last of the Lebanese Red last night, and I don't smoke dope at all.

'What *this*?' says the plainclothes, holding high an aluminium foil wrapped block the size of a Wrigley's Spearmint pack. It's a fit up, no way the hash is ours, it's too *tidy*, such a sharp-cornered lump, and wouldn't have survived the night. We're ordered to drive to the local nick where we're held in separate cells. After a couple of hours, I'm taken to the interview room where two coppers face me.

Cop A says, 'We know *everything*, your mate's owned up.'

'Owned up to what?' I say.

'The *gear*,' says Cop B.

'No, there was nothing in the van.'

A says, 'We *found* the hash, it's done and dusted! Tell us what you know!'

'Who owned up?' I ask. 'There was nothing there until you showed up.'

'You saying we *planted* the dope? That's a serious accusation!' says B.

Jesus, what a twat, this is ridiculous! I've seen police procedurals and know the hard- and soft-man interview room routine, but these dimwits are more Mork and Mindy than Starsky and Hutch!

'I'm saying nothing, *officer*, but there wasn't any dope in the van until you turned up.'

A and B scowl and order me to drop my trousers and pants so they can look at my arsehole and under my scrotum, which isn't very nice, and I'm taken back to the cell.

We all get the same shit. When Adrian Thrills, kecks down, is told in broad Lancastrian by a cop, 'Lift your knackers!' he pulls up his Y-fronts. 'NOO!' says the cop. 'Not your *knickers*, your *knackers*!'

Debbie had to wait for a female officer to stare at her parts, and pre-fiddling went unwatched to the bog to deliver a fine turd, and didn't wipe her arse, leaving a stinky ring residue for the woman cop to savour. Go, girl! Nice touch! Dave, however, was knocked about by a drugs squad drone who'd been in the same year at Dave's old school. 'You think you're so *special!*' he said, throwing him against the wall.

We've been stopped and held without cause, which is against the law, drugs have been planted, which is a crime, and fingerprinted without being charged or a magistrate's order, which is against the law. We're released six hours after being banged up, and no charges are laid: it's naked harassment from men resenting Dave's fame. Why are we surprised?

Our big-shot lawyer in London calls the drugs squad's boss to say that *everything* they did was against the law. The cops apologise in a formal letter and say they'll destroy the illegally obtained fingerprints. If we'd been poor or Black we'd have been fucked by these fuckers. Police crimes and fit-ups like this happen every day.

BREAKOUT

John Peel plays our EP tracks all the time and a couple of months later, in early 1979, we're invited to record two John Peel BBC radio sessions where we record six songs for the first time. Once broadcasted, the live demand for the band goes crazy. We've been on the front covers of the *NME* and *Melody Maker*, the arbiters of music-biz opinion, had a big splash in *Sounds*, and our live shows are getting five-star reviews.

Probably because of this attention there's an underlying hostility to us in Leeds – apparently some calling us the 'Sevenoaks wankers', a good point well made – as if we'd swarmed silver-spooned into the Mill City with wallets rammed with cash but not *from* here, it's not *fair*. Marc Almond complains that 'apart from Hugo Burnham, they [Gang of Four] were all middle-class sons of stockbrokers!' If I could be arsed, which I'm not, I'd tell Marc that Dave Allen's parents own a fish and chip shop in the Lake District, my dad's an electrician, and Andy's mum is a teacher. *Hugo*'s the most solidly bourgeois member of the band, his father a big cheese in the rag trade flogging frocks and suits from a shop near Savile Row. Wearing Doc Martens, jeans with braces and Ben Sherman's are not key indicators of class. Besides, my monkey boots are cooler.

I'm envious of the Mekons, who *like* each other, get on well, and forgive each other's foibles. Unlike us.

The noises-off negativity about our political and cultural backgrounds is balanced by the generosity of other locals, especially the free rehearsal space we've been gifted by Leeds's Soma Wholefoods cooperative. It's fabulous, an empty warehouse with huge high-roofed rooms near the canal where we can make as much noise as we like whenever we like. It's become a creative hub we share with the Mekons and Delta 5, leaving the backline up for all to use with a useful self-built PA. Hugo's theatre-group friends rehearse upstairs.

It's a brilliant place to work, the band gets tighter and the songs improve.

ARMALITE RIFLE

'Armalite Rifle' pisses me off. We'd originally jammed up an instrumental rocker developed from a heavy Free-adjacent drumbeat Hugo came up with, which Dave and Andy found parts to, but the session went south and the workout went in the dumper. A few days later, I arrive late to find the song's done, with words and everything, the only song so far for which I haven't written all the words. The track's solid with a hot guitar riff but the vocals are generic punk, shouty and obvious. My only contribution, I think, is that I'd once shared a kick-starter working title with Gill, 'Armalite Rifle', which I'd noted down having heard of a seventies Provo IRA song called 'My Little Armalite', later described by its writer Jim Dooley (according to Wikipedia) as an 'amusing and boastful rallying song', which tickles me.

While being impressed that Gill came up with lyrics at all – words are not his thing – they're tosh. Being pedantic and a martyr to fact checking I say, 'NO, Armalite's *don't* break down easy, they *don't* fit into a pram, *no* child could carry one or fire one, and Ulster cops *don't* use them.'

I say we could say more interesting things about the most popular gun in America – one-fifth of all gun-owners in the US own at least one! – and about its iconic status in the USA and with the Provos. A National Rifle Association board member, obviously hard right, once said owning one means 'F-you to the left', which it kind of does, along with F-you to democracy. Gill says, 'Whatever, what's done is done, people like it. I'm changing nothing.'

I feel better for venting.

A COMIC IN CARLISLE

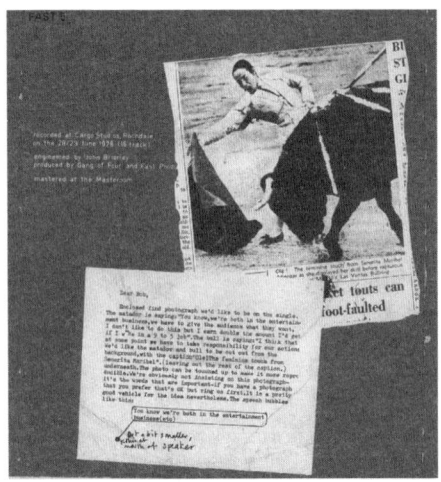

Dave's blagged a gig at Carlisle College of Art's Christmas bash. There'll be support acts, we'll get one hundred pounds, and it's a short scenic drive through beautiful countryside to an ancient frontier city bordering England and Scotland. Hadrian's Wall is a short hike away, there's an impressive twelfth-century castle, and the city's chock full of charming olde worlde buildings and wonderful pubs, etc.

We won't see any of this.

The gig's in a dreary Student Union room within a grim sixties concrete 'n' glass block that could double as a mortuary. The arty punters are sitting at rows of trestle tables with seasonal student artwork livening up the walls, Xmas-themed glitz and bunting dangling over their heads to hammer home the festive mood. There's no dressing room: we're told we can wait our turn in a chill corridor with a half-dozen stacking chairs hidden behind a mobile screen and enjoy a rider of salty snacks and slab of Tennent's. Nice.

We are seven: the band plus Jolyon Burnham (Hugo's brother; stage tech), Rob Warr (management and front-of-house sound) and Phil (lights, although there aren't any). After sound checking on a foot-high plinth stage, we settle down in the main party room as the corridor's too chilly to chill in. Art students pile in, dressed to kill and pissed up, already slack-mouthed and wall-eyed from pre-loaded budget vodka and whizz.

The first act's a hoot, a male stripper channelling Clint Eastwood in *A Few Dollars More*, sporting a wool poncho, leather-look chaps and manky Stetson, while chewing a cheroot and trying to squint like Clint, but his sour expression looks more like he's having trouble downstairs with the number twos. Clint-a-like parades up and down to Ennio Morricone's iconic music, drops his kecks, wiggles his tush, and generally minces about – very unlike Clint, this bit – and tosses off his outfit until, ta-daah!, he's naked except for a leatherette jock, his wedding tackle packed under a beer gut as round as a turtle shell, more Ernie Wise than Arnie Schwarzenegger, but the audience don't care if he's ripped, they whoop and holler, love the dadbod. Not my cup of tea, but hey, it's Christmas, goodwill to all men, different strokes, whatever.

Next on is a comic in a bad suit. He's three sheets to the wind, blue veins mapped across his cheeks, with sweat beading on a forehead topped by a Bobby Charlton combover glued flat to his pate. In the school of Roy 'Chubby' Brown and Bernard Manning, he amps up his northern-ness and gallops through a set of blue and racist jokes only a Brownshirt or rat-arsed art student could find funny. He's overcome with laughter at a gag he tells – something about a bloke with an STD – with the punchline: 'he's got bandage round back o' t' flange... looks like Kojak w'it scarf!', before migrating to one liners about Paddies and Jamaicans.

It's TOO much, this is NOT our thing – what the fuck was the promoter thinking? Dave Allen loses it, shouts 'FUCK OFF, ADOLF!' to which the 'comedian' says, 'Does your mouth bleed every twenty-eight days?' It kicks off, we're nonstop heckling, shouting down his racist gags while the room quietens; we're party pooping, he's corpsing, students are dribbling to the exits, and the mood's like watching a fight break out at a wake for someone you never liked. The Student Ents guy comes over and hands us our cash fee and says, 'Take the money, you don't need to play. Could you just please fuck off now?'

No way, we're going nowhere, there's a set to play, it's showbiz, the show must go on!

The comic gives up, abandons the stage and walks over to us. He's very upset and says, 'I told these self-same jokes to a group of Jewish mothers last week and not one complained! You know we're both in the entertainment business, we have to give the audience what they want. I don't like to do this, but I earn double the amount I'd get if I were in a nine-to-five job.'

Hugo says, 'I think at some point we have to take responsibility for our actions' – very eloquent – while me, Dave and Andy tell the comic to 'Fuck off, Adolf.'

When we get to do our turn, the room's almost empty; only a handful of diehard fans have stuck it out, the others decamping for better times in one of Carlisle's wonderful pubs, or perhaps hiking to Hadrian's Wall in the Lake District drizzle or going home to watch *Match of the Day*.

We put on a decent show capped by an extended version of 'Anthrax', Hugo and Dave totally on the groove locking down Andy's preposterously brilliant feedback as he bashes the guitar into submission on the maxed-out amp, squeaking and squalling and whining, the few punters still here getting what they all wanted. It's been a good night, all things considered.

We don't get booked in Carlisle again.

I use the comic's words on the cover of the *Damaged Goods* EP with a photo of the world's first female toreador fighting in the bullring, the bull wanting her to take responsibility for her actions . . .

ROCK AGAINST RACISM

In 1976 Eric Clapton declares his support of Enoch Powell, a notoriously racist UK politician at a concert in Birmingham, during a time of growing hard-right attacks on Asians and Afro-Caribbeans. Clapton's words outrage decent people and indecent musicians across the country, especially as everything Clapton does musically pillages Black music.

The rock photographer Red Saunders and others write to the *NME*, the most influential music mag in Britain, which sells over 300,000 copies a week. They say, 'Come on, Eric, own up – half your music is black ... PS Who shot the Sheriff, Eric? It sure as hell wasn't you!' which provokes such a strong response that Rock Against Racism (RAR) is founded with the core idea that musicians must fight back against the fascist National Front, whose aggressively nostalgic anti-immigrant platform, hatred of Blacks and Asians and anti-Semitism, is aimed at white youth suffering mass unemployment, poverty and social alienation. To counter this poison, RAR puts on national shows and events that feature Black and white musicians from disparate genres, which show that racism has no place in music, building on the already strong connections between punk rock and reggae. Other activists are inspired to form the Anti-Nazi League (ANL), giving this cultural campaign a solid political platform. Local activists form the Leeds RAR Club, where we play so often that the organiser, Paul Furness, says Gang of Four/Mekons/Delta 5 are 'almost house bands'. At 1978's huge Manchester Northern Carnival Against Racism, headlined by the Buzzcocks, we play with the Mekons and Delta 5 on the back of a flatbed truck as it crawls through the city streets.

Right-wing extremists are unavoidable in Leeds and sometimes show up at Gang of Four, Mekons or Delta 5 RAR benefit shows to make trouble, pissed-up claques of *sieg-heil*-ing skins screaming abuse at us a few feet away in the mosh pit. They kick off aggro in sync – a football hooligans' technique planned upfront – to punch and kick fans around them, gobbing phlegm and lobbing bottles. When shit like this goes down, we can't carry on like nothing's happened, it's in our faces, and Dave's first to jump offstage holding his bass like a spear, stabbing at the skins, us following, until the house security – if there is any – wades in and chucks the morons out. It's a drag.

Depressingly this happens a lot in Leeds, and I'm often wired before shows worrying about the prospect of things kicking off. These are serious men bent on organised violence, and a friend of ours is beaten nearly to death by neo-Nazis on university grounds and suffers life-changing head injuries. The Mekons get the same treatment – we're all seen as commies – and during an attack on the Delta 5 women, Julz kicks a man in the head doing a Sieg Heil salute in front of her, the skins chanting 'Repatriation's so much better' when the band sings their song 'Anticipation', the real words being 'Anticipation's so much better'. A fascist reaction to RAR is Rock Against Communism (RAC), with hard-right gigs fronted by White Power bands like Skrewdriver.

These are dark days.

One night, sitting with Mark and Corrigan and the rest in the back of the Fenton, a pub well-known as a home for lefties, punk musicians and gays, there's smashing and crashing and screaming and shouting as an NF crew steamrollers in to attack us all. Punches are thrown, chairs fly, broken bottles and beer glasses on floors sloppy with suds, as we rush to the tight bar corridor to defend ourselves, only to see the skins being beaten away almost single-handedly by a Leeds separatist lesbian in dungarees and apocalypse barnet, pummelling the fascists, her arms flailing, shouting fuck you fuck off out of it as they retreat like rats. She's incredible. What a woman! *No pasarán!*

It's a hell of a night, but I prefer P and Q.

RAR becomes a major force and in the run-up to the 1979 UK general election – where the NF puts up over three hundred candidates.* The RAR *Militant Entertainment Tour* covers the UK.† We're one of forty RAR bands, which include the Mekons, Delta 5, Steel Pulse, Aswad, Stiff Little Fingers, Alex Harvey, Angelic Upstarts, the Ruts, UK Subs, Misty in Roots and John Cooper Clarke.

We tour the country with Misty in Roots and the Ruts, two incredible bands. The fans know it's not just *entertainment*, they're thrilling events where everyone, fans and bands alike, show the unity and love between Black and White.

The shows are a blast. I like to stand out front in the thick of the crowd to catch the other bands, especially the Ruts, who monster the stage, their sound and fury signifying everything, climaxing in the full-on classic 'Babylon's Burning'. They're pro's, tight and precise, Paul Fox's perfectly played hard-rock guitar riffs – more Jimmy Page than a punk buzzsaw – propelling Malcolm Owen's

---

* Not one candidate is elected. According to Martin Webster, the head NF organiser, 'prior to 1977 the NF were unstoppable. Then suddenly the ANL was everywhere and knocked the hell out of them ... the sheer presence of the ANL had made it impossible to get NF members onto the streets, had dashed recruitment and cut away their vote. It wasn't just the physical opposition to their marches; they have lost the propaganda war too.'

† Over five hundred RAR shows are put on between 1977 and 1983.

furious vocals as he works the crowd, looking sharp in suedehead threads, jeans and braces over a red polo. He's a great bloke, but stuck on smack, and some nights so fucked up it's a fuck-up. They could have been bigger than the Clash, but only twelve months later Malcolm will be dead from a heroin OD. I'm angry and sad when I hear about it, it's such a waste.

The reggae band Misty is awesome, too, always in the pocket, despite sucking on conical reefers as fat as sausages. I don't know how they stay sharp, but they're as crisp as cellophane. John Peel's a big fan of them and I first hear their music on his late-night BBC show, the only radio slot where alternative acts and reggae music get played.*

It's a privilege to play with such cool musicians. Sometimes the things we do help make the world a little better, and RAR was one of these. I'm proud to have played a small part in it. David Widgery, co-founder of RAR, said, 'For a while we managed to create, in our noisy, messy, unconventional way, an emotional alternative to nationalism and patriotism, a celebration of a different kind of pride and solidarity.'†

At a Cromer hotel after an RAR show at West Runton Pavilion, we're playing snooker along with Muff Winwood, senior A & R exec at CBS records, legendary producer, and one-time member of the Spencer Davis Group with his brother Stevie. CBS has done a brilliant job with the Clash's debut album and we're eager to sign to a big label after being skinned by Fast.

---

* Misty's singer, Clarence Baker, was badly beaten and injured in 1979 by the Met Police's paramilitary Special Patrol Group unit during a protest in Southall against a National Front march, during which six SPG officers without identifying numbers were seen beating a demonstrator, Blair Peach, to death. No one was prosecuted. Linton Kwesi Johnson wrote, in 'Reggae Fi Peach', 'Blair Peach was not an English man/Him come from New Zealand/ Now they kill him and him dead and gone/But his memory lingers on.'
† Quoted in John Harris, 'Noisy, messy, unconventional and progressive: remembering Rock Against Racism', *New Statesman*, 13 March 2019.

Although Gill's much better than me on the baize, Muff and I play for big stakes: he wins, GOF sign to CBS; I win, we get the label's royalties from Dire Straits' 'Sultans of Swing'. His balls go on their holidays, while I clear the table, potting colour after colour after the reds and pot the black on a bank shot to win! It's a dream as I'm usually rubbish at the big table game. Sadly, the bet isn't honoured. We should have spat on our hands and shaken first. It's a bummer.

CBS offers us a big advance for a worldwide deal. It's very good. *But* we insist on a 'Rest of World' deal that splits off the USA with complete artistic control of music and artwork, because we want to license our recordings to a separate entity in the States. It's a deal breaker as CBS won't run with it.*

Muff's A & R competitor at EMI, Chris Briggs, is itching to get us on his roster and agrees to our terms if we halve the upfront money, which is fair. We sign to them in the spring of 1979, leaving us free to shop a deal with a third party in the States, and split all royalties between us equally, regardless who did what, as we work as a cooperative. We then ink a separate deal with EMI publishing, again splitting royalties four ways, and sign off the dole, we're on a roll.

---

* This approach will prove to be an excellent decision that decades later will pay off very well. Record deals are almost always in perpetuity – which is a long time – so once recordings have been made they're owned to eternity by the label on whatever shitty terms were struck before the act had any negotiating juice. This is why we and, later, Taylor Swift re-recorded early work, to be paid better, or even be paid at all, from the sound-alike work. However – sadly in the states only – by utilising Section 203 of the US Copyright Act of 1976, known as the 'thirty-five-year law', artists can opt to terminate grants of rights to record companies thirty-five years after publication of the works, and restore ownership of the US copyright in the sound recordings to the artists who recorded them. We'll take advantage of this law, terminating our contract with Warners, and see the US rights revert to us.

Our lawyer says, theatrically plonking the EMI contract in a drawer, 'You're friends now, but I *guarantee* the next time I take this out, you'll be arguing about money.'

'Nah,' we all say. 'Never!

But he'll be right.

ROCK AGAINST SEXISM

A sister organisation, Rock Against Sexism (RAS), is formed to fight sexism in the music biz. We do benefits for them but are uneasy about us being an all-male outfit, too many contradictions, even if we try to steer clear of cock-rock sexist clichés.

At an RAS show at London's Electric Ballroom, which we're headlining, we decide it's not right to go last on after all-female support the Spoilsports, so we say you go on last, *after* us and the openers, our Leeds friends in the mixed sex band called Delta 5.

It's dumb, as people think the show's over once we're off and clear the room. The Spoilsports play to an almost empty house, with only a few stragglers and their Camden mates lingering to see them. Not what was intended.

Doing the right thing isn't always the right thing.

DAD'S DEAD

May 1977. As I walk out of the year three exam room I'm taken aside by the Fine Art Department secretary who says, 'You should go home right away. Your father's very ill.'

I knew this was coming. Six months ago, Dad was told he had stage four colon cancer, untreatable, nothing could be done except palliative care. It's a disease that disproportionately affects working-class people with poor diets and lifestyles; processed food and the lack of roughage, fresh fruit and veg may be a trigger. Basically, not having a lot of money.

Dad wouldn't go to the doctor, couldn't be doing with all that but when he finally had no choice, unable to keep food down, throwing up all he ate, it was too late. A tumour had blossomed in his bowels and cancer had homesteaded throughout his body. We ask the consultant how much time Dad has left, and she says, 'He won't make old bones.'

Knowing this, I drive home fast; when I get there I'm met by Nan, who says, 'He's gone.'

Dad died soon after his forty-eighth birthday, just skin and bones, leaving a shallow hollow in the mattress where he'd lain.

I hardly knew him as an adult – he worked all hours and I was always out and about – but he was a kind man, devoted to family, who'd worked his nuts off to make a better life for us all. I'd had time with him on Sundays when I was younger, helping him work on the car. He'd show me how to fix engines, use tools and solder and give me a steer when I was flummoxed reassembling a bike engine I'd taken apart, gifting me a pleasure in making things work or mending them. The only grown-up time I had with him was a solitary late-night drink where he and I downed a bottle of Fundador brandy I'd brought back from Spain after a disastrous bike ride through France when the gear changer failed. I hadn't had any breakdown cover or any money left, so made the shift work with a beer can pull aralditied in place. He was proud Debbie and I didn't give up or ask for help. It was a wonderful session.

He achieved so much, dying in the house he'd built himself, with the mortgage paid off and not a penny in debt. And he'd been able to buy a new Ford Capri. It was a great life.

Other than the house, car, and ancient wrist watch, he had no personal possessions, and all I have of him is his signature in an autograph book.

I think of him often.

He'd have been very pleased I don't work with my hands.

DESIGNING THE *ENTERTAINMENT!* COVER

Entertainment! cover design.

I'd seen a Belgian TV guide, when gigging in Brussels with the Buzzcocks, which previewed the movie *Winnetou: The Last Shot*, a 1965 West German Western, which had a close-up photo from the promo poster for the film. It shows the actors Lex Barker (who plays the cowboy Winnetou) and Pierre Brice (the 'Indian' Shatterhand) shaking hands. The story, according to IMDb, is: 'After the Civil War, desperadoes led by a renegade named Rollins, try to drive a wedge in the friendship between the whites and the Indians.'

A sincere handshake like this can't ever have happened during the genocidal wars against Native Americans by Europeans but is a rich territory for a *dérive*. I take the TV guide home, always saving interesting pictures, phrases and words to recycle for artwork and song lyrics. The movie's based on the writing of Karl May (1842–1912), one of the bestselling German authors of all time, selling over two hundred million books, potboilers about a mythic American West later reassessed in communist East Germany as proto-critiques of capitalism. Einstein and Hitler were both fans, but probably not in the same book group.

I think a lot about what the image signifies: the handshake, the racial stereotypes, the friendship against the odds, the promise of equity and justice 180 degrees from the reality of murderous ethnic cleansing and betrayal. Rich visual territory for our debut album.

Since EMI had conceded absolute control of artwork to us – this was a crucial condition – I do the outer and Andy the inner sleeve designs for *Entertainment!* It's more efficient to work separately and we have different methods, Gill's inner relying on photography and text, and my outer a mix of drawing, collage and text.

I don't want the sleeve to have any photographs of the band, because what we look like isn't important, although it surely is, but I want the cover to be a visual manifesto of what we're about. Heavily influenced by my love of comic strips and the Situationists' use of *détournement* – which the *Oxford English Dictionary* says means 'transforming artworks by creatively disfiguring them' – I add text around my hand-drawn image traced from the photo, making the cowboy's face white and the 'Indian's' red, having done this sort of thing at Leeds. It overtly references André Bertrand's Situationist comic-strip pamphlet *The Return of the Durutti Column*, later creatively ripped off, and repurposed, by Factory Records. Situationism, Wikipedia says, 'expanded the Marxist critique of capitalism, particularly its tendency to replace authentic experience with "individual expression by proxy" through the exchange and consumption of commodities.'

Situationism was good in the development of a revolutionary tactic to reinvest our cultural past and overtly use popular imagery to subvert it and make the familiar strange, rather than trying to *épater les bourgeoisie* – to scandalise the middle class. I riff on this thought on the *Entertainment!* and *Damaged Goods* sleeves.

On the back of *Entertainment!*'s outer sleeve are drawings I make from a newspaper photo showing the 'fattest man in Switzerland' with wife and kids in his gigantic trousers, although this may not be his family, he might not be the fattest man in Switzerland nor anywhere else, and they could be someone else's pantaloons. I use photocopies, Sharpie line drawing, and torn coloured paper stuck in place. It's a grandchild of one of my paintings, '*Pour Marx*', a drippy Union Flag painted in household gloss with the words 'THE ART WITHOUT BOUNDARIES IS CONFINED TO THE NATO BLOC AND ITS ALLIES'. Phew! It was pretty good, the title quoting Louis Althusser, the French philosopher and criminal wife strangler, with its obvious French/English wordplay on 'pour' and 'poor', not that Althusser had a sense of humour. But I was deflated when I saw it hanging in Sheffield's Mappin Gallery: it looked just like a *painting* in the echo chamber of art where cultured people who all agree with each other agree to be challenged by things that aren't challenging, like anything by Jeff Koons. I decide to concentrate on Gang of Four and focus my creative energies there.

Gill's inner sleeve design shows photos of things seen on TV with an oblique commentary, analogous to the lyrics on '5:45', 'How can I sit and eat my tea with all that blood flowing from the television? . . .'

Decades later, why are we still sitting and eating our ~~tea~~ dinner with all that blood flowing from the television?

When will it ever end?

DR FEELGOOD

We owe a lot to Dr Feelgood, who I see whenever I can, in love with the sound and the fury of their shows, Lee Brilleaux centre stage, a picture of debauched masculinity in a once-white suit stained with booze, ash and slop. He'll have a fag and a pint in one hand as the other white-knuckle-fistedly grips an SM58 mic as he spits out in a mist of phlegm their underclass songs of jealousy, doomed love and low-rent dreams. A waterfull of sweat runs down his face while he sings, the threat of violence and retribution always there, the air of a sociopathic double-glazing salesman who'd just got his cards.

At his side, Wilko Johnson's incredible, lurching about the stage like a human pinball, attacking his strings with fierce four-fingered flicks, stabbing with stiff arms his Telecaster like a pike, careening from one side of the stage to the other, glaring glass eyed with a thousand-yard stare from a face frozen white by the sulphate, his jaw grinding double time as the speed does its work. An awesome spectacle that in the early days we cloned as we worked on how to connect with crowds and own the stage.

Loving Lee's swag, I dig out oversized demob suits at jumble sales, the bigger the better, the stains and wear made by men back from the wars trying to make a life in a land unfit for heroes. Andy will forever channel Wilko, scampering stony faced from stage left to right, bashing the strings so hard blood's regularly spattered across the pickups, his nails split and ragged as if after torture.

One of our few covers is Dr Feelgood's classic 'Roxette', and when we do it right, everything feels good in the world.

Postscript

2005, I'm at a *Mojo* Awards dinner where we win the Inspiration to Music Award, a wonderful night, in a room packed with rock gods like Jimmy Page, and I see Wilko across the floor, who I confuse by shaking his hand and saying we owe it all to you. He hasn't a clue who we are.

BAKED!

Our lighting guy, let's call him Gary, is a hardcore stoner baked twenty-four/seven, permanently puffing on a spliff or skinning one up, or chomping with the galloping munchies on a soft white bread and marmalade sandwich, like Paddington; or all three at once.

One a.m. in a Birmingham hotel, I'm tucked up warm when the fire alarm goes off. Fuck's sake! It's DEAFENING. Not a drill! Not the first time this has occurred – prats on stag dos or pissed-up rugger buggers away from her indoors love setting off alarms and fire extinguishers, it's *hilarious* – so it's more a nuisance than concern, but one time it could be real. Dozily decamped to a hotel car park and shuffling in a blanket to keep warm, me and others in the entourage are told by a wired hotel rep in a yellow tabard to STAY CALM, don't panic, the fire brigade's on its way, make sure nobody's missing in your group blah blah blah. We do as she says and see that everyone's here save Gary, no doubt off his tits in a sinsemilla daze. I'm not very fond of him, nor an altruistic or nice person, but somehow stupidly volunteer to get him out of the hotel before he's burned to a frazzle in an inferno, not that there's any sign of smoke, or that he'd notice if there was. He'd think it was the Hawaiian buds seeds playing up.

The alarm still blaring INCREDIBLY LOUDLY, I sprint up the stairs to Gary's room and pound on his unlocked door, which swings open to reveal a pothead's *Marie Celeste*, stale coffee in a cup, a room service tray sticky with ketchup and fetid fries, a half-empty pack of Jammy Dodgers, wine gums, Rizlas, roaches, a half-munched kebab and stinky clothes decomposing across the floor. The TV displays the stoner favourite, the static BBC Test Card F shown when no programmes are being broadcast. This is an image of a smiling young girl playing noughts and crosses next to a grinning clown dolly, super creepy; some dopeheads believe that during the night she, or maybe the dolly, will wink, which is creepier still. I wouldn't stay up all night on the off chance of a wink, but maybe Gary does. I look under the bed, but he's not there, definitely not in the room.

A whiff of hashish wafts in from the bathroom, where Gary's lying fully clothed in the bath, water up to his chin in a parka with the hood pulled low down on his forehead over bloodshot eyes opened just a crack, a fat blunt fuming in his lips.

'The FUCK you doing?!' I say. 'It's a FIRE ALARM! You could FRY! You got to GO!'

'Well,' says Gary, slowly, 'I fi-gure [BEAT] if there *is* a fire [BEAT] I'll be OK [BEAT] if I stay in the *BATH*.'

'Jesus H. Christ! Just fucking *DIE*,' I say, and leave.

There's no fire. Gary is saved.

BREAKING IN AMERICA

(Photo: iStock)

We can expect a pleasant evening in the Tri-State area today, clear blue skies and an 80°F high down to a 55 low overnight, with a light easterly breeze. Low pressure may bring in rain tomorrow, but showers will be light and localised. Otherwise, it's a fine late summer's day and it'll be a fine weekend!

We're living the rock 'n' roll dream, in the US for the first ever Gang of Four tour, fizzing with excitement and eager to gatecrash the world's number one music market, even though we doubt many people here have heard of us. We are six: the band plus Rob Warr, our manager, who's still doubling as our front-of-house sound man, and Jolyon – Hugo's brother – who's our sole roadie and driver now at the wheel of Frontier Booking International's splitter van, which we picked up this morning in Manhattan.

Handing us the keys earlier that day, Ian Copeland, our booking agent at FBI, said that although the company Ford Econoline wasn't 'pretty', it was 1,000 per cent reliable, showing a worrying lack of confidence, and we shouldn't anticipate any problems from State Troopers who might be bugged by the handwritten cardboard sign taped to the back window that reads 'License Plate's [sic] Applied For'. Should there *be* any issues, he assured us, call anytime, which means we're on our own: this is a time before the invention of mobiles, email or personal computers and there's no way to contact *anyone* while we're moving.

We're playing at Philadelphia's Hot Club tonight, the first show in a month of a dozen solo club dates and thirteen support slots with the Buzzcocks, playing two sets a night on half the dates, more than *thirty* performances in twenty-five days, with one day off. We've never done double sets before, but it sounds cool, we love playing.

'Fuck's sake!' says Jolyon, thumping his head on the wheel. 'The fucker's fucking fucked!'*

It's not like Jol, a cool stage tech who can sort anything, to panic. The agency Ford's spluttered to a stop midpoint in the Lincoln Tunnel, a critical link between Manhattan Island and New Jersey, and we're blocking one of its two-mile-long outbound lanes. The hard ceramic-tiled walls are amplifying the passing traffic roar and

---

* Jolyon is unknowingly quoting Anthony Burgess's description in *A Mouthful of Air* of the many uses of fuck: '"Fucking", it is true, can be used as a neutral intensifier in "fucking good" and "fucking stupid", but to be "fucked" or participate in a state of "fuckup" is to be in a state of distress. I once heard an army motor mechanic complain of his recalcitrant engine by crying "Fuck it, the fucking fucker's fucking fucked."' (London: Hutchinson, 1992).

the death metal sound of standstill commuters behind us honking and hollering abuse.

The van's roomy enough but stinky like Hugo's curry, beer and weed-infused Transit. I'd hoped for a plush stretch with lots of legroom, tinted windows and high-end hi-fi, like you see on TV. Nope. The cassette player's broken and the bench seats are stained and shredded. But it could be worse: we could be mithering about the cold, rain and wind back in our dank Leeds rehearsal room.

We're used to things not happening and waiting for something to happen as it's 90 per cent of what being a gigging musician is. Sitting in a broken-down Ford is depressingly familiar. I'm disappointed, but have faith Rob will sort things out, which he usually does.

He doesn't need to do anything. This is America, the hope of the world, where stuff happens fast. In minutes, a huge tow truck reverses at speed toward us from the mouth of the tunnel, hooks us up and drags us out to be left marooned at its maw on the shoulder of the New Jersey Turnpike as a river of pissed-off salarymen gun by, giving us the finger as they go.

The payphone's down, there's nowhere to take a leak, and I'm not looking forward to the prospect of Gill and Dave, both of whom were in a bar before we left, pissing into an empty Rolling Rock bottle. We can only sit and bicker, waiting for whatever. Jolyon, a petrol head, is poking around under the bonnet trying to figure out what's wrong. 'It's brown bread,' he says. 'Donald.'

Philadelphia is only 100 miles south but may as well be on Pluto. If Jol can't get the motor going we'll need fresh wheels, but 5 p.m. Friday on the hard shoulder of the Lincoln Tunnel's Jersey-side sphincter is no time or place to hire a van. And we don't have a phone, money or friends.

I'm prepared for setbacks and open *Zen and the Art of Motorcycle Maintenance*; Robert M. Pirsig's meditations on his fictionalised bike journey and what it might philosophically mean are very relevant, I think, stuck in a stinky van circling the drain. A book's the best on tour, I'm always reading. But fiction's nothing to Gill, incompatible with his party animalism and lack of interest in others. He snatches it away, throws it in back, and says, 'You've read it before!'

Although we've been friends since our teens, I've still never known Andy read a novel or a non-course work text other than *Bury My Heart at Wounded Knee*. Three weeks from now, this book will be with him when we play at the American Indian Centre in San Francisco, the heart of the radical Native American movement. This was the home of First Nation activists – the *Indians of All Tribes* – who'd symbolically occupied Alcatraz Island for nineteen months between 1969 and 1971, tagging the desolate prison buildings with 'Red Power' and 'Custer had it coming'. On the wall behind the stage we'll play on is a poster with the iconic photo of the great Teton Dakota chief Sitting Bull and text that reads 'LANDLORD'. We'll all be proud, but especially Andy.

Right now, Hugo's dialling through AOR radio to find something worth listening to. It's annoying, I prefer ads to the Allman Brothers and don't like enduring fragments of tracks by Maria Muldaur, Journey and Supertramp. I want to hear Velvet Underground, MC5, Richard Hell, the Ramones, the Meters, Parliament or Chic. But US radio stations don't mix it up: they either play white or Black music, pop cultural apartheid. It's not like the UK. The van only has an eight-track cart so Hugo can't play any of his cassette mixtapes, so radio's all we've got. The only way to opt-out of vanilla AOR is to sit in silence, which me and Andy are keen on but outvoted on, but we're happy when Hugo finds a fine funk station. This hassle will be history when we all get our hands on the revolutionary new Sony Walkman, launched last month, which means we can listen to our own sounds, in a sonic world of our own.

Dave wakes up and asks if he can get a taxi back to Manhattan. This riles Rob, who says, 'We haven't got any money. We must play Philly. If we don't, we don't get paid, and *you* don't get a bed.'

Impeccable thinking from a man with a philosophy degree who's a master of 'IF . . . THEN . . . logic'. Not gigging would be a disaster as we've only got two hundred dollars cash float, just enough for gas and a burger each. No one has a credit card.

Rob's budget covers two twin-bed rooms for the six of us in an economy hotel, so every other night we have to share a bed, in my case with either Hugo or Rob, who are reasonably clean people that I hope don't snore or have transgressive nocturnal erotic impulses. It's sub-optimal but better than dossing in the van, and far better than sharing a room with Andy and Dave, or being in the same hotel as them, or the same city, as the two of them aren't good to be near when drink's been taken.

We'll only break even on this tour if nothing goes wrong. We can't beg EMI for help as our deal with them is for 'Rest of World excluding the US and Canada', and the company won't cough up tour support for a territory it can't sell records in. Our UK advance only covers wages of thirty pounds per week per person this year, and we'll be financially fucked if we don't get signed in the US: it's the only way we can make proper money. But responses from American record outfits have been bad. Capitol Records has passed, saying our music was 'too left field for the present marketplace in the US' – probably true – while A & M writes in corporation-speak, 'We will not be interested in a more extensive investigation of your work at this time.'

It may be academic, as we're getting nowhere slow. However, bored with nothing doing, Jolyon turns the engine over again and it restarts! Rock 'n' roll! Sweet! We're convinced our luck's turned as we gun onto the fourteen-lane NJ Turnpike, the van driving like a dream. From now on, our troubles will be out of sight.

No, they aren't. A half hour later, the engine chokes again, and we freewheel from the tsunami of traffic onto a freeway feeder road. We are truly fucked. But Rob won't give up, having seen a motel's neon light not too far away, which he hikes towards to find a payphone to call the Hot Club. We sit and mither in the dark until Rob reappears to say he's spoken with the club promoter who knows a man with a van already en route here to pick us and our gear up and take us to the venue. 'It's good news,' Rob says, 'the gig's still on and the van'll be here soon. It's only a three-hour drive to Philadelphia, we'll arrive around midnight, they'll hold pulling the plugs until one . . .'

No one's listening except Dave, who asks, 'Aren't we meant to be onstage at eleven?'

It's hard to believe Dave has *read* the tour itinerary – a mark of shame – rather than balling it on receipt and binning it, as the rest of us do. Rob, surprised by Dave's unexpected attention to detail, says, 'Yeah, but they'll hold the doors, there are two support bands, it'll be fine,' which worries us all. Rob's optimism is a sure sign of doom.

A Veedub camper van pulls up behind us. It reeks of weed, curry and cat piss, with a Furry Freak Brother at the wheel and a hippy-chick friend riding shotgun. She doesn't say a word, too absorbed in skinning up a blunt, while the driver – who may be able to talk and might even have a name – mumbles something but we can't decode his stoner drawl. We can only take our guitars and sardine in the midget RV like a lame Guinness World Record attempt, and abandon our splitter on the roadside, the keys left on the wheel. The Econoline will be towed to a garage where they'll find sand's been poured into the gas tank to choke off the fuel supply when it's moving, which is why it dies but restarts after a rest when the particles have settled. The tank will be removed and sluiced out. We've been pranked by Squeeze, the previous users of the van. It's a hoot.

The flower child up front non-stop feeds the driver fat-nosed reefers, the Sensi seeds snapping, crackling and popping, clouding the cab with smoke, we're all coughing and choking in the smog, our faces mulched to the windows, none of us toking, the midnight show would tank if the band's baked. As we draw closer to Philadelphia with time running down, we cut song after song from a set originally planned to be all of *Entertainment!* plus maybe covers of 'Rosanne' by the Mekons, and 'Day Tripper' if we get an encore.

We arrive at the Hot Club with just twenty-five minutes to go before they pull the plug at 1 a.m. It's mad. Police and fire control vehicles are parked out front with pissed-off cops cajoling the steaming punks who've spilt onto the cool sidewalk from the oven-hot club while inside the sardined punters are fried, lairy, and wet with sweat. The crowd hollers and brays as we come through the stage side door and push through them onto the low corner stage, totally wired, desperate to make a noise, it's our destiny.

Pylon, the support act, have been heroic and played two sets to fill time, knocking out the only eight tunes they have twice but in different orders, the crowd apparently loving their last one the most. I wish I'd seen their show, they'd been incredible. We owe them big-time as they've left their backline up for us to use and Curtis Crowe, Pylon's drummer, says he's delighted to see Hugo pummel his kit.

A fireman and a cop stand at the back of the room, chewing gum, tooled up and antsy, performatively checking their watches every few minutes. They'd ordered the promoter to 'Shut this place down, now!' until it was clear this might start a riot, so they'd backed off but insisted on a strict 1 a.m. curfew, no exceptions. We have to play, if only for a quarter hour, and when we kick off with 'Ether' the reaction's insane, the punters explode, pogo and scream, going ballistic as we blast through a mini set of five that rips off the roof, ending in 'Damaged Goods', the only one they can know, the crowd singing every word. We perform in a trance, like we're being played by the music rather than the other way around, only a beat between tunes, BANG BANG BANG, until time's called. The moment Gill's final chord fades, the power's pulled and house lights stammer on overhead. It's over.

We're stood stock still onstage, shattered, soaked in sweat, to be hugged and glad-handed and high-fived by the crowd as they shuffle out.

The cop outside says, 'Hell of a show!'

'Yeah,' I say, 'true that.'

We edge through the melee into the tender Philly air and slump down against a cool brick wall to chug ice-cold beers. The promoter says, 'Awesome, unbelievable!' and gives us the full fee.

We can pay for the motel rooms. It's all worked out very well.

Postscript

Curtis Crowe, Pylon's drummer, will write that when Gang of Four went on,

> The entire room took a step back. It was like a strong wind through a wheat field. No ... it was a lot fiercer than that. It reminded me of those slo-mo atomic blast documentaries where you can see the shockwave as whole forests rocked back. The clock ran out after only five songs. Never having said hello or goodnight, the band dropped their instruments and walked off. Every single person in the room got their money's worth. Everyone. Whatever tensions have been building in the crowd had been knocked out of them like a hard punch in the gut. They shuffled out exhausted. Even the cops and the fire department looked dazed.*

---

* A message from Curtis to me, published in Gang of Four 77-81 box set, 2020

Seven days from now we'll play here a second time. The Hot Club is hot, sold out, and the word's out. Ticketless fans cluster on the sidewalk outside the venue and hover at the stage doors while we're on to hear the noise. It's fabulous, who knew America had even heard of us and that our music would resonate so much on first hearing? After the show, we press the flesh and talk and talk to the fans. They want to know when our debut album will be released in Britain and if a US deal is in the works. Not yet, we say, but fingers crossed, the labels will be at our LA show. We're going to be great. What could possibly go wrong?

Post Postscript

A year later we'll play Emerald City in Philadelphia, a glitzy disco once called the Latin Casino, a supper club but not a casino, which hosted crooner titans like Frank Sinatra and Sammy Davis Jr. Post-disco, FBI uses it as a venue for new wave and punk bands like us, Blondie, Talking Heads and XTC.

The Latin Casino features in *The Irishman* where Robert De Niro's character accepts an award. Martin Scorsese exactly recreates the room where we once performed.

Emerald City's razed to the ground in 1982 to be replaced by Subaru of America's corporate HQ that will be demolished in turn in 2019.

THE RAT

The Rat. (Photo: © Kathy Chapman)

Kenmore Square's seen better days. Shut-up shops shoulder a pizza place, small record shops, and a Supersocks discount sock and T-shirt store. Among them is the Rathskeller a.k.a the Rat Club, Boston's primo alt-music and rock venue, where everyone from the Cars, the Police, Talking Heads and the Ramones have played. A front-lobby door in the middle of a painted brick wall opens onto a low-roofed, black-painted chamber with a raised stage at its far end; an in-your-face venue where bands must play great or go home, the hub for local punks and music cognoscenti.

We've trained up to Boston, lugging just guitars and sticks for two sold-out nights here, hoping we can borrow the support band's backline, like we did with Pylon last night, as we can't afford to hire any kit. A hot local band called Mission of Burma will open for us and we find all four – Roger Miller (guitar/lead vocals), Clint Conley (bass), Peter Prescott (drums) and Martin Swope (tape manipulation/engineer) – at the club when we stumble in, lounging among a pyramid of beat-up flight and traps cases. Sure, they say, of *course* you can use our kit, and then super-generously say we can crash at their Brighton house, which is fantastic, as we're skint. That night we'll sleep at theirs on floors and sofas, better than sharing a *matrimonio* with Hugo or Rob.

Soundcheck over, and the house PA set, Rob and Jolyon arrive with our actual backline. They've been driven here from the City of Brotherly Love by a wise-cracking local fixer called Tom Potts, who owns the van and *lives* rock 'n' roll, he says, and is immediately on the firm, which he pronounces as *foim* in a strong Philadelphian accent where water's *wooder* and coffee's *cooughee*.

After a rapid onstage equipment change, we head over to Mission of Burma's place to chill pre-show. Tom ferries us there in the van's windowless metal rear perched on flight cases with foam blocks as improv second row seats, and Tah-Dah! opens a chunky cool box with iced Buds to cheer us up. He non-stop chatters and jokes, knows everyone who's anyone in Philadelphia. 'Everyone's *buzzing* about the jawn last night,' he says, 'youse guys were *humungous*.' We hang out at MoB's place and talk music, food and the Frankfurt School until showtime. They're nice guys – *everyone* here's nice – and their band's *hot*, man, they're *good*, they make a brittle noise that pumps up the packed punters who go mental when we kick off. We play like it's Judgement Day, we're mobbed when we're off, the fans clutching Damaged Goods EPs for us to sign.

Peter Prescott says watching our show was like being hit by a train, meant as a compliment. Despite our splitter-van blues Ian Copeland's done good, we're not used to A-list support acts like MoB and Pylon, who Tom says were the nuts at the Hot Club and stopped a riot before we showed. Our second night at the Rat's is as good as the first. I love Boston!

This tour's going to be *something*.

Postscript

The Rat shut for good in 1997 and was ripped down.

The Hotel Commonwealth, a 148-room luxury hotel, stands on its site.

NEW YORK NEW YORK

(Photo: Wikipedia/public domain)

The famous Algonquin Hotel lies at 59 West 44th Street, where Dorothy Parker toped and coined her bon mots, and where movie stars and literary gods like Arthur Miller, Tennessee Williams, Audrey Hepburn and Elia Kazan hung out. You may enjoy first-class cocktails and agèd brown drinks served in the world-famous bar, its sophisticated ambience enhanced by an accomplished lounge jazz pianist teasing sus minor 7th and 13th with a sharp 9 into Great American Songbook masterpieces. A must-see in NYC.

Sadly, we're not staying here but down the road at the bargain basement Iroquois Hotel, 49 West 44th, a low-rent dive Ian Copeland favours to house the FBI roster of bleached blonde popsters, demented punk rockers, and new wave misfits. The B52's (who still have an apostrophe) discovered and recommended it to Ian, who lived here himself for a while when he first moved to the Big Apple, before a tsunami of money from sold-out shows for the Police and Joan Jett et al. afforded him Long Island luxury and a swish midtown apartment. The Iroquois' sole claim to fame is that James Dean lived here in the fifties for a couple of years before he made it, doubtless attracted to Times Square's *Midnight Cowboy* sleaze a few blocks away, where a walk-up nosh-off in a door well was a breeze.

We're in town for two nights at Hurrah, our first concerts ever in NYC, the uber-hip club that's the first in the city to promote punk, new wave, no wave, and industrial music*. Ruth Polsky books the bands, at the top of her game, charming, smart, and funny.†

It's a big deal, we're excited, the four of us jabbering and joking in the lobby as we hustle to check in. The receptionist pays us no heed, we're just another scabby bunch of Brit bigmouths dreaming of greatness, he's heard it all before and is multi-tasking, scouring the *National Enquirer* for news of aliens on the moon while ear-holing a trannie radio behind the desk that's tizzing out dog-frequency sports-report chatter as he scribbles in the house book and tosses over the room keys to whoever.

---

* Sid Vicious got into a fight here in 1978 that won him two months jail time in Rikers Island; Bowie recorded the video for his single *Fashion* in Hurrah, a sure sign of ultimate hipdom; and our shows here are amazing. People *love* us! Every other punter seems to be in a band, and halfway through the set someone shouts 'David Byrne's taking notes!' I think he was.

† Ruth is tragically killed at thirty-one, her career on a wave after becoming the booker at Danceteria, when an out of control taxi mounts the sidewalk and runs her down outside Limelight in New York. What a waste.

I ask if I can check out the basement fallout shelter. He says, 'Take a hike, it's perma-locked, the key's lost, who gives a fuck, when the birds fly, bend over and kiss your ass goodbye.'

I say, 'It'll be a bastard if the Soviets launch their Scuds today. Where should we go then?'

He says, 'Fuck *off*.'

My room's on the fourth floor which means lugging heavy equipment – we always unload the backline from the splitter, so it's not stolen – up the sticky stairs or loading it into the elevator that inches up and down at snail speed. Riding up once with Robert Fripp, of King Crimson and David Bowie fame, he says, apropos of nothing, 'I once had sex in this lift.' He'd have had plenty of time.

My suite has a bedroom, Polly Pocket-sized lounge/kitchenette, mouldy sofa, wine-stained carpet, wheezy A/C and a mini fridge, so ideal for entertaining and canapés.

The hotel doesn't have a restaurant or bar, or room service of any kind, but who needs it? Like other midtown Brits and tourists, Gill, Dave, Hugo and I sashay down to O'Donoghue's Irish Pub, at No. 156, for an early evening pint of Guinness, which isn't bad and it's a decent drinking den with a back-mirrored bar blazoned with shamrocks and Celtic calligraphy, just like pubs in Dublin aren't.

Not all Ian's acts stay at the Iroquois. The Gramercy Park, downtown, is classier, pricier and nicer. Rooming there's a sign that business is good, and it's where the Buzzcocks will stay. Pete's already written some hits. One day, we will, too.

IAN COPELAND

Time for a word about Ian, our agent in the US who founded Frontier Booking International aka FBI specialising in repping the new wave acts now breaking America and packing clubs, theatres and sheds across the country. He'd moved to New York from Macon, Georgia, where he'd discovered local acts like the B52's, REM and Pylon. The agency is able to rep almost every happening band *du jour* – the Police, Joan Jett, Squeeze, the Go-Go's, Iggy Pop, Buzzcocks, Talking Heads, *us*, etc. – because they know Ian and his crew *love* the new music and have serious juice with promoters, working insane hours from a swarming ant-nest office. (In years to come, the lovely Courteney Cox will work on reception, and later move in with Ian; Courteney's mother had already married Ian's uncle, Hunter Copeland, in 1974.)

Ian's dad is Miles Copeland Sr, a one-time jazz trumpeter and now senior CIA intelligence officer in the Eastern Mediterranean – an obvious career move – and his two brothers Miles and Stuart are manager and drummer of the Police respectively. Brought up in the Lebanon, Ian was in a badass bike gang before volunteering for Vietnam, a sergeant at nineteen, so relaxed his nickname was 'Leroy Coolbreeze'. He tells us he and his platoon had just dropped acid back at base on R & R when they were ordered to take on attacking North Vietnamese soldiers, after which he was awarded the Bronze Star for heroism, though he's offhand about it and says he spent much of the time holed up in a bomb crater watching overhead tracer fire light up the skies. Awesome when you're tripping.

Hugo first met Ian years ago when he was a schoolboy booker of bands at Cranbrook School and Copeland was an agent at John Sherry Enterprises in the UK. Hugo asks if his missing finger was shot off in combat, but he shrugs and says, 'No, I lost it fixing the chain on my bike.'

Ian's charming, clever and funny with a laconic delivery and accent forged south of the Mason–Dixon line, and, uniquely, we pay close attention to him. It's down to him that we have a hopefully break-even US tour, which mixes support with the Buzzcocks and select club dates, despite our debut EP being available here on import only and *Entertainment!* hasn't even been released yet in the UK. A key objective is to get a deal with a US label. Ian knows what he's doing.

What could possibly go wrong?

CLUB 57

Club 57 at 17 Irving Place and 15th Street is the top venue in Manhattan for new wave and punk acts with a flat acoustic that flatters guitar bands and pulls a passionate East Village crowd who know their shit.

It's rammed, hot as hell, and the anticipation's electric. Everyone's itching to see the Buzzcocks. Before we go on there's a backstage brawl between a Manchester tech and a local, the scally headbutting and breaking the Brooklyn boy's nose, blood fountaining, boy taken to hospital . . . it's very familiar.

We know our job, we're the warmup, we've done it a lot before and love what the Buzzcocks have done for us; without their sponsorship things would have been very different. But when we go on, we realise straight off it's not like the UK, the billing's seen here as more like a double bill, the crowd *wants* to see us. We play all of *Entertainment!* – material that's almost all new to the punters – more or less in order, more or less well, and get off. They go nuts. New York, New York.

The next day we set off in the now sand-free gas tanked splitter to look for America.

DINNER WITH JERRY

Jerry Wexler is the greatest man in post-war pop, the man who came up with the phrase 'Rhythm and Blues' and worked with many of the greatest artists of all time, from Aretha and Dusty to Dylan, and everyone in between, the man who founded Atlantic Records with Ahmet Ertegun, signing Led Zeppelin on Dusty's recommendation – and the man who produced hundreds of the finest records of all time including 'Respect', 'Shake, Rattle and Roll', 'Son of a Preacher Man', 'Stand By Me' . . .

Jerry says he loves Gang of Four, and Warner Bros in North America are likely to be signing us on his say-so. He says we're doing something unique and important, and it doesn't even sound like a line.

The day after our Club 57 show in NYC, we're invited to Jerry's Park Avenue residence for dinner, just us and his wife. How can we be here, dining with God? We five – me, Dave, Gill, Hugo and Rob – arrive at this swankiest of Manhattan addresses and are escorted up to the apartment in a personal lift by a huge, solicitous and besuited man – surely not a lift operator but a ninja bodyguard or a Navy Seal on R & R – who operates the red-knobbed up–down lever. It's an under-egged role for a bodyguard, if he is one, but I'm not asking as he looks like he'd deep-six you if rumble his true gig.

Jerry and his fragrant wife Renee Pappas meet us as we exit the lift, 'So *pleased* you could come,' they say – as if we'd have declined!

– shaking hands, a soft pat on the back as we're led in for an aperitif, a Negroni for all save Dave, who'd prefer a beer. 'Domestic or import?' asks the white-gloved help, but there's regrettably no Tetley's, perhaps Sapporo? You can't have it all, even when you do. The apartment has exquisitely curated mid-century and American heritage furniture, beautiful fabrics and signature art adorn the walls, gorgeous ceramics – Picasso? – bless a sideboard and light spills from a contemporary chandelier of leaded glass *kunst*. Renee has a wonderful eye, the apartment's her creation and a visual feast, and it's no surprise she later becomes an aspirational interior designer *de la luxe*.

At table, Jerry and Renee are fine hosts, we're fed and watered as if we matter, and conversation unfolds smoothly; they've been well briefed, which is a great compliment.

'You studied art,' she says to me, 'I'm sure you must like Cezanne?'

'Of *course*,' I say.

'You must see *ours*, one of the later works, a small piece.'

She guides me over to a classic from the *Mont Sainte-Victoire* series on a far wall and says, 'It's wonderful, though I'm not sure it's in the right place?'

Jerry gently corrals us all into his office, the walls dripping with gold and silver and platinum discs glittering like the Amber Room in St Petersburg, a forest of photos of him at work with Aretha and Bob and Ray Charles and . . . everyone. We talk music and culture and the evening glides to an end.

Our boat's come in.

BREAKTHROUGH IN FRISCO

11 September 1979. Now close to the end of the tour, we're supporting the Buzzcocks at the Temple Beautiful, 1839 Geary Boulevard, San Francisco, a punk-rock venue in a one-time nineteenth-century synagogue, just nine blocks from the iconic Fillmore West. Next door you'll find the converted Scottish Rite Temple, the HQ of Jim Jones's Peoples Temple acolytes from which over nine hundred would 'commit an act of revolutionary suicide' with Jim, drinking cyanide-laced Kool-Aid and dying in the Guyanese jungle in November 1978, a dark addition to the San Francisco block's mojo.

A wooden stage at one end of the Temple Beautiful is overlooked by a seated balcony on three sides, which hangs over the mosh pit, the chamber topped by a fine domed roof decorated with a massive seven-pointed star. The Clash played here earlier this year, and it's an epic venue for a sold-out Buzzcocks/Gang of Four double bill, a first time in the city for us both, and we're no longer an unknown known. The word's out: these guys can *play*. And, of course, so can the Buzzcocks. I never tire seeing them play their wonderful buzzsaw pop songs, watching them from the side of stage most nights as I cool off after our turn.

We've played every night bar one for almost a month, with and without the Buzzcocks, our own shows mostly double sets on at nine or ten and back again at twelve or one. It's been a fantastic experience and made us stronger, you can see it in group photos, and a window on how the Beatles must have felt after their thirty-hour week Hamburg residencies: they were *tight* and *together*. Nothing beats doing relentless live work, you learn to work the stage and the crowd, face down the creeps, and sweat the good songs while losing the losers. We are on it, show honed, hot and heavy, ready to do our thing.

The city's still wickedly hot when we hit the boiling stage, 80°F on the sidewalk outside at 8 p.m. but over 100°F under PAR-can lights, each as hot as a one-bar fire. We play on after burners, almost on autopilot, barely pausing between numbers, SONG SONG SONG BANG BANG BANG, perhaps our best show to date and a critical breakthrough in front of a fabulous wild crowd who go ballistic. 'MORE!' they scream. 'MOOORE!' they roar. We could play all night but must cede the stage to the mighty Buzzcocks, it's their gig, and stumble to the dressing room to collapse on the floor with our heads swaddled in ice-stuffed towels, pounds lighter, our chests steaming as we cool off. Did that really *happen*?

I love rock 'n' roll.

ANTHRAX

This is the first song Andy and I write where we feel we've got where we want to be, away from genre straitjacket. I'm a fan of Jean-Luc Godard's movies that challenged formulaic Hollywood and French film storytelling and encouraged the viewer to construct their own narrative from often disparate elements, most notably in his late great film *Numéro Deux*, where he used split screens and off-screen commentaries to deny a single authorial voice.

This seems like a modern way to describe how we live; things can't always be decoded from a single point of view, and, among conflicting inputs, a story's sense changes depending on where you sit.

I've typed up some words, a paean to waking up jittery and regretful inspired by Raymond Chandler's brilliant hangover description: 'I woke up. An axe split my head.' Me and Andy talk about this for a while but don't record anything until we're in a rehearsal room, as Gill only has an acoustic guitar in our Kelso Road digs.

I write down the song plan: heavy, funky drums and bass throughout, two slabs of freewheeling improv guitar alternating with vocal sections where I'll sing fixed words and Andy will ad lib, commenting on what we are doing or where we are or what equipment we have, or anything that comes to mind. The only rule is not to react to what I'm singing, so not a call-and-response number, which will make every performance different and not handcuff meanings. It's only when the song's recorded at Cargo Studios, and is included on the *Damaged Goods* EP, that Andy's vocal part becomes frozen, which is a shame.

Andy's virtuoso feedback is an homage to Hendrix, working the tremolo, worrying the on/off switch, bending the neck, bashing into the amp, sometimes smashing the guitar when the neck breaks under the assault, a simple two-note figure bringing in Hugo and Dave's enormous Can-like funk groove. We finally got somewhere.

FLY ME TO THE MOON

A sharp-suited man turns left when he boards the plane and is wafted to a wide seat and warmly greeted by a fit air hostess in a tight skirt who smiles and says, 'Champagne?' presenting a tray bearing chilled Bollinger and *platillos* of potato pancakes smeared with Beluga whose scent is guaranteed to excite any business exec's jaded palate. He flirts with her, deceiving himself that his unctuous chat-up schtick presses her buttons, and pats her arse as she sashays away. *Yet another groper twat!*, she thinks. He kicks off his shoes and leans back to consider today's *cordon bleu* menu; it's a longish haul to the East Coast, maybe the Kobe and the Château Latour?

In back, I'm squeezed in the five-seat misery stretch between a hyperactive seven-year-old, who's fidgeting and whingeing to a bag-eyed mother cradling a mewling babe, and on my right a hefty Shiite cleric nervously fingering beads while muttering prayers for salvation from certain aviation doom. I've chosen irradiated lamb chunks and mash paired with a presumptuous mini bottle of Aryan anti-freeze, which makes my teetotal neighbour fiddle even more fervently with his props. I'm open to a double-double G & T that might knock me out until I wake up on the runway, although I know an alcohol doze lasts only long enough for regrets before the decades to kill before arriving at JFK. It's time to get stuck into a doorstop like Umberto Eco's new tome, *The Name of the Rose*.

It's best not to sit near Dave or Andy, ruinously lively booze-buddies who camp in airport bars until the final gate call, always last to board and arriving beer-breathed and pre-loaded before non-stop toping from the duty-free Blue Label they'll crack open on board. They can be heard ranting and rambling as we fly through the skies, and at times a hostess may ask Rob or me if we could ask our friends to moderate their language, the F-word and C-word is upsetting other passengers? They're no friends of mine, I say, *noli me tangere*, I'm not my brother's keeper!

The last few round trips to the US we've flown Air India and Iran Air, picking up bucket-shop tickets for FA on the last leg of flights from Tehran or Delhi to New York, trips from LHR to JFK in coach because many Indian or Iranian passengers deplane in London despite having paid for a through flight to the US, the economics of which escapes me. The unused leg is dumped at budget cost to be hoovered up for zilch by rockers like us. I daydream about how awesome it would be to travel up front with legroom that might suit anyone other than Toulouse Lautrec, exquisite food and drink, and an absence of under-fives. Kids are demons on planes.

Back home, our travel agent says he can swing first-class flights for coach-class prices on major Yank carriers! How so? By bribing the check-in people at Heathrow or Los Angeles. Of course!

Our first rodeo, we're told to bowl up an hour before the Pan Am flight takes off, lugging cabin luggage only, to a specific check-in counter with twenty pounds per person in cash, the airline rep prepped for our arrival by Mr X. This late in the day, no-show's seats can be released and empty seats reassigned, so flyers in coach can be legitimately upgraded to first class at the check-in person's discretion, as now all unallocated seats are available, and no-show chairs are freed up. These seats would otherwise be empty, which would be criminal as the plane's fully staffed and supplied. It's a victimless crime. The bung works wonders, and we're all boosted to first for just a score each!

Check-in and passport control – in these olden golden days, queues are short – takes minutes and then we all – the band, Jolyon, Phil and Rob, lairy blokes in leathers and Levi's, Motörhead and Pep Boys T-shirts – SPRINT through the airport to the departure gate (in these innocent times, there are minimal security checks) to arrive huffing and puffing as a final boarding call is made.

I turn left and am steered to a wide seat to be greeted by a smiling air hostess who says, 'Champagne?' handing me a chilled Bollinger and selection of finger food. *How did this sweaty punk blag this?* she thinks. *He must be famous!* I kick off my monkey boots and lean back to consider today's choices from the *cordon bleu* menu; it's a longish haul to the East Coast, maybe the sea bream and the Chassagne-Montrachet?

Postscript

The bung is a slightly richer fifty dollars per person at LAX, but offers a more civilised experience than LHR, all upgrades done well before the flight. One time, a helicopter service will ferry Hugo and the road crew from JFK to Manhattan. Once on the 747, we may be given the desirable upstairs pod to ourselves, where we have much fun and can't annoy the movie stars, nepo brats and financial racketeers in the cheap seats downstairs who may have actually purchased a ticket, although I doubt anyone who turns left pays with their own money – the rich and famous are always on the blag. It's an excellent service and unbeatable value.

Pan Am and TWA go broke.

TOO MUCH WHISKY AT THE WHISKY

The Tropicana Motel. *(Photo: Robert Landau/Alamy Stock Photo)*

Palm trees waver in the fiery breeze warming the Tropicana motel, 8585 Santa Monica Boulevard, whose rooms horseshoe a black-painted pool which so many guests have fucked or been ducked in over the years. The receptionist says to women checking in, 'Hey, don't swim in *that*, you'll get *pregnant*, heh, heh.' This is Rock 'n' Roll's Valhalla: Led Zep, Blondie, Jim Morrison, the New York Dolls, the Ramones, the Police ... *everyone's* stayed here. Tom Waits has a Trop bungalow up back, though I never run into him, he's only around in the lonely hours. The Stooges roomed here when they recorded *Fun*

House round the corner at Elektra and Andy Warhol/Paul Morrissey's *Trash* was filmed here on the astro-turf lawn which surrounds the pool, of which Stanley Kauffmann wrote, '*Trash* is disgusting, not for what it is on screen but for what it is in the minds of the people who made it', a thought that could apply to many of the motel's muso guests. There's always another band plus entourage frolicking poolside, which makes the dark hours lively, but don't complain to the receptionist, who'll say you don't like it, go elsewhere, LA's full of hotels for *straights*.

We say hi to the Dead Boys who watch us unload, and then Hugo and I drop into the Trop's destination eatery, Duke's Coffee Shop, where we bump into Debbie Harry and Chris Stein. Hugo asks if Clem's with them and Chris says, 'Burke the berk!' and heads back to their room. Duke's is the best breakfast joint in LA – thirty-two varieties of omelettes – where I stuff my face mornings with steak, three eggs, and home fries with freshly squeezed OJ, bottomless coffee and a fruit bowl. Breakfast's the most important meal of the day on tour as I don't eat near showtime, I'll want to puke, and lunch is for losers.

We're thrilled to be at the epicentre of the entertainment biz at the finale of an inaugural tour where the reviews and receptions have been epic, we've *arrived*, we are HOT! Tonight, we play the Whisky a Go Go, the iconic Sunset Strip gig that's a fast-track to fame, fortune, and talking about rehab on chat shows. Andy's blown away we'll perform at the same five-hundred-capacity room where Hendrix jammed and Zep blew off the doors in an early double bill with Alice Cooper. We'll do two sets each night, all four sold out, with a squadron of record companies on tonight's guest list eager to drop life-changing big bucks on us that could allow us to raise our weekly wage from the measly thirty quid we're subsisting on, with a Warners deal apparently already being talked about.

The first show's at ten, it's a blast, the audience goes crazy, loving whatever we do, rampant and tight on stage with ear-splitting screams after each number all unknown to the crowd aside from the *Damaged Goods* EP tracks. After one encore we're off, ecstatic, wheezing and wet, towelling down and chilling in the luxe dressing room. The club looks after us *well*, waitresses filing in with comped cocktails and beers and cocktails and beers... The room downstairs fills again to capacity with hyped punters who'd lined up around the block keen to get a top spot close to the high raised stage. The anticipation's intense, on again at zero hours, we're cocky and confident as waitresses file in with comped cocktails and beers and cocktails and beers...

It's a disaster. Hugo and I are hammered, Gill can't see straight, and Dave's off his tits.

When we go on, the room erupts, it's like we're the Stones, but Dave runs face first into a upright steel column on stage right and WHAAAM! smashes his nose, blood spurting and congealing on a now sloppy and unplayable bass, his tee soaked in gore. Gill hasn't looked at the running order taped to his wedge and is playing a different song to Hugo and me, or perhaps it's the same song but in a different tempo, arrangement and time signature, or I've gone deaf, and then TWAAANG! Dave's heavyweight bass E string snaps in two, the only time this has and will ever happen in his career. We've no back-up bass and can't continue until the support band reluctantly loans us theirs. A quarter hour later, the bloody stage having been mopped and Dave's bleeding staunched by golf-ball clumps of toilet paper stuffed in each nostril, we start over, playing very badly to pissed-off punters in a hollowed-out room, the record execs having bailed for post-show expense account blow and to talk shop over mixed drinks at the Rainbow Bar and Grill on Sunset. No one hangs backstage, there's one left to schmooze.

The next night we're brilliant, totally on it on both the early and late shows, holding back on inter-show cocktails and beers, but it's too late, baby, now it's too late. We fly back to Britain without a US deal, having messed up bigtime. It'll be months before Jerry Wexler bulldozes our signing to Warner Bros. Thank God he didn't see us at the Whisky.

Postscript

The Trop will be demolished in 1987. A Ramada Inn stands in its place.

LESTER BANGS PAYS HOMAGE

He came in drunk.

Lester Bangs, one of America's all-time great rock journalists and one-time editor of the legendary *Creem* magazine, has stumbled into our Hurrah club dressing room in NYC. It had been a fierce sold-out show. We're buzzing but overwhelmed. This is LESTER BANGS, like Zeus descending in the form of a man; we can hardly speak.

Dave finally says, 'You liked the show?'

'You guys ...' says Lester, heisting a six-pack of beers from our mini-fridge, and bouncing out, '... are SHIT!'

MEKON MARK WHITE'S LYRICAL WORLDVIEW

Visualise a poets' Venn diagram that locates Mark in the overlap between Philip Larkin and John Betjeman, a resolutely *English* voice grounded in petit bourgeois life, with its emotional and sexual disappointments, magnolia dreams, and sticky with regrets. Mark's stories are about men floundering in their limitations, gloomy about their prospects, and lumbered with lives overdetermined from birth.

He sits in a long tradition of dissent and troubled eschatological visions; centuries ago he'd have been at home among the Civil War Ranters, Levellers and Diggers. His 'Fight the Cuts' is a distant descendent of John Ball's 'When Adam delved and Eve span/Who was then the gentleman?', raging against inequality, injustice and oppression. His lonely narratives, like 'Where Were You?', are the broken whines of a romantic loser who'd do anything rather than do anything to get it together with his distant love.

Mark's landscape is of Pooterish witnesses drowning in alienated anonymity, predestined to fail, bystanders in their own lives, faces pressed hard against glittering shop windows of privilege; consumers of the venal parade of flummery, obscene wealth and entitlement that makes modern life such a shitshow. Despite this, there's a nugget of hope that ordinary people might have their day and good may prevail, the oligarchs, kleptocrats, and ruling classes might even become the biters bit. One of the finest wordsmiths in recent music.

THE MEKONS

I see the Mekons many times, my best friends, an absurdly great absurdist act. We share stages, rehearsal rooms, concert bills, perform as one on flatbed trucks at demos, entertain each other. At their first ever show Mark's pushed into view on a sofa labelled 'spaceship', which still makes me smile at the memory. It was the best bit of that evening. They're always fun, the music propelled by Jon Langford, a renaissance man who's always up to something, doing this and that, making art. He drums with a shrug, a bit behind the beat like Charlie Watts, but in the pocket should he choose. Jon, Andy Corrigan and Mark White know how to win over crowds with well-timed comic patter and windy gags. It's a pleasure to be in the room.

I steal one of Corrigan's gags, his intro of Tom or Kevin with 'Give a big hand for a young man who's been learning the guitar and fresh from Hendon Police College ...', though the reference is lost on American audiences. Tom Greenhalgh and Kevin Lycett play with an offhand attitude to timing, tuning and chords, which makes every set thrilling and new, and I'm thrilled every time I hear their Velvets-adjacent masterpiece 'Where Were You?' with Kevin frowning at the fret board as he attacks the strings, as if the guitar were a personal enemy. Tom sings on a few tunes, his vocal tone like Chet Baker with sinusitis.

It's a miracle to have such friends.

THE SALAMI DEFENCE

Portugal, 1980. We're co-headlining a series of concerts with Steve Harley's Cockney Rebel. It's an unlikely pairing, as Harley's a sham-glam popster with faux Bowie pop hits like 'Judy Teen' and 'Make Me Smile (Come Up and See Me)', and the creep behind an outraged petit bourgeois artist petition that demanded the Sex Pistols be dropped by EMI. Which they were, to Malcolm McLaren's delight. Whatever, Harley's music wasn't my – or by that time many other people's – cup of tea, as his audience was becoming more *selective*. We'd be first on but had equal billing; it was soon clear that most punters would come to see us.

The first show is in a bullring near Porto. It's a warm summer's night, cicadas are chirruping, flags flutter in the summer breeze.

The backstage dressing rooms are in a corrugated iron shed divided in two by a thin metal wall between the compartments, sharing lighting and power from a grumbling generator that's struggling to deliver enough volts, both rooms dim in feeble light. But it's OK, we're enjoying the gloom, joshing while we down cold beers and Vinho Verde, tuning up and talking through the set, waiting to be called to the stage. It's nice.

Suddenly, the room's plunged into total darkness. There's no power. Dave ducks out to find out what's happened and sees that Steve Harley's next door section is now blazing with light, our juice has been killed to give Harley the amps!

Dave's outraged, picks up a metal stacking chair, and starts to bash the thin metal dividing wall against which, on the other side, he knows Steve's sitting. BASH CRASH BASH CRASH! He does this until light's restored in our room and Harley's fat fuck tour manager, who I'll call Keith, lurches through the door, his purple face glistening with coke-head sweat, China white legs and gut framing his *turistiche* shorts.

'The fuck's going on?' he says, squaring up to Dave with chair in hand, ready for another swing at the wall. 'This don't happen on one of my tours!'

Violence is in the air. Dave eyeballs the tour manager, daintily puts down the chair, and then swan dives BLAM! onto a catering table laden with cold cuts, cheese, mayonnaise, pickles, nibbles and fruit.

The table collapses WHOMP! on the floor, and food and snacks and platters splatter everywhere. Dave gets up , covered in salami, pizza slices and gloop, and, wiping mayo from his face, points at himself and says, 'THIS is what happens when you turn off OUR lights!'

STEVE HARLEY SABOTAGES OUR SHOW

We're on a shared coach with Cockney Rebel en route to Lisbon chatting with Harley's band who tell us last night's bass player was sacked for upstaging Harley, because his rocking back and forth in time with the music had *robbed attention* from him. This may or may not be true, but a deputy's sitting in on bass at the next show. Harley is skulking up front near the bus driver and will only communicate with his troops via the TM, and not at all to us.

Keith, doubtless still reeling from Dave's brilliant Salami Defence, seems wary about interacting with us, lacking authority because we're not a *support act*. He's dripping with sweat, like a lardy Zinedine Zidane, and says, 'No hard feelings, yeah?' No. There are. The onboard vibe's fraught but restrained until we arrive in Cascais, where tonight's show's in an outdoor sports ground.

Stars twinkle in a deep Prussian blue night sky, cicadas are doing their thing, it's warm and dry. Gorgeous. Portugal on tilt.

We're on first again – we've got to say something to our hopeless booking agent about alternating closing as we've got equal billing – and it's sensational, we're totally on it, the crowd goes crazy, it's wild, they know all the words to 'I Found that Essence Rare', they love Gill's guitar on 'Anthrax', and 'Damaged Goods' becomes a sublime singalong. We walk off expecting to go straight back on for an encore.

But before we've even got to the side of the stage, bright-white house lights WHAM on, and intermezzo muzak booms out, shouts of complaint from the crowd. What the fuck?! There, right *there* in plain sight next to the house lighting control, stand Harley and Keith. It's sabotage. We are seriously pissed off.

Revenge is a dish best doled out whenever opportunity knocks, which it does in our next show, in a Lisbon sports arena. Another great gig in front of an excited and hip audience. After, we play cards in the dressing room, which is less a dressing room than a brutalist mausoleum or car park or set for a Beckett play, all bare concrete walls and triple-height ceiling, directly behind the stage entrance. Cockney Rebel's dressing room with a door is ten metres away and they'll need to shuffle past us to go on.

It's austere but nice. Fluorescently bright and airy, a cool ozone breeze wafts in from the Atlantic, as we chill out supping Super Bock beer on ice and joke as we play three-card brag, a low-stakes game we play for hours on tour, with brown-coin bets and a maximum fifty-pence pot.*

Midway through a hand, Keith sidles up, rests his sweaty palms on Hugo's shoulders, and says, 'Uh, guys? If it's cool . . . mind clearing the area? . . . So Steve can get onstage in artistic privacy? His routine . . . He needs to get his head together pre-gig. You know how it is with Big Stars?'

Hugo gives him the look. *Keith* wants *us* to vacate *our* dressing room/brutalist shrine/car park/Beckettian set so *Steve* can get his *head together?* Not on your effing nelly!

---

* Not that this apologia cut any ice with David Thomas earlier the same year, when we were on tour with Pere Ubu. He wouldn't gamble, even if the maximum pot was fifty pence, insisting we play Black Maria instead. A friend once upped the pitiful brown-coin ante to twenty-pence and declared 'To Hell with Poverty!', which I used later for a song.

Keith jumps back, sweat popping on his brow, plate-sized stains erupting in the pits of his Hawaiian shirt – and says, 'OKAY! OKAY! Forget I said a thing!' and retreats.

Harley's gone too far. Gill has a good idea and says, 'Why not play pass the bottle? Form a circle and play Super Bock catch?' This fun game demands sharp hand/eye coordination and concentration that none of us possess, and many bottles are dropped and shatter on the concrete floor.

Steve has to tiptoe to the stage through shards of broken glass sparkling on a floor foaming with beer suds. He won't turn on the house lights again.

MAKING *ENTERTAINMENT!*

A smart rented five-bedroom houseboat can be found moored on the north side of Battersea Bridge on the Thames, where we'll stay while we record our debut album. This chic riverside pad on Cheyne Walk has a fine view of the lovely but wobbly Albert Bridge* and on the south side of the river sits the iconic huge-chimneyed power station once pictured on the cover of Pink Floyd's *Animals* LP. The river's tidal here, and in the mornings the houseboat settles at an angle in the black riverbank mud when the water's low, and I wake up scrunched at the bottom of my bed, confused and stiff, the chemical toilet's whiff singeing my nose.

Jolyon collects us each morning in a minivan and ferries us to the studio. We're working at the Workhouse, Manfred Mann's place on the Old Kent Road, a traffic-clogged main drag out of southeast London. It's minutes away from the site of the Peckham slums where I once tottered, long demolished but replaced by squalid housing now also awaiting demolition in a borough floundering in unemployment, deprivation and desperation. Not much has changed since I was small.

The Thomas à Beckett at 320 Old Kent Road, aka the Henry Cooper, is where we go when we take a break. A boxing landmark, the pub had

---

* Once nicknamed by Londoners 'The Trembling Lady', marching soldiers had to break step halfway across to stop the bridge shaking in sympathy.

Henry's gym on the first floor where heroes like Muhammad Ali, Joe Frazier and Sugar Ray Leonard sparred when they were in town. Though not with each other.

More excitingly, David Bowie rehearsed upstairs from the bar when he was working on the *Ziggy Stardust and the Spiders from Mars* album. Along with the diesel, dirt, and leaded petrol fumes, we're inhaling rock 'n' roll royalty's air. Better still, the pub has Atari's sensational new *Breakout* arcade video game, a ludic triumph that we'll waste hours on. It's all we need to chill.

Andy, Rob and I will co-produce the album, which we want to be uncompromising, honest and minimally messed with; making something that's radical, outside of a genre straitjacket, and talks about the tormented world we live in. The studio engineer isn't forthcoming about what the racks of outboard boxes do and makes no suggestions, other than proposing we use an Aphex Aural Exciter to add harmonics to the voices, which we reject as trickery. He's polite but unenthused by our stuff, and often looks like he's thinking about jobs for the weekend, pet food or what's on the telly.

Recording's straightforward. We play the songs as a band until we get a take that we're happy with, and record keeper vocals after, adding few or no overdubs. We'll use only minimal FX so we don't iron out the songs and will sing in our British accents, avoiding American pronunciations that have cursed generations of UK artistes. The songs on the record aren't assembled or manipulated in post, especially as two-inch twenty-four-track Ampex tape is a bastard to edit with a razor blade. In the pursuit of authenticity, we rig a bespoke reverb using a mic dangled in the toilet's pan that's picking up sound from a speaker fed by audio from the studio. Sadly, it sounds like shit, so we go down the simpler path of electronic reverb and delay effects, like everyone else does. Authenticity's sometimes unrealistic. The record takes three weeks to make from start to end, a wonderfully productive time. We're left to our own devices and no one from EMI visits other than our A & R man, Chris Briggs, who loves what we're doing.

At the wrap playback – beers, cheap fizz and finger food in a label manager's office at Manchester Square – EMI staffers are lukewarm, one saying, 'It's *different*?' – meaning it'll never sell – and another, 'Is this a *demo*?' – meaning it sounds awful. But Chris is gung-ho, determined to fight our corner and talk the company round. One says the mix doesn't sound like a *mix* – too *skinny* – and asks if a remix is in the frame? Another says. 'Is "Essence Rare" the single?' but we say no, it's too mainstream, which is stupid, but we've got *principles*.

I'm talking to a sales guy who asks what I meant by the closing line in 'Ether', '. . . There may be soil under fuckall.'

'No,' I say. 'it's "There may be oil under Rockall".'

'Mmm, I still don't get it.'

I think he prefers Cliff.

Whatever the sales guys think, the record sounds just like I wanted it to. Crisp, aggressive and uncompromising, *Entertainment!* sounds like itself, there's no *decoration*; songs that cut to the chase, like Chicago blues.

Dave and Hugo's rhythm section is immense and original, bringing the funk to punk, and I'm amazed that my best friend Andy, without traditional guitar skills or training, can invent something game changing. His guitar's incredible. However many times we play 'At Home He's a Tourist', or 'Anthrax', or 'Ether' – basically any of the tracks – I'm knocked out we've made this music. My words and Gill's guitar over the groove are like yin and yang, tussling but on the same road, he and I are as one, and I'm pleased my words *mean* something and may merit talking about. This album's pushed all four of us to the limit.

I hope people like it.

Postscript

Pete Waterman will buy the Workhouse in the late eighties, but it burned down soon after, destroying the twenty-four-track master tapes of *Entertainment!* that had been stored there. The site was bulldozed in 1996 to make way for an Asda supermarket.

'YOU CAN'T WRITE POEMS ABOUT TREES WHEN THE WOODS ARE FULL OF POLICEMEN' – BRECHT

This is the end of days of the analogue age. Digital drum machines, sequencers, mobile phones, PCs, and samplers don't exist. Songs are recorded on two-inch-wide twenty-four-track tape and mixed down to stereo, with song edits made by cutting tape with a razor blade and sticking the sections together with sticky tape. Nothing can be shared online – there's no online, the Arpanet/internet has only military and academic applications – and a decade will pass before Tim Berners-Lee invents the World Wide Web. Fans and musicians swap DIY cassette mix tapes, and song mixes for review have to be biked or snail-mailed.

The most common way of writing is singing along to a piano or guitar. The composer(s) then presents the finished song to their bands with music and lyrics in the bag. The group's work will be to polish the tune, teasing out parts that'll work with the chords and melody. It's an easy way to work, but the songwriters make almost all the money.

It's not our way. We write songs as one in our warehouse rehearsal room, no one prepares anything in advance, and Gill only plays guitar when he's there, not even keeping one at home. He and I don't do anything musical outside the room, like we did when we roomed in the same house.

We write like this: Hugo and Dave come up with a beat – the

simpler the better – and Andy and I improvise guitar and vocal parts over the top until we find the germ of something we think has legs. I then write the words. Or the reverse: Gill may play a riff – the simpler the better – and the rest of us will work to it. I always try to sing in my native accent as I hate hearing Brits sing cod Yank.

For example, 'Return the Gift' started from a Gill alternating guitar note Da-duh-Da-Duh-Da-Duh-Da-Duh, as simple as page one of Bert Weedon's *Play in a Day*. Dave, Hugo and I lock on to this mechanical line, and Dave pushes the riff, satisfyingly ending the phrase with a funk flourish that brings it back to the start. He comes up with a heavy second part, a simple climb up the neck, for the chorus. I sing monosyllabic gobbledegook at first and then a word or phrase fits, in this case 'Head-A-Way-From-The-Years-You're-on-the-Pricelist'. 'Return the Gift' was in the notebook as a potential title, and the rest of the words came easily. It's an old-school starter: first work out the tune and the beat and the words will follow, Paul McCartney first sang 'Scrambled eggs' before landing on 'Yesterday'.

Another example is 'Ether'. I'd scrawled a note to myself that read 'Uncomfortable the good life's probably at someone else's expense while things are done in our name that we don't know about or condone'. It's a call-and-response number, and against my part Andy sings about Northern Ireland's H-Blocks where IRA prisoners were imprisoned.

In 1978 the British government was found guilty of 'Cruel and inhumane treatment' by the European Commission. IRA suspects endured 'the five techniques': prolonged wall standing, hooding, subjection to noise, and the deprivation of sleep, food and drink. This would be the playbook used in Guantanamo and Abu Ghraib, although waterboarding, dog attacks and sexual humiliation were added as icing to create the so-called torture *Super 8*.

In 1955 the UK claimed sovereignty over an uninhabitable guano-caked crag, called Rockall, 300 miles into the Atlantic Ocean, 'the most isolated small rock in the oceans of the world' (according to James

Fisher in 1956). Royal Marines were winched on to the seventy-foot-high outcrop to raise the Union Flag, the last land grab of the British Empire. The government said this was to stop the Soviets spying on Britain's guided nuclear weapons tests, but also claimed rights to all resources, i.e. oil and fish, for twelve miles around the shit-encrusted crag, disputed ever since by Ireland, Denmark and Iceland.

That closing line of 'Ether', 'There may be oil under Rockall!' may be true.

My notebook's full of scribbled words, ideas and potential song titles, with notes linking disconnected things being prone to narrative pareidolia, seeing connections between elements and patterns that aren't there and then linking them. The words aren't autobiographical or about relationships but lifted from something I've read, like the first line of 'Natural's Not in It' is the title of a 1938 book by Henry Durant, found in a second hand bookshop, called *The Problem of Leisure*.

I aim to write simple declarative sentences in plain English. While a non-believer, an unoriginally top-ten text is the first line of the Bible's John 1:1 'In the beginning was the Word, and the Word was with God, and the Word was God'... only one word – 'beginning' – has more than one syllable in a sentence to explain the start of all things! Brilliant!

I avoid storytelling and similes, although sometimes one sneaks through, like 'I'm as bored as a cat' in 'Glass', which I kick myself about, it's *lame*. I like disparate points of view, like Godard uses in the split-screen *Numéro Deux*, where Andy bounces off my voice when we feature call-and-response vocals. The rule is, you hear his solo voice, they're his words, but we never work together on lyrics, Gill leaves me alone, just as I wouldn't dream of giving him notes on his guitar. I try to write about the world as it is, the deceits we collectively salute, how commodity fetishism has overwhelmed us in an oligarchic society whose ruling class claims economic, racial and social inequalities are not ingrained but ordained by God. And be funny. And not use metaphors too much.

I *love* the words to songs like 'Telegram Sam', the pop perfection of

'SOS', and the narrative brilliance of 'Ruby, Don't Take Your Love to Town' or 'Wichita Lineman', but only a mug would compete with T Rex, ABBA, Mel Tillis or Jimmy Webb.

I remembered seeing a poster that read 'We Found the Essence Rare' and thought the collision of ontology and shopping was cool. For a long time, I thought the image was of a beautiful woman dripping with diamonds, draped in fine clothes, a chic chick in haute couture. I realised this was an invention when the music writer, Kevin Dettmar, found the source and tells, in his excellent *Entertainment!* monograph in the '33⅓rd' series published by Bloomsbury, how 'Essence Rare' was a perfume launched by Houbigant in 1928 to compete with Chanel No. 5. It was priced at about $3,700 a bottle in 2024 values. The scent sold well during the misery of the 1930s Great Depression and was relaunched in the 1970s. Perhaps I'd seen its ad in *Vogue*, which read: 'We searched until we found the Essence Rare. We searched. Until we found a fragrance that starts softly, develops beautifully and never seems to end. And then we made it in perfume.'

My lyrics had been triggered by a false memory image that hadn't existed about a product I'd never heard of, and copy I'd made up.

THROWN OFF *TOP OF THE POPS!*

EMI is pissed off by our refusal to release 'Essence' as a single and insistence on 'At Home He's a Tourist' being put out instead. It's a racket with a propulsive four-on-the-floor groove we think's like disco, although it isn't, a guitar intro like a train wreck in the Lincoln tunnel,* and lyrics about the alienation of daily life. It surprises us all when it gatecrashes the UK charts at no. 58!

Andy's mad guitar workout, smashing and bashing the squawking strings, hammering the pickup switch, off the beat here, back on the beat there, is a thing of beauty. The title line landed from nowhere. Sometimes everything seems ersatz, like a stage set, through a scanner darkly. It's not original – I've been reading Heidegger – the anxiety about what it is to be in the world. But fake's aren't fake if you've got the source code; like Truman Capote said about Holly Golightly, 'She's not a phoney because she's a real phoney.' Phillip K. Dick would disagree: she *is* a phoney because she's *not* a phoney. Hmm.

Although the single's barely charted, we've *automatically qualified* to be on *Top of the Pops*, the most influential TV network pop music programme in the UK – maybe the world – which is a fast lane to the Top 20!

* How a live gig of ours was described in a *New York Times* review.

This is because a *TOTP* rule says that artistes – other than in the no. 1 position – can't appear on the show two weeks in a row if their single stays in the same spot. New entrants like us – at no. 58! – are invited to play instead, and this week the chart hasn't changed much from last week... a very BBC way to do things but cool from our POV: we're on the way to a HIT! I'm excited to have a chance to *mime* to our jagged song and lip sync into a solid aluminium tube masquerading as a mic while Gill, Dave and Hugo pretend to play guitar, bass and drums that are theatrical props only. It'll be a cinch.

However, the Beeb lobs a hand grenade. Auntie says the word 'rubbers' in the chorus line, 'The rubbers you hide in your top-left pocket' is 'inappropriate for a family audience' and we must change the word if we want to go on the show! We debate about what to do. Should we tell the *TOTP* producer to shove the show up his fundament and raise our heads high in artistic purity or pander to this blackmailing petit bourgeois censorship?

We decide we'd be mad to miss a game-changing TV opportunity over the use of an American-English slang word I'd used instead of the British-English 'johnnies' because it flowed better, and which no one uses in the UK anyway. We cave and say, OK we'll change 'rubbers' to 'packets', i.e. 'the packets you hide in your top-left pocket', as it carries the same meaning but won't embarrass mums and dads uneasy about explaining what a condom is or what it's for. Learning how to unfurl a French letter on a banana will be a parental challenge for gloomy future times. The BBC say this is a good call, an excellent new word, the floor will be yours with this edit/censorship.

However, a baroque BBC/Musicians' Union closed shop deal's in place that's designed to keep orchestral and session players in work, their majority membership. Acts can only *fake* a performance on the show to an *authentic original* recording, and any variation from version one – like dropping in a substitute word – demands a whole *new* recording that must be approved by the MU to ensure the re-recorded track employs the same session musicians as the original, i.e. in our case to make sure that session musicians who weren't ever employed *would* have been used and paid again *had* they been used in the first place. Offending words can't be bleeped out as it would reveal the BBC's censorship – which they wouldn't *dream* of doing – and would also deny session musicians who were never employed the opportunity not to appear on a track they didn't play on anyway.

So, we must fast-track re-record the song using the people who played on the original or equivalent seniority subs – i.e. the four of us – who'll be paid a scale performance fee by the BBC.* A union rep has to be paid to witness the new session to ensure the rules are obeyed so that he can then approve it as a compliant *new* recording we can then fake playing to with integrity. This has to be done quickly on Monday so that we have a new recording to mime to on Wednesday, when the show's recorded for Thursday broadcast. Short-order time's booked in the Workhouse studio where we go through the motions of re-recording the backing track.

The MU guy is camped in the Henry Cooper pub next door with Chris Briggs, our silver-tongued EMI A & R man, and is delighted to get a fee for sitting in a boozer browsing the *Exchange and Mart* over a lager top. The sham session over, the rep's presented with a family-friendly recording the Beeb can use, i.e. a dupe of the existing track with 'packets' subbed for 'rubber', me having recorded this new word very professionally, if I say so myself. Everyone's happy.

Wednesday, we're onstage at BBC TV Centre to pre-record the show to the bowdlerised track.

---

* It's a win–win for the sessionistas, two sessions where there was once one, but a lose–lose for rock bands who'll find their recording debt hole with the label is deeper.

However, it's all good until it isn't. Gill's well-oiled and decides to piss off the director by wearing a 'Troops Out Now!' T-shirt he can't possibly wear on TV, as the Troops Out Movement is an Irish Republican sympathiser group *verboten* on the Beeb in the current climate of fear where IRA bombings on civilian and military targets in Northern Ireland and the mainland are bloody daily events. The T-shirt goes.

The director, a floppy-haired and chunky-jumpered poshboy – *everyone* senior in the BBC is a besweatered posh boy – is an aficionado of dynamic sweeping camera moves who wants onstage action where cameras glide through jiggling fifteen-year-old girls from *Smash Hits*. He's pissed off by Andy's mischief and blows his cool at Gill's next move – Brechtian DefCon 1 – which is to cut the guitar strings and arrange them in a mangled cluster at the guitar's machine heads, revealing the show's artifice, inauthenticity, means of production, etc. Gill, scowling, stands stock still as the music rolls. 'Will he move at all?' the director asks, and we say, 'No, he won't.' Bad vibrations.

However, the director isn't nearly as pissed off as the show's producers, who are *mortified* to discover we did what we said we'd do and replace 'rubbers' with 'packets'! This carries the same immoral implication as rubbers, i.e. men may have *johnnies* on their person when they go out hoping to get lucky.* This filth could traumatise The Man on the Clapham Omnibus, not that any posho BBC producer would dream of using a bus and sitting next to people who went to secondary moderns or work in a shop. Rob and Briggs point out that the BBC agreed up front to this inoffensive word change *and* that this hyper-sensitivity only seems to apply to us, citing as an example that no one canned the recent broadcast of the lewd 'Cool for Cats' by Squeeze, which includes the line, 'I'm invited in for coffee and I give the dog a bone.'

---

* Non heterosexual leg-over doesn't exist at this time.

The argument fails. The producer says not only is the word 'packet' offensive but the change from rubbers is so *obvious* people might notice and conclude that the BBC has *censored* our song *which it would never dream of doing*! You must, the producer says – this *suggestion* is non-negotiable – re-record the song again and replace 'packets' with 'rubbish', as this *suggested* word *sounds like* rubbers so no one will hear the difference! This is an end-game situation, as – sans time machine and *Star Trek* transporter – re-recording and mixing a track in a south London studio is impossible to do inside an hour. Rob says, 'No, this is censorship, you can't tell us what words to use, we're sticking with "packets", the word "rubbish" is rubbish, and the line wouldn't make any sense: why would anyone stuff trash in a jacket pocket?'

The producer sighs and says, 'You know quite well that "packets" means *French letters*. This is a family show. "Rubbish" is non-negotiable.'

He's told to go fuck himself, and we're kicked off the show.

As we exit the building Sniff 'n' the Tears rush in to take our slot – they must have been called some time ago, all this chat was BS – and mime along to their crap song 'Driver's Seat', an appearance which does the scab seat sniffers no good, their song peaking at no. 42 in the UK.

'At Home He's a Tourist' tanks and is banned on BBC pop radio.

EMI thinks a newly signed act called Duran Duran will be a better bet.

Postscript

The no. 1 single the week we're kicked off *TOTP* is Anita Ward's 'Ring My Bell', a whiny ask for a happy ending. DING DONG DING!

Post Postscript

Three years later, our chart single 'I Love a Man in a Uniform' is also banned from UK TV and radio play because the song mentions the army during the Falklands War.

B-SIDE

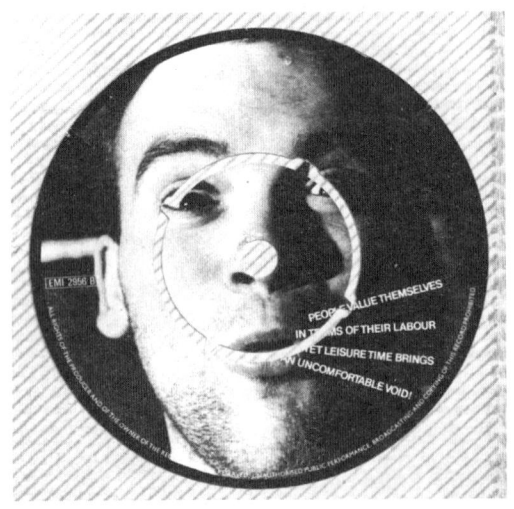

They say it is love. We say it is unwaged work. They call it frigidity ... Neuroses, suicides, desexualization: occupational diseases of the housewife.
                Silvia Frederici, *Wages Against Housework* (1975)

On the flip side of 'At Home He's a Tourist' is 'It's Her Factory', a song inspired by the 1970s feminist Wages for Housework campaign.

This is the only song Hugo ever sings on, and he nails it with furious lyrics that are mostly his, sometimes improvised live to include a new attack on women and women's rights somewhere in the world. I contributed only the title.

Gill plays sloppy but cool drums, which Dave locks on to with a crisp bass motif, while I play a tune on the melodica, a nod to the great reggae artist Augustus Pablo who *owned* this extinct instrument.

Over the years, we'll see women's rights so hard fought for and won rolled back in America, Iran and Afghanistan, the three great theocracies, so the song still resonates. I wish it didn't.

WE BUILD A PA

Webster Chicago voice recorder.

Support bands are often charged by chiselling main acts to 'use the PA' or the mixing desk, and since our fee is usually only a tenner, we sometimes play for nothing other than bar drinks on the house. We vow never to do this shit if we get bigger.

We talk this over with the Mekons, who endure the same nonsense, and come up with a plan: if we had our own PA we'd be quids in on supports and could use the system whenever we headline in a pub or a club. We could make something as fat as the

Saxon Sound, the awesome big-box reggae sound system with its stomach-churning low end we admire so much. We can build it in the Wharf Street warehouse rehearsal space that the hippy Leeds Soma Wholefoods collective is still letting us use FOC, which is very good of them.

Corrigan steals Harry Olson's audio reference book *Music, Physics and Engineering* from the library, which he thinks will tell us what we need to do, although it doesn't, as there aren't any useful exploded diagrams like you'd find in a 'Reggae Sound System Haynes Manual', if one existed. Should there be one, there'd be a chapter on how to roll a massive conical spliff like Bob's sucking on the cover of the classic Wailers album *Catch a Fire*.

Corrigan busks it, drawing up schematics and writing up a parts shopping list: plywood, black paint, two-by-one timber, speaker drivers, speakers, wire, and a fuck-off power amp. Having virtually no money, we scavenge dump and construction sites in the Golgotha of Leeds for materials.

Mark White and I find an old wardrobe waiting to be burned, its eight-by-four three-ply back panels just right for bass bins. Hugo is a champion shoplifter and steals a power drill, tool kit, drill bits and screws.

Corrigan shops for tech at M & B Radio, a government-surplus shop under the railway arches at Bishopsgate Street, which is piled high with superannuated test equipment, radio ham spares, knackered military technology and kit so old its sell or buy date is past its sell-by date. Twenty pounds buys us not so much: a fuck-off but fucked Second World War British Army power amp with fragged valves and fried wires, replacement valves, recycled speaker cones, and a pair of heavy speaker drivers attached to thick steel armour plating that had been mounted beneath the wings of a Hurricane fighter plane. We imagine them used to broadcast surrender messages to the retreating Wehrmacht: '*Berlin ist gefallen! Der Führer ist tot!*' It's a bargain.

Corrigan – who doubles as GOF's sound engineer and a Mekon front man – also buys something to record our shows. He finds just the thing, a 1947 Webster Chicago wire recorder that's going for a song (five pounds) and uses thin steel wire to record onto, instead of tape (for many years, I thought it was a seismograph). Sadly, it sounds terrible, recording only frequencies over 1 kHz, no middle or bass at all, so it's dumped.

Corrigan and I know how to solder, so we rewire the amp, which is simple as it doesn't have transistors or printed circuit boards. The fuse is missing, its empty clip fat enough to house a chipolata, so we improvise one out of a fag end with a thick metal paper clip wrapped around it. We pop in the replacement valves and *voilà!* it turns on when we flick the switch!

Everyone in the Mekons/Gang crew has a job, scavenging, cutting wood, painting, etc., under Corrigan's supervision. Gill and Jon Langford soften the three-ply wardrobe wood with steam from a kettle so it can be bent into shape for speaker flares, behind which are mounted the speaker cones and Second World War drivers. Painted matt black, it looks and sounds awesome. The PA is a triumph, Corrigan is a genius! However, when we take it out for the first time, we have a problem: it's too big to get through the club's doors.

Back in Leeds we dismantle the flares and cut them down to size, and use the skinnier PA at our next gig. The amp works brilliantly for a couple of songs until it bursts into flames, popping the house fuse, our show over. The promoter's not impressed. We don't get paid.

We decide to use house PAs after all.

Besides, we're doing fewer supports.

ANNUS MIRABILIS

25 September 1979: back home from the US tour, a few weeks after the Whisky a Go Go debacle, *Entertainment!*'s released in Britain. The reviews are incredible and the album's described as one of the best debuts ever, a tour de force, a masterpiece. Even now, it's still referenced like this, hard to credit.

The banned 'Tourist' has tanked but the album is *happening*. The London office we share with the Slits and the Pop Group is swamped with requests for interviews and TV and radio sessions. Gig offers flood in, we headline the Lyceum in London and have a prestige hometown date – headlining this time – at the Leeds University Refectory Hall. We play every gig we can get, touring the UK, Europe and the States, over ninety sell-out shows, supported by wonderful bands like the Raincoats, Red Krayola, Mission of Burma, the Mekons, the Beakers, the Bush Tetras, Pylon and REM.

The US tour supporting the Buzzcocks and as a headline club act made us, we've become an *act*. There's no substitute for gigging, there's nowhere to hide, songs work or they don't, lose the losers and play good or go home. Our shows thrill, winning audiences with our attitude, alt-music, and pinball stage moves, barely taking breath between tunes, a world away from shoegazing. Friends who see us say, 'But it's not *like* you.' 'No', I say, 'It's *theatre*, who'd pay to see the real me?' Offstage I have conventional tastes, nothing to see here and express a different side of myself onstage, darker and exaggerated. It's a blast.

Out and about and before and after shows I prefer not being recognised and don't go on about what I do. But the others adore being the centre of attention, especially Andy. He laps it up, he glows with joy when he's in the thick of it, playing to the fans, and is always up for after-show adventures with Dave. I enjoy hearing about what they do, but glad I wasn't with them.

Jerry Wexler's our champion at Warner Bros and says we're an important band the label needs on the roster, and that Hugo's one of the best white drummers in the game right now. He should know. We sign in the spring of 1980, licensing *Entertainment!* to Warners in the US and Canada, to be fast-track released a few months later. The album wins rave reviews and a lead spread in *Rolling Stone*, the most influential music publication in the world. The same title commissions a major feature from the world's greatest rock journalist, Greil Marcus. He's the author of *Mystery Train* and writes insightful and keenly argued essays about everyone from the Band and Dylan to Elvis, placing music in a cultural and social context. He joins us on a UK tour and writes about the experience, nailing what we're about, a magisterial piece. He's a fantastic bloke, he and I share many views and interests, and we'll be good lifelong friends.

Our next US tour's on a different level to the first: coast to coast, bigger audiences, more dates. We move from place to place on a custom tour bus with a dozen beds, comfy lounges with audio/video at front and back, bijou washroom and onboard toilet. The rule is no number twos on the bus, *gross*. The mid-bus beds are the size of coffins, stacked three high in two sets with a narrow corridor between. They've got cute blackout curtains for privacy, and I like the one in the middle: the top bunk risks rising farts and the bottom row gets the road bumps.

I like travelling like this. After post-show glad-handing and drinks, I climb into my bus coffin and bed down for an overnight drive to the next city, a few chapters of whatever before I'm lulled to sleep by the muffled talk and laughter from the front lounge and the constant du-donk du-donk du-donk of the wheels as they cross the concrete slab sections of America's crappy highways. When I wake up, we'll be parked up in a club or theatre parking bay or hotel car park, if we have day rooms. I like to take a walk to sense something of the city we're in, dressing quietly so I don't disturb the bad boys, Gill and Dave, who'll be sleeping off the late night partying up front hammering through last night's beer and wine rider.

I sometimes ride shotgun by the driver to escape the noise – I hate background music – sitting in a high seat which allows me see far down the road, now and then chatting about the weather or traffic.

Tour bus drivers are a special breed, often ex-military or ex-cons, or both, always alone at the wheel and curtained off from company behind them. Loners, they doze through the days and when we play, driving as we sleep, hooking up with trucker buddies on CB radio and talking in code about the road and threats ahead. A message crackles from our driver's receiver: 'Fox in the henhouse exit 9 on-ramp!' '10-4' says our driver, '10-10 in the wind.' He turns to me and says, 'Good call, passing a bear at this speed would be a pisser!' Our conversations are like this:

'You see *that*?' he may say, pointing at a car zigzagging through the lanes alongside us, 'That fighter pilot's *overtaking* us.' The motor pulls away into the distance. 'See! I *knew* it!'

We play and play and play, everything's going our way, but it's time to write new songs, the set could do with freshening, we need a new LP to move on up.

The only downside is Rob quitting as manager, as EMI Records has poached him, making him an offer he couldn't refuse. He's been great, guiding us from nowhere to somewhere, patient, imaginative, and good with money. I can't blame him, I'd have done the same in his shoes, there are no hard feelings, and we'll be lifelong friends.*

We start on album number two.

---

* Rob will later return to management and look after Scritti Politti, The Human League, and ABC.

WITH THE ANGELS

The Paradiso, Amsterdam, locally called the *Poptempel*, is the coolest gig in Holland, a 1,500-capacity converted church where everyone who's happening plays. It's in the middle of town, not far from the Rijksmuseum and its Rembrandts, good to see before a gig. It's ugly outside, more railway terminus than old church, but inside it's a delight. Huge Romanesque stained-glass windows overlook a wide stage and dancefloor; there are two balconies with tiered seating on three sides, one of them high up in the gods for people with keen eyes or too stoned to open them. Loose joints and varietal weed can be bought from a helpful hippie vendor, and a haze of marijuana smoke drifts over the steaming crowd rammed on the dancefloor and jumping and screaming for more.

Our show over, the house lights are on, and Elgar's 'Nimrod' from the *Enigma Variations* – our exit music – is booming over the PA as sweaty punters shuffle to the exits.

We skip to the dressing room, hyped, yammering about how great the show was, what to do and where to go, the night's young and full of promise. But standing in the centre of our room is Big Willem, the notorious head of the Amsterdam chapter of the Hells Angels. The size of a beer truck, he's dressed in full Angels colours, a 'President' patch on his leathers, a fearsome sight. At his side stands his sergeant-at-arms, holding straight-armed toward us a mirror in his left hand on which sit four fat lines of blow/crank/not blow/not crank/who knows, and in his right holds upright a long bowie knife that glimmers in the showbiz ball mirror lights. The Angels are big fans.

Three prospects stand behind them, attentive. They sport '81' patches, the '8' and '1' standing for the letters HA, but they haven't earned their winged skulls yet. It's a tough gig.

'Hey, beefcake!' says the smiling capo, embracing Hugo. 'Fucking great fucking show! Take this!' The sergeant-at-arms, who steps forward and presents the powdered mirror to Hugo, is already known to us. He's The Man with No Face, a local biker legend. He's clearly been in a serious accident, or been done over, or in a fire, or had chemical burns, or all four, flake-white scar tissue stretched like clingfilm across his cheekbones and forehead with a cute bumpette where his nose had once been, a two-wheeler Voldemort. Jesus wept!

These are serious men, much feared here. The city of Amsterdam recently paid them 172,000 guilders (three hundred thousand dollars in 2024 values) towards a chapter clubhouse outside the city so they'd stay away and keep their mischief in-house. Not good.

Hugo, eyeing the Memphis rails which could be *anything*, says, 'Uh, no, not my thing . . . I think I'll pass . . . but cool, yeah, thanks for the offer!'

The chapter president clutches H tight. 'No worries, beefcake. We fix you up later! Whatever you fucking want! *Anything.*'

The Man with No Face jabs the mirror towards Gill, Dave and me, the bowie knife blade looking bigger, sharper and shinier by the minute. We squeak excuses to pass on the blow/smack/meth/whatever as politely as we can, our formerly masculine voices raised several octaves to castrati.

The president nods to TMWNF who passes the gear to the hovering prospects who hoover up the dust, the rigid hierarchy doubtless determining which of the three has second dibs on the fourth line.

We need to tread softly. The interns are on a training day, falling off a badass biker learning cliff, and will be desperate to earn their colours. It's a little tense. I'd seen earlier from the stage how the Angels in the audience had created negative space around them, a black hole no one wanted to be sucked into and brush with the outlaws. So far, it's cool, but I bet the Stones at Altamont thought things were until they weren't.

We'd been told that when Iggy played here last week, he'd said something like, 'All you Angels are faggots!' during the show. Unwise, although you've got to admire his godlike Iggy-ness. But the insult obliged the Angels, however much they adored Jim, into a punishment hiding. Their honour was at stake. They made him go back onstage after a few slaps and say sorry, didn't mean it, mistaken identity, Angels rule etc., etc. This either did or didn't happen, but I'm not ruling it out. And saying nothing.

'We go for a drink, NOW!' says the prez to me and Gill, Dave and Hugo having bailed, falsely claiming they needed to sort out onstage stuff and that, a roadie's job. We were too slow and leave with the boss, the sergeant-at-arms and the rocker interns, on a works outing.

We go to a nearby bar which is rammed, but the boozy crowd parts before us like the Red Sea before Moses. At the counter, the barman's frantically pulling pints, on his own, working his cojones off. 'YOU!' yells the chapter boss, the bar falling silent. 'BEER! For me and my friends! NOW!' The barman turns and signals he'll serve us just as soon as he's done this round, sweat beading on his forehead, while nearby drinkers down their Amstels and edge to the door. This isn't acceptable to the prez, who picks up a heavy glass ashtray and throws it – WHOMP! – to hit the barman midway between his shoulder blades, knocking him down, beer glasses flying. FUCK!

'BEER NOW!' he shouts at the bruised bartender, jumping up fast from the sticky foamy floor, 1,000 per cent focused on the men with wings. The Prospects nod, mentally noting how to act when service is slow, a key learning point.

Only a few people stay in the bar; most slope off as we chug chilled Grolsch and make polite small talk about bikes and bands, praying nothing kicks off. Thankfully, nothing does, it's all very civilised. I doubt the pair of Rijkspolitie coppers watching us from their Mazda outside will help if it does.

We respectfully thank the president for his generous hospitality, wave our goodbyes – *Tot ziens!* – and head back to the hotel. It's been a lovely evening.

BRIEF ENCOUNTERS

Make America Great Again

We're in the Deep South and stop for a bite. I ask for a burger and fries from the redneck server who's wearing a Reagan '80 button that reads 'Make America Great Again!'
    She says, 'Wheah yoo fraam? Yuh shuah tawk funnay!'
    'London, England.'
    'Oh,' she says. 'Yuh speak English verr will!'

Service with a Smile

An electronics store on Avenue of the Americas, NYC, has a digital wristwatch on display in the window, the first I've seen, a display only the size of a matchbox, very cool. I go in, ask to take a look, and say to the counter guy, 'How do you set the time?'
    'The fuck do I know?'
    A smart consumer, I say, 'How long's it insured for?'
    'Till you get out in the fuckin' street!'
    I buy two.

Attitude

Corrigan and are in a White Castle where he orders a quarter pounder. The server says, pointing at Andy's silver cock-and-balls earring, the one he and Mark White bought with our food money in Leeds, 'What's the significance of that?'

'I'm homosexual!' Corrigan says.

'Mmm,' he says, and shrugs. 'Good luck to ya!'

IGGY AND MICHAEL

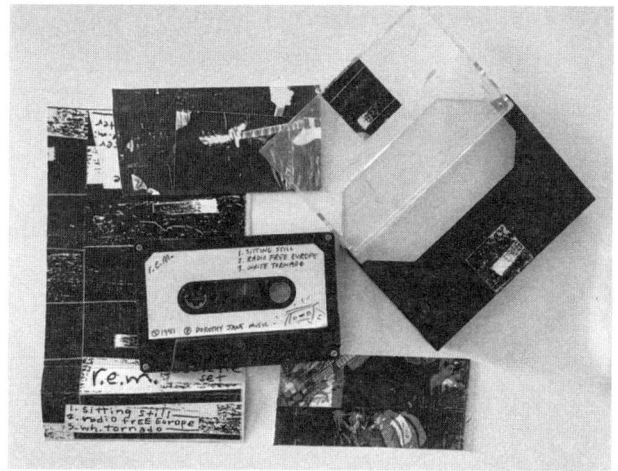

REM demo tape.

It's November 1980 and we're co-headlining at the Santa Monica Civic with Iggy Pop, a hero of mine who I last saw supporting the Ramones in New York a couple of years back.

The techs are putting up the backline and I'm scuffing about the stage thinking about how to approach the show tonight when Iggy limps up to me palm outstretched and says 'JON? ... JIM!' and we shake – *I'm shaking hands with James 'Jim' Osterberg aka Iggy Pop who knows who I am!*

'Weeell,' he says, in his signature drawl, 'would you *mind* if I have the stage-level dressing room? I'm too OOLD to get up the stairs.'

'Uh, of course, *Jim*,' I say. 'It's all yours.' I'm embarrassed we're going on last, and who wants to follow Iggy?

I watch every second of his act from the wings. The OOLD guy – early thirties – sashays on with his iconic pimp-on-a-catwalk strut, shirt off, ripped, the audience holding its breath, shouts 'One-two-three-four – Ow!' and the band blasts off with the Stooges classic 'Shake Appeal'. Iggy doesn't stop moving, prowling his turf, aggressive, snarling, camp, working every inch of the boards, crowd surfing, a stagecraft masterclass up there with James Brown. As I watch I think if this counts as a job, I've got one of the best jobs in the world...

A couple of months later we're touring the States supported by REM, *another* great band from Athens and close friends of Pylon, and after the soundcheck Michael Stipe and I are talking about how Iggy does it. Many nights, REM cluster side stage watching us at it, it's the School of Rock 'n' Roll work experience, just like I do to them, although I much prefer watching from front of house. Thinking of what I've borrowed/stolen from Jim, I say, in one of the only bits of performing advice worth sharing, 'Imagine you're a wolf marking the boundaries of your territory with piss, prowl the stage, it's *yours*.' Michael shyly gives me a cassette demo tape REM's using to shop a deal – they've made a couple of dozen of them – and says, 'Hope you like it.' Do I like it? I LOOVE it! The cassette includes teeny colour-photocopied paper inserts, cut-ups of band shots and has three tracks:

1. Sitting Still
2. Radio Free Europe
3. White Tornado

IGGY AND MICHAEL

I play the tape to an A & R man at Warners who says he doesn't hear any songs. 'You've got no *ears!*' I say. REM will soon sign to the Copeland's IRS label, and, in 1988, will be signed for big bucks to Warner Brothers. I feel weirdly proud when they get huge, not that I've anything to do with their success, just a bystander in their magic. I still have the cassette, which I cherish.

I GET MY HEAD KICKED IN

We're mobhanded in a Chapeltown terraced house at a cool blues party. The whole crew's here: the band, Linda, our office manager, Jolyon, Phil. Tomorrow will be the first day of a three-week UK tour, we're playing all over, it'll be a blast, fun times ahead. We're the only white people here but we've been before, good people run this place, the host says, 'Wah gwaan,' as we enter, waving us in with a Red Stripe in one hand and a bull-nosed spliff in the other, the room foggy with ganja, 'How yuh stay?' To which I'd say *mi irie* if I could say it well, but would sound like a prat even if I could. The DJ's playing heavy dub whose deep bass moves without pause through your body, the 30 Hz sinewaves as long as a bus generated by fat sub-bass woofers buried deep under the decks. The toaster's words are lost on me, I can't decode patois, but the sound's excellent.

We're all chilled, Linda's on the dancefloor shuffling and grooving until there's a kerfuffle, some out-of-town guy has hassled her, touching her up and dissing her as a slag. She's pissed off and wants some air outside, going down the narrow staircase only good for single file. She's gone longer than we expected until we're told one of the stranger rude boys has punched her in the face, knocking out a tooth, words had been shared, disrespect given that required retribution. Gill and I go to help her, Gill first down the stairs, but one of the gang follows him, between me and him, a beer can in hand that he starts bashing and crashing into Gill's skull as they descend the staircase, WHACK THWACK SMACK on his head, Andy with hands up for protection as they stumble down the dark passageway. I'm right behind, trying to pull the rude boy's hitting arm, but it's too tight to land a punch. We fall out of the house door into an empty street among parked motors. Gill's sprawled on the ground between two motors, covering his face as two guys kick at him where he lies. I grab one, pull him around and try to boot him the balls, a really dumb thing to do in a fight, but don't connect and I'm off balance, and BANG, smacked in the face and dropped to the ground. My guy's buddy leaves Gill where he lies, and both give me their full attention, putting the boot into my head again and again until I'm out cold.

Someone calls 999, an ambulance and cop car screech in, I'm rushed to hospital. Apparently the barney triggered local trouble, the word being that this might be a race thing, maybe a BNP or NF incident or white guys crashing a blues dance looking for aggro. Who knows what's being said, so our lot have to get away before it escalates, and Linda will need her teeth seeing to. The cops are hopeless and won't get out of their squad car without backup, won't chance it as these are violent times. After a while a paddy-wagon arrives, but there's no one to arrest, no one's seen anything, nothing to see here, no one will talk to the filth.

I'm operated on at Leeds's St James's University Hospital. My cheekbone's broken around my right eye socket, the bone collapsed into my jaw, so they make a neat cut on my temple behind the hairline to insert some tool that can pull the bone out and back in position. My right eye's damaged, the white now incarnadine red, and my vision may be affected. I'm released next day to be driven barely conscious down to my Muswell Hill flat where I will be in bed for a week or more, luckily without a brain bleed, blindness, or entering a coma. I don't know much about what's going on but I'm well looked after by Debbie.

I must be quite a sight, head half-shaved, the operation stitching looks like a ham lobotomy, a lopsided face with cherry-coloured eye and black and blue bruising shading to yellow as it wanes, my puffed up face a living Mark Rothko.

I mostly recover, although the bundled nerve serving the right side of my face that's fed through the middle of the cheekbone has been permanently damaged, this side of my face will always feel funny. It could be worse. I could have lost my sight.

The tour's cancelled and rebooked as soon as my cheekbones have bonded. We're playing at Cambridge Corn Exchange, I've taken my cheek protection mask off for the show when halfway through the set Gill lurches Wilko-style full tilt across the stage and runs straight into me, his guitar head WHAMMING into my face. It really hurts, but nothing breaks, nothing to see here . . . FFS!

TOO MUCH DRINKING MAKES GILL ILL

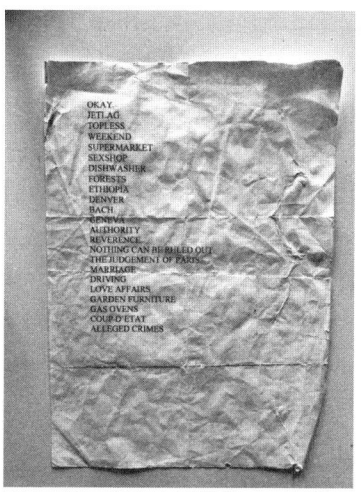

Song titles.

A decaying block of once attractive art deco flats can be found a few streets from the Whitechapel Road in the East End, its thick-painted Crittall windows unopenable and the cracked glass panes made safe against rain by cardboard. The concrete walls are pitted and fungal from water, which overflows from blocked gutters and drips from a broken downpipe. Burst bin bags in the stairwell spew a moraine of trash and filth down the treads and a pile of soiled nappies has been carefully arranged like Ferrero Rochers on the stairwell's turn below a graffito of a spurting penis that reads 'Suck my Cock, Tracey'. Andy has a flat on the third floor and this is where we write songs together now we're in London, except when we don't, for another studio album, although we're finding it hard. Andy's desperate for a hit, me too, but thinks we need to be more *melodic* and *accessible*, which might be true if we were different people in a different band.

It's proving hard to produce anything as our lifestyles aren't compatible. I like to work predictable daytime hours Monday to Friday, like a job, I don't sleep well at night and wake early, at my creative best in the morning, and try to keep evenings and weekends free for friends, family and going out, which gives me inspiration for lyrics. Whereas Andy wants to work whenever he feels like it, be spontaneous, go on until we've got somewhere. I'm not sure this is possible as night-time fun times out up West are inevitably followed by dog-day mourning in the mornings; his hangover's vicious before the Solpadeine kicks in.

Our theoretical daily MO: I arrive at midday to sit with Gill in front of a TASCAM 144 four-track cassette recorder, practice amp and guitar, and a SM57 microphone, programming simple beats on the Roland Drumatix TR-606 drum machine and play or sing along. Something either happens or it doesn't.

An A4 sheet is Blu-Tacked to the wall that reads 'Banned' over a list of no-go subjects or words such as dollars, cash, love, metaphors, adverbs, etc. Money references especially annoy me. Gill, who wants to input more lyrics, routinely uses them to traffic light human relationships, but we've already been there, and I say us talking about cash is like a dog returning to its own vomit.

Another stuck up sheet reads: 'Song titles'. Gill finds this useful as he can't think of any words without a starter. Keith Richards says, in his memoir *Life*, that Mick Jagger can't write lyrics until Keef gives him a title either. Only when I gave Gill the one-word title 'Paralysed' as a catalyst could he write his brilliant words of self-disgust.

He's focused but antsy, getting worse in the afternoons until the sun's edged over the yardarm, 6 p.m., when he'll fill a large glass to the brim with chilled white wine, a rule he keeps to except when he doesn't, visibly relaxing when he's chugged the first Chardonnay and sips at a second, at his best now, articulate, chatty and funny for maybe an hour or so until he pours a third glass that's my sign to bail – it's the tipping point – and work's finished, he's already thinking about eating and drinking out.

One day, there's no answer to my knock and he doesn't answer the phone so I assume Gill's sparko after a heavy night and head home. The next day, he tells me he'd been kept in an overnight bed at the nearby Whitechapel Hospital, an emergency admission. He'd felt rough and thrown up a cup of cherry-red blood and called a cab to take him to A & E but the taxi driver, seeing Andy with a chevron of gore from throat to groin, screamed and ran away, he must have thought it was a crime scene, which Gill thought funny, although the ambulance paramedic didn't. He was visited at his hospital bed by an alcohol advisor who said he had a dysfunctional relationship with booze and appeared to be dependent on alcohol, which was bad for his health and mental wellbeing, so should radically cut down or ideally quit drinking. Gill said no, drinking wasn't a problem, he didn't touch booze until the evening, knew his limits – basically twaddle. Andy can't have told the doc how much he knocks back each day or about sundown-rule exceptions, i.e. when he tours, flies, gigs, goes to the pub or lunches.

He and I now no longer socialise much, and I hide bottles if he comes to mine. He won't leave until every drop's gone. Fun no more.

BRIBING THE COMMIES

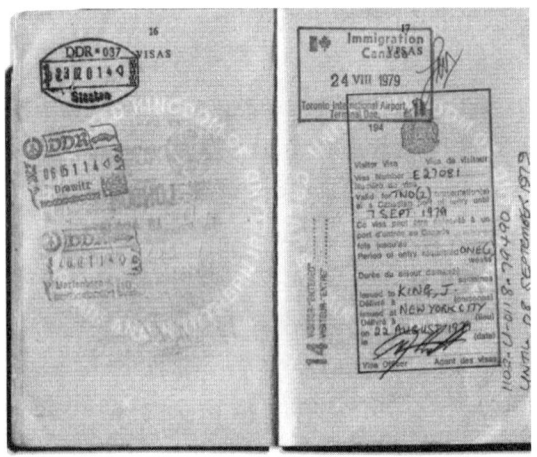

Passport.

The heavily patrolled barbed-wire fence is adorned with machine-gun emplacements, followspot watchtowers, and minefields in a 200-metre-wide buffer zone that runs the length of the German Democratic Republic (Deutsche Demokratische Republik, DDR), a hardcore Soviet stooge state bordering West Germany. DDR guards will shoot to kill anyone trying to flee the workers' paradise on this Cold War frontline which would, should the war boil over, be vaporised in a twink by the fat tactical nuclear missiles that nestle in the dense forests either side of the Elbe. This would be a MAD smackdown between camo'd Scuds and smooth cruise missiles, whose winners will be the first to lose in this lose–lose scenario. Only a few roads connect West Germany with West Berlin, 100-mile-long rat runs rigidly controlled at each end by the commies with exit roads along the way staffed by soldiers in armoured cars to stop Westerners straying off piste.

Don't stop anywhere on these autobahns other than at an Intershop area, where only hard currencies like Deutschmarks or dollars are accepted and you can buy discount Veuve Clicquot, knock-off fragrances and pricy petrol, or even – if you're desperate – stop for a bite of bad food served badly. Be mindful of the Ramones advice in their classic 'Commando':

First rule is: The laws of Germany
Second rule is: Be nice to mommy
Third rule is: Don't talk to commies
Fourth rule is: Eat kosher salamis

Wise words. We're heading to West Berlin, an enclave within the DDR that's run by the British, French and American militaries, who all have a zone to look after. Camouflaged vehicles pootle about everywhere and the Cold War enemies park up their tanks and armoured cars near the depressing crossing points and spy-swap bridges made famous in thrillers. It's a hangover from the Great Patriotic War – *everything* here is a hangover from the Great Patriotic War – when Eastern Europe was occupied by the Soviet Union and Stalinist puppet states were installed, and West Berlin is an anomaly, a capitalist Eden hemmed in by a high wall that's treated as a state by the Tankies* and as a part of West Germany by the West.

* 'Tankies' is the what hardcore Communists are called who didn't quit the party after the terrible Soviet invasion of Czechoslovakia in 1968. People on the so-called 'New Left', like me, held them in contempt.

Western tourists can cross to the other side via Checkpoint Charlie but must first buy twenty-five Ostmarks at parity to the Deutschmark, a rate ten times less than scalpers will offer you on the commie side, although this is illegal – *everything* is illegal here, even if it's not, and it's estimated 2.5 per cent of the adult population grass up their friends and family to the Stasi, so keep schtum and don't trade cash! Besides, there's nothing worth buying here other than vodka or schnapps, and the food's diabolical. No wonder the East Berliners have such bad skin.

Greil Marcus, the wonderful writer and great friend, tells me he was in Berlin as a teenager when the wall was erected in August 1961. A single coil of barbed wire had divided the East and West sectors until one day workmen overseen by DDR squaddies lay a line of bricks, which by nightfall is shin high; work continues the next day, and it's clear a wall's being built. People in the West sector shout abuse at the guards, realising they'll soon be cut off from friends and family in the East, and others living in the Soviet sector begin to panic when they realise they'll be trapped, with many jumping the wall to flee while it's still low and security's still patchy; there's a famous photo of an East German soldier doing the same.* A few days on, the wall's too high, and the DDR will be a walled-off cage for decades.

Since young Berliners are exempt from military service, the city's become a humming hive of alternative creativity packed with squatters, anarchists, punks and pacifists, and it's wonderful to be in the place where Bowie recorded his brilliant Berlin trilogy that we played non-stop in Cromer House. It's May 1981 and our gig's at SO36 in Kreuzberg, Berlin's equivalent to CBGB, an ideal place for Gang of Four to play and as good as it gets, a stinky dive with a super-cool vibe.

* This is featured in the 1982 Disney film *Night Crossing*.

Hugo, Dave, Andy and I are queuing at the DDR border in a flash rental Merc, driving ourselves to West Berlin, Hugo at the wheel. Our two techs, Jolyon and Phil, are travelling separately with the backline in a four-tonner, having set off much earlier as their van's bound to be examined closely to make sure no escapee's hiding in a fake petrol tank or false-bottomed flight case.

There are zigzag tank traps, machinegun nests, observation towers, and a high fence topped with razor wire which makes real the East/West conflict. This is no game. Chest-level vehicle barriers can squish drivers to pulp from door-height up should any try to ram through, and thirty-feet-long six-tonne concrete blocks mounted on hydraulics can be instantly rammed across the road, able to stop even a fast-moving fifty-tonne lorry.

We pull up alongside a DDR soldier toting an assault rifle who's checking drivers' creds. *'Die unterlagen?'* he says – we hand over our passports – *'für das auto?'*

Hugo, at the wheel, rummages in the glove compartment for paperwork. Uh-oh. We are idiots. We don't have any hire or insurance documents or logbook, and don't know who hired the car – it wasn't any of us – nor which company the car was hired from. Fuck's sake!

An officer comes over to wave away the Easty private and leans in the window. *'Dokumenty?'* he says in Russian, and points at Dave's Ramones T-shirt. *'Nettes T-shirt.'* Nice T-shirt.

'Yes!' Hugo says, warming to the hustle, *'Dokumenty!'* – and points at the AA sticker on the windscreen, then grabs three Gang of Four T-shirts on the back seat and hands them over. We are waved through.

'The Cold War will end with merch!' Hugo says.

The gig's brilliant, crazy: the punks and new music fans here have great taste, they know the songs word perfect, singing along, screaming, shouting, applauding our moves.

A demonstration kicks off nearby as we play. It sounds like trouble, a nee-nawing orchestra of cop sirens, angry crowd chants, metallic megaphone orders '*Nach hause gehen! Zerstreue dich jetzt!*', and the sound of high-pressure water cannoning into the anarcho-squatters who scream and swear as they lose their footing and fall, the noise constant through our set. A few puffy-eyed people stumble into the gig, tears running down their faces, coughing and spluttering, the signature peppery whiff of teargas lingering on their clothes adding a spicy bouquet to the foggy dope- and fag-smoked room. We play all the songs we know, repeat some in encores until we're burned out and get off.

We're invited to a drunken after-show party hosted by an East German dentist couple who'd risked their lives to escape the Soviet zone, hiking to a less-patrolled section of the forested border where the mines were sparsely scattered and the fence could be scaled by ladder. Respect.

Someone gifts us four bright blue FDJ (*Freie Deutsche Jugend* – Free German Youth) shirts that have been smuggled from East Berlin. Excellent schmatta but illegal to wear in West Germany as the rags are seen as symbols of anti-democratic activity.* We all wear them later in the year at a Hurrah club show in NYC. I hope our anti-Tankie intention's obvious.

It's a good do, and I chat with Jayne County, who's moved here and now identifies as a woman having had surgery to fully transition. I admire her a lot, she's a charismatic in-your-face performer whom I last met when she was Wayne County with her band the Electric Chairs, who'd supported us at Camden's Electric Ballroom, an awesome show. They were *loud*. I wish I'd brought my copy of her brilliantly offensive single 'Fuck Off' to autograph, which has the wondrous lyric 'If you don't wanna fuck me, baby, fuck off!'

She's all woman.

---

* Three-quarters of East Germans aged between fourteen and twenty-five are in the FDJ, a set up designed to control all aspects of their lives and promote Tankie communism. It also arranges discos.

ABBEY ROAD

A couple of months earlier, we're recording our second album in a large white-fronted Georgian building set back from a busy north London road, not far from Lord's Cricket Ground, a five-minute walk from St John's Wood Underground Station. The traffic on Abbey Road is constantly held up by tourists from all parts stopping on the zebra crossing which fronts the studio while they try to take a photo aping the cover of the eponymous Beatles album made here. Grumpy motorists stuck at the crossing wave and shout to shoo away the cameramen and women standing in the middle of the road to get the money shot, which is dangerous and annoying. Everyone does it.

A cluster of sightseers is looking over the low wall at the front across a modest car park to the building, where they can see a short metal staircase rising to double doors, over which is an illuminated sign which reads ABBEY ROAD STUDIOS. There's no clue that this is the most famous studio complex in the world, which houses the most famous studio in the world, Studio 2, where the Beatles produced the greatest collection of work in pop music history.

There's also no clue that we're making our second album here, IN STUDIO 2! We've set up in a corner of this huge, high-ceilinged, wood-lined room, big enough for a mid-size orchestra but over-specified for a four-piece rock band whose equipment fits into the back of a Ford Transit. The control room that looks down on the room has a new desk only recently installed to replace Abbey Road's unique TG12345 mixer with reverse throw faders, like the controls in an aeroplane cockpit, to adjust audio levels, on which the Beatles' oeuvre had been recorded and mixed.*

We want to make a record with a funky, heavy feel, and to work with a producer who can help us get in the groove and hired Jimmy Douglass, a production legend famous for the funk monster Slave and had also worked with AOR and R & B giants like Aretha Franklin, the Average White Band, Bette Midler, Bryan Ferry, Dr John, Foreigner, Hall & Oates, Roberta Flack, Roxy Music, the Rolling Stones, etc. Nothing he'd done was like our thing, he sees it as a challenge, and says he'll do it, amazing us all; he can't need the money, not that the production advance he's getting from EMI is life changing. He says our shit is the shit, which is nice.

Me and Gill will co-produce the record with Jimmy and we can't have everyone at the desk. From now on Andy and I will be jointly credited for songs rather than split the publishing four ways. This is because we've been collectively sluggish writing new material, trying to produce songs built up from a Hugo and Dave foundation groove, which works brilliantly when it works but more often morphs into directionless jazz-funk or Free-adjacent workouts followed by a downcast trudge to the Fenton.

Developing songs from jamming's been a writing roadblock because Gill lacks foundation guitar skills and is unable to play scales or lead lines and can't or won't follow by ear other players. Trying to write like this is the triumph of hope over experience; it rarely goes anywhere. Andy's at his brilliant best when he comes up with a riff that Dave and Hugo can work with or when he freewheels over the top of a continuous groove, improvising and bashing, and the only

---

* This historic and unusual mixing desk was given away to a north London school to end up being dumped in a skip.

thing that matters is being in the same key as it's all about him. 'What We All Want' is written like this, a groove monster with my locked-in vocal counterpoised with Andy's improv Hendrix-inspired lead guitar over Dave's relentless popping funk bassline – his love of Can and Funkadelic coming through – and Hugo's rock-solid floor-tom-heavy beat BA-Boom-Boom-BA-Boom-Boom!

'What We All Want' is Jimmy's favourite track, but he doesn't like the words; in fact, he doesn't warm to *any* of my lyrics, says they're 'schoolboy' subjects or too political, I ought to write about shagging, partying, near-shagging, shagging while partying or being dumped, it's more chart friendly. Without doubt true. Being dumped while shagging and partying would tick all the boxes, but I'm done with that.

We fight about words. I'm not budging and lay it on with a trowel saying what I write about is what I care about and what people actually talk about when they're not partying or shagging, i.e. almost all the time: relationships, nuclear Armageddon, alienation, what's in store, etc. These are dark times, and the next day I show him the UK government's *Protect and Survive* 1980 pamphlet, just published to help households know how to best survive the imminent war, which I pillage for the song 'In the Ditch'. And I show him a book of Bertolt Brecht's collected poetry that once inspired me to write 'Not Great Men'. Jimmy's not interested as the Ostie German didn't write about chicks, and he prefers talking to Andy, who doesn't read literature or share government H-bomb survival tips.

My cool relationship with this big-shot producer warms a tad when we start recording 'Cheeseburger' and Jimmy says he digs my words, which is either true or it isn't. I tell him I harvested them from a late night Gill and I spent in Barney's Beanery, a bar with pool tables a few blocks up from the Tropicana in LA. We'd been wasting time shooting pool against all-comers, winner stays on, i.e. us. – not sharks but we'd got in gear – and were running the baby table for long stretches without shelling out. We're well-practised as most of the time spent in a band means twiddling your thumbs while waiting for a stage or a bus or an interview call, and eight ball's a great way to kill time. It's much easier than snooker, which I'm hopeless at. Being colour blind doesn't help; I can't tell the brown balls from the red against the green baize. Gill thinks the game's a lock when we're taken on by a half-drunk trucker duo. They think they're all that, splitting the balls with cannonball breaks hoping for lucky pots, playing cushion shots that go on their holidays, all the while spilling their life stories over cold Schlitz beers and twenty-dollar bets to make the games more interesting. They're not as good as they think, and it's fun taking their money, although we both suspect maybe they are, and there'll be a last-ditch double-or-quits hustle twist where we get skinned. But they don't and we're a hundred dollars up at night's end. I write down what I remember they said the next day: 'I move from one place to the next ... I hope they keep down the price of gas ...' etc.

At the track's start we drop in a cassette recording Gill and I made of a fast-food chef's shout-out in the Red Flame restaurant in New York – *Cheeseburger to go!* – and the song's a happening thing, even if it's not AOR chart material. As Gore Vidal said, it's not enough to win, others' must fail.

The session runs from 10 a.m. to 8 p.m., all four of us first laying down backing tracks, after which Dave stays away from the studio and has fun in the smoke, while Hugo comes in to eat sirloin steak lunch and dinners in the works canteen – excellent fries – and drinks Pernod and black in the evening, which is a vile drink. Jimmy, Andy and I record guitar and vocals, and fuss over the songs and the sound and the mixes. No one from EMI comes by. I'd expected at least *some* corporate intervention but there's none and we do it our way. 'What We All Want' turns into a monster, and 'Paralysed' is Gill's masterpiece. I'm proud of the album, which takes us five weeks to make from start to finish.

At the playback, EMI's pluggers say they can't hear a *single*. Hmm. The album is called *Solid Gold*.

CLUSTERFUCK

Andy, Busta, Hugo and me.

> What can God do against the stupidity of men?
>
> Sean O'Casey

Our road crew has been refused entry into the US! It's a disaster. Our useless management had forgotten to apply/couldn't be arsed/ thought blagging at immigration would be a money-saving breeze – *just say you're on holiday but make sure you stand apart in different lines at immigration, and don't talk to each other once you've deplaned.* While this worked at JFK, driving back into the US from Canada is way tougher, especially if you're sporting 'Manny's Schlepper' shirts and concert blacks, which broadcast I AM A ROADIE from a mile away. The land crossings on the World's Friendliest Border™ are notoriously the World's Most Unfuckingfriendly Border Crossings™ for musicians.

At immigration, a swivel-eyed uniform will deep-dive interview you as he/she/they riffle through your passport, holding it up to the light like it's a bagged dog turd, missing nothing, squirrelling for a slip-up or mis-squeak or logic error – 'So, can you *prove* you were never charged with Crimes Against Humanity?' – sniffing out a lie in its bodyguard of truth; while at the same time tooled-up dog handlers with hyper spaniels snuffle around the tour bus for blow and weed. It's worse than East Germany! You only have to bung merch to Stasi guards to get through!

Since everyone expects the third degree, touring bands routinely park up before the bridge to dump moody shit while the driver vacuums and wipes and bleaches and vacuums and wipes and bleaches every surface, a challenge for CSI aficionados, before rocking up clean to the crossing point, leaving Canuck trashcans rammed with glassine bags, skins and wraps.

But the dimwit crew had driven up *all together* in a single hire car to the Champlain–St Bernard de Lacolle border crossing to say, 'We're planning a driving vacation in the States?' ... but immigration say, 'Okaaay... so what's with the tour itineraries... and the guitar spares... the soldering iron? ... You guys, jeez!' Their passports were stamped REFUSED ENTRY, and they're told they'll have to fly home from Canada.

We'd flown separately from Montreal to New York – our visas are totally kosher – to do promo stuff and schmooze at Warners and we're chilling in the Iroquois when we get the bad news, which makes Dave *snap*.

He says, 'That's IT! I HATE this shit! The office couldn't run a bath! I've had it, I QUIT!'

He stomps off, followed by Hugo unsuccessfully trying to talk him down. He's the only one Dave will listen to – he doesn't hate him like he now does Gill – but won't change his mind, packs his bags, jumps in a cab to Kennedy, and flies home.

We're über-fucked: *no* bass player, *no* crew, with the next leg of the tour on the Pacific edge kicking off in Seattle in only two days. Cancelling these shows would bankrupt us: the cupboard's bare back home, we depend on the money we'll make from this 1981 tour. It hadn't started well. When in New York we dropped by Warners to talk about album promo stuff, and they said *thrilled* to see you but *why* are you here? Our management hadn't told them we'd be touring the US, another cock-up.

The tour's been a wild success with sold-out shows breaking percentages, *Solid Gold*'s a critical hit, fabulous live reviews etc, but we only go into profit on the back end, i.e. when we hit the West Coast. Dave's playing has won huge praise, it's heavy and focused and funky, channelling the Meters and Funkadelic and Can, the engine room of our sound. But he wasn't looking forward to the dates and feels unappreciated and thinks Gill and I get almost all the attention – which is probably true. But his anxiety and bad karma aren't helped by nightly getting smashed with Gill after shows and only grabbing short bed sleeps until the long braindead drive to wherever. Although Andy and he are conjoined bar buddies, they're always in each other's faces, their mutual bile only diluted when softened by booze. But their relationship went south once Dave read an interview where Gill said the music's all down to him, falsely claiming he wrote the bass parts – it's ludicrous, Andy's a terrible bass player – and feels he's being kicked into touch.

Trouble's been brewing for a while. A few months ago, Dave disappeared post soundcheck at a sold-out Liverpool Eric's gig and took a train back to London. We thought he'd OD'd or been arrested or injured, our tour manager ringing local hospitals as we sat on our hands in the dressing room hoping he'd show, until we admitted defeat and had to go onstage to say the show's off, Dave's gone AWOL, no idea where, he may be in trouble or sick or dead, blah blah . . . but the scouse crowd wasn't having it, they'd been sardined for hours in a steaming room waiting for us to go on, yelled abuse and lobbed beer and stuff at us as we made our apologies. I can't blame them, it was shite. Next day, we have a summit with Dave – he was crashing at my north London flat – he's wet-eyed and remorseful, he'd had a crisis, he was fragile, 'forgive me'. We did. Nothing more was said. Nothing is ever said.

Then, a few weeks ago, playing in communist Yugoslavia, things had got ugly between Andy and Dave. We've drawn a big crowd here as our music's been linked to the struggle for democracy and an end to repression, and our concerts in Zagreb, Ljubljana and Belgrade have morphed into chances for young people to demonstrate against the grey-haired commie regime. One show, a phalanx of jittery riot cops rocks up, a water cannon parked up in a side street, itching to bash anti-state punk rockers' heads, desperate to deny them a walk-in part to history. The emotion's *insane*, we feed off it, it's *intense*, the set's one of our best ever, and we go off together with the crowd baying 'MORE, MORE.' It's mad, deafening, a constellation of lit cigarette lighters twinkling in the dark. Hugo and I, standing together in the stage-right wing, go back on and take a deep bow, drinking in the applause, waiting for Dave and Andy to appear from stage left, but no show, so we bow over and over – where the fuck ARE they? – we're marooned, twitchy, there's something up, close to bailing when Gill stumbles on, nursing a fat lip, followed by Dave, bruised and scowling, facing each other off, their love/hate relationship pivoted to the dark side, as both pick up their guitars and straightaway blast into 'Essence Rare', which is *sensationally* aggressive and blows the roof off, and at its end dropping their axes and marching off. The fans go nuts, it's total theatre. Backstage they're held apart till more booze smooths the storm.

A stagehand tells us Andy and Dave were brawling backstage, off their tits, rolling on the floor, fists flying, after Gill had accused Dave of being 'rockist' – because he'd put a foot on the monitor! – and

Dave saying, 'FUCK YOU! It's not YOUR band! It's – NOT! – YOUR! – FUCKING! – BAND – YOU – FUCK!'

The next day, the two of them catatonically hungover, nothing more was said. Nothing is ever said.

Dave didn't forgive or forget. And now he's gone for good.

Desperate, Hugo calls Steve Baker, our A & R champion at Warners, for help. Gill thinks it's a waste of time, we should pack it all in and fold the band, there's nothing we can do. Steve says, 'Giving up's for pussies' – *trés* American – 'we've still got forty-eight hours to fix this, take a breath, I'll make some calls, try to find a dep.' We say whatever, go ahead, and only a few hours later Steve says Jaco Pastorius, Bill Laswell, and Busta Jones are all keen to sit in. 'What do you think?'

What do I think? I can't believe it, these players are *legends*! Jaco Pastorius, one of the greatest jazz bass players of all time! Bill Laswell, the legendary jazz/fusion/no-wave bassist in Material! WTF! Steve says money's no issue – Warners will pick up the tab, what a mensch – but Jaco and Bill have now passed because they'd need more time to learn our stuff. Whaat? Our stuff must be *infantile* to these guys! But Busta – whom I'd seen owning the stage last year at Hammersmith Palais with Talking Heads on their *Remain In Light* tour – says he's in, totally up for it, and will join us in an NYC rehearsal room to learn the set in a day. Busta's worked with Albert King, Bob Fripp, Chris Spedding ... and played on David Byrne and Brian Eno's *My Life In a Bush of Ghosts*, an incredible CV.

Gill, still wallowing in a hangover swamp, isn't convinced and says if Busta hasn't nailed 'What We All Want' inside the first hour, he'll bail, Gang of Four is toast.

At the studio, Busta says, 'You guys may be worried but I ain't worried – *I am the man!*' and he is, nailing *three* songs in the first sixty minutes and has the entire sixteen-song set plus 'Sweet Jane' down inside twelve hours, turbo-funking the songs and machine-locking with

Hugo, every song massive and in the pocket. By day's end, he and I are tight, instant friends. He's funny, talented and super cool. Amazing.

The day after we fly to Seattle, wired and nervy, career on the line, to play the Showbox. The pent-up frustrations, anxiety and disappointment of the last few days are forgotten the moment we start. Gill and I explode on stage, him careening from one side to the other, bashing into each other, me moving from mic to mic, and Busta, for the first few seconds frozen by the drum riser, looks at Hugo gap-mouthed, who grins and shouts, 'GO FOR IT!' Busta whirls out like a dervish, covering every inch of the boards, the three of us doing everything everywhere all at once, fighting to own the floor, the crowd loving it. Busta's *insanely* good – he must have sold his soul at the Crossroads to play like this – driving us on and on and on, not one fluff, a foundation for Gill's guitar work to reach *unbelievable* heights and somehow making my words *mean* more.

At the after-show, I'm told every musician in the city was here including Kurt Cobain, who later says Nirvana started as 'a Gang of Four and Scratch Acid ripoff', which is very cool. We will talk about the Showbox show for years as a gig Everest. In moments like these, being in a band is the *best*.

Postscript

A week later, we're playing Perkins Palace in Pasadena when a naked man jumps on stage midway through a song and embraces me, it's hilarious, Busta and I corpse, laughing so much we can't play until the streaker – who is pre-Chili Pepper Flea! – is gently led away by a roadie. It's the first time we meet. Busta will sit in with us in the States through 1981 but leaves in the autumn, saying the Rolling Stones had asked him to join them, although this never happened.

We had much fun with him, colossal shows, and loved him like a brother. But his psyche and health were ruined by his chronic coke addiction; every cent he made went up his nose and he died of heart failure aged forty-four. What a waste.

SARA LEE JOINS

We need a new bass player and see it as a chance to reset. Someone says what about Sara Lee? She's phenomenal, has played with *everyone*, once almost the house bass player at CBGB, learns songs fast, a consummate musician and a nice person, too. It's a fluke to find she's playing the Leeds Festival in Robert Fripp's League of Gentlemen, which he's soon winding up, and Sara might be looking for a new gig. We go see the show and are knocked out, she's *good*. Talking after, we make the pitch, and she says, 'YES!' straight off, she loves what we're about, it's right up her *strasse*.

As we're in Leeds, we invite Robert and the band up to ours for tea and biscuits. Making our way there, Bob looks out the car window and says, maybe remembering our conversation in the Iroquois's lift, 'I went to an orgy here once . . .'

Sara's brilliant, we close the deal, and she joins when the LOG tour burns itself out. It's all good.

SONGS OF THE FREE

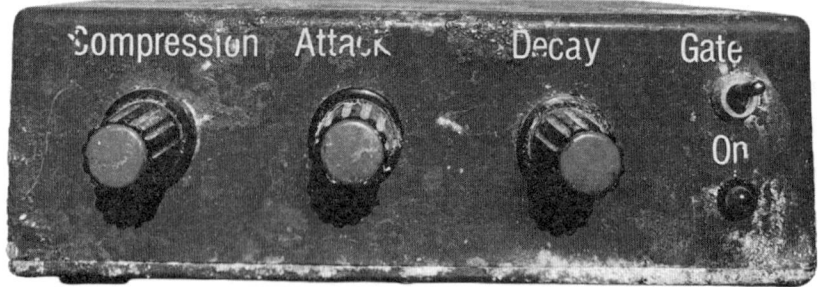

(Photo: Mike Howlett)

We're all disappointed by the failure of *Solid Gold* to sell in 1981, despite its golden reviews, and thought we'd lucked on a hit with the 'To Hell with Poverty' single we made with Nick Launay, the studio recording that most reflects what we're like live, built on a huge guitar riff Jimmy Page would have been proud of over a driving groove, and lyrics I was proud of. We thought it might chart, but it didn't. EMI's pluggers couldn't be arsed to work it, too busy with Duran Duran and Queen. I can't blame them.

We're treading water, the recording advances from Warners and EMI are only enough to pay our wages, and at this point critical praise and peer respect don't stop us thinking we're *failures* stuck in shitty flats we can't afford to quit and can only stay solvent from concert income. Respect doesn't pay the rent. We've fired our useless management, Hugo taking over the day-to-day until we find someone who can do the job, which is itself causing tensions as doubling up as a musician and administrator means he and I talk less about music than petrol receipts and carnets, and it's a drag. I much prefer the otiose arguments I used to have with him about whether *Harvest* is better than *Twelve Dreams of Dr Sardonicus*, not that I have a view either way, they're both brilliant.

We need a hit. Commercial acts make the opposite whinge: they're not taken *seriously* as *musicians*. A while ago, in the dressing room post-show in Boston, MA, the Cars' guitarist lurches in – a local band that has become one of the biggest acts in the States – and kicks off, finger stabbing, off his tits, hair gone freelance, and says, 'Everyone thinks you're so fuckin' *cool*, so fuckin' *fresh*, but I think you're fuckin' *shit*, how come no one talks about *us* like this,' etc, etc. I say, 'Hey, tell you what, swap catalogues then, you have my *respect* and I'll take your *cash*! On second thoughts, just fuck *off*!' As he fucks off with a vassal, I think what was *that* about, a *nil sum* game, the Cars v. Gang of Four? Fuck's sake!

Maybe GOF songs and commercial success are like oil and water? I know our music's leftfield and my lyrics aren't mainstream, but does this mean we're a quasi-jazz act, making discs to promo shows, rather than the other way round? Writing empty words about nothing isn't me... EMI said *Solid Gold* lacked a song with a hooky chorus, which was true – only one of the tracks had a chorus at all, but this never hurt Funkadelic...

With Dave gone and Hugo managing, the writing's now down to just Gill and me. So we change how we work, hunkering down in an eight-track studio in London's Mount Pleasant that's owned by Jon Astrop and Phil Saatchi, funk bass player and shredder guitarist respectively. We write by multi-tracking. I've got a Korg 606 drum machine for simple beats, and sometimes ask Jon to lay down a bass line, which means we don't need to call Sara or Hugo in too early. This works for me as I don't need to wait for Andy to show.

We're chalk and cheese now where we were once yin and yang, and rarely hang out together: he's a social monster, loves living the life, getting pissed, eating out, hates mornings; whereas I'm more insular, find restaurants a yawn, like to read, go to the movies or see dance at Sadler's Wells, at my best in daylight. We compromise on working together afternoons and early evenings. I can come in during the morning and lay down rhythm tracks and keyboard parts, sometimes helped out by a bass groove from Jon, and sing over them. This method allows me to write words and music, and I work up songs like 'We Live As We Dream Alone' ready for Andy to add guitar when he comes in.

We soon have enough material – some even with choruses – to make a third album, and want a more R & B funky feel so reach out to Mike Howlett, the one time bass player in the legendary hippie band Gong, and the producer behind A Flock of Seagulls, OMD's 'Enola Gay' and Martha and the Muffins' huge hit 'Echo Beach'.

He says yes, loves the band and he's happy to co-produce the record with me and Gill. He proposes we work at Ridge Farm, a residential studio in Surrey so we can be away from nightlife and social and domestic distractions, focus entirely on the work. An excellent idea. We first work on the songs with Sara and Hugo to get the parts right and then all move into the studio in March 1982. We're onsite every day, working firm hours 10 a.m. to 8 p.m., six days a week. Mike works in a structured way, teasing each track to find the *thing* that'll make it work, a riff, groove or lyric. It's very different to how we worked at Abbey Road, which was like working on tilt, always visitors coming and going, drop-ins and drinking, and random people in the control room – Jimmy Douglass swears even Mick Jones sat in one day, but I don't recall this. It either happened or it didn't.

Mike mirrors Hugo's basic drum parts on the awesome new Roland 808 drum machine, which is way better than my crappy Drumatix 606, so we play as a band locked to its seductive sound, not that we'll use it on the record.

The 808 will kickstart a transformation in music making, a tech breakthrough session drummers will curse when their studio work evaporates as feel and uncertainty and tempo changes are kicked into touch by programmers who want beats without flux or feeling. John Bonham would have been on his uppers.

The sessions proceed seamlessly, with deep discussions about the songs but without conflicts, all working as a team, the absence of arguments weird but heartwarming. Mike says 'I Love a Man in a Uniform' could be a hit, a song with a conventional verse bridge chorus structure, even a key change after the middle eight, and my words tell a story about a macho man without civilian prospects who joins up to feel better about himself, an unreliable witness corrected by the female backing vocals sung with brilliance by Stevie Lange (otherwise known as Stevie Vann) and Joy Yates. During the session, the talkback mic that allows comms between the studio and the room's left on in error while Hugo whacks his snare CRAAAK! which sounds fantastic through the dinky pickup. Mike thinks we should use this as a brilliant drum analogue to a gunshot, and asks Simon Smart, the studio engineer, how we can replicate the super-compressed sound.* Simon says the circuit board's buried in the bowels of the state-of-the-art mega-expensive SSL desk so we can't use it. But he can make a box with exactly the same circuitry for ten

---

* Compression is a recording/broadcasting process that squashes the audio into a tight dynamic range and smooths the sound, so it plays better on small speakers like shitty iPhone cans. It makes loud things quiet and quiet things louder. Singers enjoy using it creatively, so *breathing* can be a musical thing, and artists like Michael Jackson have brilliantly played with its possibilities.

pounds. So he does. The CRAAK! sounds wonderful after 'Shoot, shoot!'

We decide to call the record *Songs of the Free*. While writing the lyrics I'd been reading Michel Foucault on the concept of 'carceral culture', about how social control becomes internalised, with many of the songs lamenting our collaboration in late capitalism's relentless occupation of every facet of our personal lives and monetisation of our dreams; monitoring each other like prisoners in Jeremy Bentham's thought experiment panopticon.

Andy and I almost never talk about words – I always write them alone – but when we come to the album outer sleeve artwork, up to now also my solo territory, he's very engaged and excited to get involved. I'd given him Joseph Conrad's *Heart of Darkness* for his birthday – I don't know why, he never reads fiction – and he LOVES it, spotting the inspiration for some lines on 'We Live as We Dream Alone'. Conrad's book was one of the first to raise awareness of European colonial horrors and genocide in Africa, and pictures London's docklands at the heart of a vast mercantile engine that links Western freedoms with misery and exploitation, and Andy suggests we write liner text for the album that brings this out.

'I Love a Man in a Uniform' is the standout single. EMI is delighted, the pluggers have *finally* got something to play with, commercial and BBC Radio 1 DJs say it could be a smasheroo, it's getting boffo airplay, it looks like we may have a HIT!

But … in April 1982 the Argentine military has invaded the British Falkland Islands aka *Las Malvinas*, and the teeny colony, a sheep-glutted rump of empire 8,000 miles away in the South Atlantic, is occupied by thousands of soldiers, leading to war in the South Atlantic. Who knew it was there? Prime Minister Thatcher dispatches an armada of warships carrying thousands of British troops to win them back. The Argentine navy's flagship cruiser *General Belgrano* has been torpedoed and sunk, killing 323 sailors, and Royal Navy ships are under constant attack from the air. It's deadly serious.

A few weeks after 'I Love a Man in a Uniform' is released, the record's doing very well, predicted to chart, and a club hit throughout the UK. Media is *sold* on the song, it's sexy and hip they tell us, and we're invited to play it on a peak time TV show. *However*... arriving at the studio, the producer says, 'We LOVE you guys, it's a TREMENDOUS song... but you can't play it, you've got to do something else...'

We say, 'Whaat? It's the single! The one we're here to promote!'

'Sorry, guys,' she says, 'but *our boys* are going into Bluff Cove [a landing point in the Falklands for the British Paratroopers] tonight and we couldn't possibly play your song about the army. It's not patriotic.'

'But... But... the song's not *about* the Falklands.'

'I'm sorry, play something else or pack up and go. Not negotiable.'

We play something else but it's a waste of airtime. 'I Love a Man in a Uniform' is taken off air in the UK and banned by the BBC.

The single tanks.

LOVE AND MARRIAGE

Debbie and I wed in the ancient church of St Peter's that nestles in the heart of the pretty village of Shoreham, where as a teenager I'd daily driven to court her. My USP had been the offer of a back-seat ride to fun times on a Honda 50, so long as she got off and walked should a hill be too steep, irresistible. While April has so far been the cruellest month with rain, frost, and snow showers, today a mackerel sky promises a change for the better. As we take our vows clouds scatter and shafts of sunlight shoot through the stained-glass windows, bathing the apse in a kaleidoscope of colour.

The wedding reception's a joy, held outdoors on an emerald lawn, sipping generously gifted champagne in warm spring sunshine under a cerulean blue sky scattered with high cirrus clouds. Good friends have come: Mark White, Hugo, Sara Lee, Ian Copeland, Mike Howlett, Kevin, and Jenny. Andy – who Debbie's known since the age of eleven, years before I met him – is my best man. His speech is clever, funny, and affectionate; we all smile and laugh and we're touched by his words, the high point of our friendship.

I haven't had a stag party – not my thing – but instead, last night, Gill and I play snooker at a country club. His mother puts us up, and Mrs Gill leaves me a pre-nuptial Valium and mug of water on the bedside table, which is very kind of her. When the celebrations are over, Debbie and I drive off in our gorgeous Citroën DS23 limousine. It's been a wonderful day. She is so beautiful.

I'm a lucky man.

EDDI

Gang of Four publicity pic. *(Photo: Warner Bros)*

Songs of the Free's released in May 1982 and gets fine critical reception.

'I Love A Man in a Uniform' being banned's a downer and EMI has written off hopes of any chart action . . . but the upside is we're signed to Warner Brothers in North America, we're only with EMI for the 'Rest of World', so political bans at home are worth zip in the US, where we're getting strong airplay on college, Black and Mexican radio, and it's a club hit. The US label's fizzing, thinking we've finally turned in a commercial recording and we may become a breakout act.

We're excited, too; maybe they're right, here comes the summer, a busy time ahead. We're booked on the BBC's *The Old Grey Whistle Test* in a week's time followed by fifty or so US gigs in summer and autumn tours that will kick off three weeks from now. In the process we'll appear on the cheesy US disco music programme *Dance Fever* – like *Top of the Pops* in flares and with good teeth – *and* we're on the US Festival bill in San Bernardino, California, along with the Police, the Ramones, the B-52's and Talking Heads; 400,000 people are expected to attend the three-day festival, one of the biggest turnouts in rock 'n' roll history.

However, the new songs won't work without backing vocals and we have to find a backing singer for the live shows who can cut it onstage, hit the right notes, and not be an arsehole on the tour bus. But not having a manager is tough. Hugo has to do the finding, but it's really late in the day. Things could go south before we board a plane. He puts an ad in *Melody Maker* and shortlists five candidates, with auditions scheduled in Blackwing Studios, London SE1.

The talent's brief is, uh, learn the parts to four songs from *Songs of the Free*. Easy. The auditions don't go well, the first says, 'I haven't had time to learn any of the songs, but you play them and I'll pick up the parts.' Hugo says, 'No, this isn't how casting works – don't forget your coat.' The next, a belter who must be a wildcat strike convenor in real life or a protest-march rabble-rouser who shouts 'Maggie Maggie Maggie! OUT OUT OUT!' has a foghorn voice like Cilla Black on ludes. 'We'll be in touch,' Hugo says, but won't. The third doesn't know the words and hasn't written them down: 'NEXT.' The fourth, in platform shoes and diamante boob tube, maybe thinking it's a cool rock-chick look, like a female Noddy Holder, squawks like a panicked chicken so loud I'm worried I'll get tinnitus. She's awful. Not wanting to be unkind, I say, 'Have you gigged before?' 'No, never.' 'What do you do?' Hugo asks. 'I work at *Farmer's Weekly*,' she says, at which Hugo and I corpse, struggling to control ourselves. We shouldn't laugh, but really, stick to the day job. 'We'll call you,' Hugo says, but won't. Things are grim.

Our final prospect is a young Scotswoman called Eddi Reader, down from Irvine New Town. She'd phoned Hugo pretending to be her own agent by putting on what she thought was a posh voice – 'Aaam *represssentine* a tal-ented sing-err who maaay be rrait for this opporrrtunity' – which Hugo barely understood but booked her in anyway. Beggars can't be choosers.

I'm losing the will to live, wondering how to play the new songs *sans* backing vocals, when Eddi walks in, shy, avoiding eye contact, nervous.

'You play in a band before?' I ask.

'No,' she says, 'but I've busked in Glasgow and all over, played in a circus and with performance artists, and sing all the time.'

My heart sinks. Fuck's sake, she's not going to do *mime*, is she? Another timewaster?

But she has the voice of an angel! What pipes! Not only that, but she's learned *everything* on *Songs of the Free* from first track to run out, she knows our music better than we do and reminds us how the songs are structured when we've lost our way. She's a sensational singer, way better than me, what a discovery! We're in the presence of greatness, she's going to be a STAR, so we offer her the job on the spot: rehearsals next week, BBC TV the next, US tours, etc., etc. until the year's end.

Gang of Four is her first pro gig but who could tell? She's got class. We do *The Old Grey Whistle Test* with her – joined just this one time for the show by a second singer, Heather Thomas. Eddi's vocals are *out standing*. A few days later, her first concert with us is in Edinburgh, it's fantastic, she shines before a crowd that's wild, loves what she does, and totally up for it, even if she's not from the Auld Reekie.

Eddi's father is here to check us out , make sure we're sound. Jim's a welder, a man of the world who's worked the rigs and in Germany, like the *Boys from the Blackstuff,* he's seen it all, won't stand for any nonsense. Back for a post-show dram in the hotel bar with Gill and me, he says, looking us in the eyes, index finger-stabbing the air as he talks. 'You take care of my wee girl like she's your sister, OK?'

'For sure!' I say. 'Deffo!'

We throw away a Glenfiddich bottle's cap – Slàinte Mhath ! – down the whiskey to the dregs, swap edgy music and drill-rig stories, share Tommy Cooper jokes, and earn a firm hand shake and nod when we say our goodbyes, woozy but not blootered. We've passed the test. He's a good man you wouldn't want to cross.

Looking after anyone other than myself will be new, as band life is every man/woman for him/her self – but I'll do what I can. A week later, we're in the Iroquois Hotel, midtown Manhattan, the day before our first show in New Haven. Eddi, her first time ever in the US, has ten days' advanced per diems in her pocket – two hundred bucks – and says she wants to walkabout and see the skyscrapers and everything. Since Gotham's a dangerous place and she's an ingénue, I remember my vow to her pa and say, 'Whatever you do, don't talk to *anyone*! AVOID EYE CONTACT!'

'Okey doke,' she says, and heads off. She returns a few hours later in a waterfall of tears. She's blown her money betting on a street-hustle game of Find the Pea, a Janet and John scam!

'The hell you thinking?' I say. 'It's a con! The pea guys are crims!'

'Well,' she says, 'a fellow in the crowd won a hundred dollars! It must have been OK.'

'Fuck's sake! He was a SHILL! And YOU were the MARK!'

Hugo and I have a word with the tour manager and agree we'll make up her losses, but only give her per diems daily from now on, and say someone will have to escort her until she's got her street feet, although no one will.

A few shows on, bussing from one place to the next, covering hundreds of miles every day, I see her writing in a notebook, something I do too, jotting down thoughts, quotes, things I hear people say, etc., for songs, and it's always interesting to find out about other people's creative MO, so I ask if she's writing lyrics.

'Nae,' she says, in broad Scottish, 'ah write doon sassenach wurds ah dinnae ken 'n' whit thay mean,' or something like this. I don't understand what she's saying but see what she's up to when she hands me her little book. It's a self-penned English slang dictionary, with entries like this:

Div = Foolish person
Wally = Foolish person
Berk = Foolish person
Bins = Spectacles
Gigs = Spectacles or concerts

It's better than Samuel Pepys.

Eddi is professional, funny, and good company, and we play more than fifty shows with her. But in 1983, she leaves us for the Eurythmics, an ideal backup for Annie Lennox. I'm sad to see her go, and we'll remain friends. The brilliant Dolette McDonald joins us in her stead, a charmer and a wonderful singer who makes me laugh.

Creative life is all about endings.

Postscript

Eddi will become hugely successful in her band Fairground Attraction, winning many awards for her global hits. Later, as a solo act she will put the words of Robert Burns to music and be given the MBE for her services to Scottish music. She deserves it all. Those pipes!

SMURFS

Tonight we're playing at Magic Mountain, a theme park northwest of Los Angeles in Valencia, California, a great gig where we've sold a lot of tickets. We're all buzzing with anticipation.

As we drive up we can see our name in a huge sign across the arched entrance, which reads:

WELCOME GANG OF FOUR AND SMURFS

My wife, Debbie, and Sara Lee are here, too, as we have a few days off between US shows. Being sun-loving Europeans and not nipple-phobic Yanks, they're sunning themselves topless by our accommodation's pool, glistening with Ambre Solaire, goddesses, the sound of KROQ-FM and cicadas in the wind.

I'm digesting the latest *National Enquirer* scoops on the recliner when the doorbell chimes. It's UPS with a package, which the delivery guy hands me and looks up to see Aphrodite and Athena luxuriating poolside with their tits out, double takes, and turns to slap me with a high five, saying, 'Way to go!'

I'm living his dream.

WE SHOULD BE DEAD

I'm slow-driving up the Holloway Road in north London on my beautiful chrome-yellow tanked Café Racer Honda 750 F1, under the 30 mph speed limit, in the lane reserved for motorcycles, buses and taxis. No one needs drive fast on a big bike in town, it's uncool, the bike's burbling with happiness, my hot wife's on the back, what's not to like? A car pulls out only twenty feet away from a side road – stops across my lane – I slam on the brakes – it's too late – there's nowhere to go – WHAAAM! – I crash into the car full force, smashing headlong into its side, the bike's rear wheel flipping UP UP to launch Debbie UP UP and OVER the car roof to bounce into the tarmac on the other side, knocking her out. I don't know what's occurred, I'm out too, lying flat in the road next to my totalled bike and sideswiped car, bystanders don't know if we're dead or alive. An ambulance takes us to hospital to be checked out but amazingly we're only badly bruised with no bones broken. It's a lucky escape, saved by our helmets.

When I come round the nurse says, 'You OK?' and I say, 'How's my bike?'

We're discharged after a few hours, neither concussed, just badly bruised, my left thigh empurpled and darkening. I'm in good shape, so we don't cancel a slot on BBC TV's *The Old Grey Whistle Test*. We play a bunch of songs and I stay glued to the spot. I can hardly move my legs.

Next day, I'm stiff but mobile, and for the first time since sixteen, without wheels. I need a new bike fast because if you stop riding you lose your mojo forever; the future will be carpet slippers and a pipe, moaning about Young People and the price of sausages.

I decide to get exactly the same model bike as before, because I loved the F1 so much, and see one advertised – same year, same tank, but black – and buy it over the phone, sight unseen. It's a fine machine, drives just as the old one, but it's like going out with a girlfriend's twin sister, it's weird, wrong, it's got to go. Trouble is, I can't afford to buy another bike without getting rid of this one.

So, I think maybe I should get the bike *stolen*, as selling the replacement would be a hassle as I'm away gigging all the time. Someone says this would be *fraud*, mate, it's not a sound idea, so I rethink and just park the new bike, without the rain cover on, outside my shitty Stoke Newington house in north London. Pre-fixer-upper Stokey is a crime hotspot and the bike is stolen inside two weeks, despite being D-locked and chained.

But the insurance company is very slow, and fusses about crash and theft claims made only weeks apart.

I grit my teeth and ask Bennett for money that's mine anyway, a chance to get some of the cash owing me as Glotzer's always shifty and says, 'Paperwork SNAFU... bookkeeper's got rabies... LA's sunk into the Hellmouth,' etc., etc. He's probably blown it all on blow or paid off someone who'd paid off someone who needed to be paid off.

'How much you *need*?' he asks.

'Everything I'm *owed*! I *need* to buy a new bike.'

'How much?' he says.

'Ten grand sterling?' I've no idea where this number came from.

Bennett says, 'Our accounts aren't *finalised*... paperwork SNAFU... bookkeeper's got rabies... LA's sunk into the Hellmouth... so I'll make it simple, write you a *personal* cheque, comprende?'

I don't know why this is simpler than writing a cheque from the GOF account but say, 'Yeah, whatever,' and he writes me one for fourteen thousand dollars.

Other than per diems and a hundred pounds a week, it's the only money I'll get.

Postscript

I buy a touring Beemer boxer twin. It's gorgeous, and we drive to Spain on the biker heaven *route nationale* trunk roads down the left-hand side of France to the border town of Saint-Jean-de-Luz, over to San Sebastian in the Basque Country, and east via high hairpin Pyrenean roads to Catalonia. My mojo's back.

A LONG CON IN LA

Gill, Hugo and I meet Bennett Glotzer at the 7720 Sunset office where he reps Frank Zappa, and the brilliant punk *superfrau* Nina Hagen, who'll come to hate him as much as I will. She's an exiled East German whose Ossi hit single 'Du hast den Farbfilm vergessen' – pop tosh about forgetting to take colour film on holiday – was a brave backdoor critique of the DDR and whose album *NunSexMonkRock* is a triumph. We never meet her, which is a shame.

Glotzer, a thick waisted slaphead who looks like a cross between Uncle Fester and a Tellytubby, glad hands us and says, 'I *LOVE* you fuckin' guys, stoked you came by, grab a frostie, a Sprite, whatever!' as he parades us around the shop swearing and yabbering all the while, saying things like, 'Luck's 10 per cent opportunity and 90 per cent preparation' or, 'Talent's 10 per cent inspiration and 90 per cent perspiration', etc. His HQ's a wasp's nest of activity rammed with ripped young men and hot babes with sunbed tans in budgie-smuggling shorts and micro skirts barking on phones, scurrying between photocopy and telex machines, and stuffing paper and promo pix in envelopes amid a pachinko parlour clatter of typewriters and background music; takeout Szechuan, sandwich trays and pizza boxes are stacked high on the desks, Jesus, everyone must work all hours.

It's *buzzing*, we're sold, where do we sign?

Ten years on, Hugo learns that the 'staff' were all actors hired to play 'Office Assistants', a low rent payday for thespians whose ambitions can't have been higher than corporate hostility or intimate hygiene ads. Apart from his boob-tubed 'PA', only one person actually *works* for Glotzer: Camilla Fegy, whom he calls 'Gorilla' but I don't know why, or what she did.

Before we see Bennett, Hugo tells Andy and me that Mo Austin, who manages Warners, and Lenny Waronker, its President, took him to one side and said they'll work with *anyone* but PLEASE don't go with Bennett. But we ignore this, thinking it's just sour grapes after Glotzer had scored millions for Zappa winning a big deal lawsuit against Warners.

We've been desperate for good management, floundering after failing to replace Rob Warr when he walked, then hiring/not hiring Ian Copeland as our manager, which wasn't permissible as you can't be an act's agent and manager at the same time, followed by hiring/not hiring Chris O'Donnell, Thin Lizzy's manager, who'd said, 'It's all about *planning*,' and then disappeared. Hugo's tired of managing the day-to-day, it's too much work that causes constant friction between us about logistics and money and direction and we have to find someone fast. He and I were keen on AC/DC's managers Cliff Burnstein and Peter Mensch, but Gill dislikes the band and doesn't rate Burnstein, I think because he looks *exactly* like *Animal*, the mad Muppet drummer. We point out that AC/DC haven't done badly under him, but Andy says no, he wants to go with Glotzer. We have to make a decision, and we're impressed by his roster: if Nina and Frank think he's OK – and Zappa's a neurodiverse details-obsessed guy, unlike me with a short attention span and bored by detail – then Glotzer must be kosher.

Never missing the opportunity to miss an opportunity, we ignore Mo's advice and sign with Bennett – the kick-off of a short long con. Soon, we'll all be fucked.

HUGO'S GONE

We intro Bennett to Ian Copeland at FBI, now one of the most powerful booking agents in the US, and our champion in the US. We want them to put their heads together, talk about what we can do better. But there's an instant froideur between them.

Glotzer: 'You gotta be *strategic*. No more fucking about.'

Ian: 'Fucking about? How so?'

Glotzer: 'These dumbass fuckin' shows! The same fuckin' places over and over and fuckin' OVER!'

Ian: 'The fifty-plus *dumbass shows* the boys played last year all sold out and made money. But they don't get airplay outside of college radio, they're not breaking out, clubs and theatres are the best we can get. And "Uniform" is dead in the water.'

Glotzer: 'Precisely! No fuckin' strategy!'

Ian: 'Man, we're booking agents, not magicians ... so your new *strategy* is what? To have a *strategy*? To be more famous? Shit, wish I'd thought that.'

It's not going well. As they leave, Bennett and Ian man hug and both pretend to stab each other in the back, a prescient gag. Before he goes, Ian whispers, 'He'll skin you alive.'

Bennett then reveals his *strategy*: dump Ian and FBI. 'Copeland's sitting on his hands,' Glotzer says, 'not working the phone, spends all his time on the Police, Joan Jett, the Go-Go's, whoever, the big earners. You're *nothing* to him! You'll do better elsewhere!'

Glotzer goes on and on and on like this whenever we talk: 'Copeland only cares about the Police, it's his two brothers that count, not you schmucks, you're *roadkill!*'

We surrender and split from Copeland.

It's stupid. Ian, who only a year before had come to my wedding as a friend, won't take my call when I phone to say no hard feelings and will never speak with me again.

Bennett says you got to make another record, playing more shows will get you nofuckinwhere. I say gigging's the only way we can make decent money and he says, 'This is small time! You gotta change your mindset! Trust me, I know this is right!'

So Gill and I knuckle down to writing, working at Andy's flat with a 606 to write drum beats on and a four-track cassette recorder, so don't need Hugo and Sara until we've got new material down.

Sara's cool and has other stuff to do, and Hugo carries on with UK day-to-day management as Bennett doesn't have an office outside LA. Hugo now has nothing to do on the music front so whenever we talk it's only about logistics and bookings and van rental and gaffer tape, it's so *boring*, we argue all the time about trivia, about nothing.

Gill's dismissive of Hugo's abilities as a drummer, always critical and aggressive when they talk, and thinks Hugo's opinions are worthless. He doesn't share Jerry Wexler's view that Hugo's one of the best young white drummers working now. Gill says Hugo's holding us back, like I suspect he also says about me.

Writing's a drag. Hugo and I argue even more – it's classic transference.

Bennett says you got to dump Burnham, you don't need a drummer on the payroll, and you fucks argue all the time. Gill thinks the same, but says *I've* got to fire him.

'*Me?*' I say. 'Why not you? You're the ones who want him gone!'

Gill, who never misses a chance to diss Hugo, says, 'It has to be you. You and Hugo are *incompatible*, I'm with Bennett.'

A lot of the friction *is* down to me, I'm an arsehole sometimes, but rows are rarely about what they're about, our conflict's rooted in frustration, the band's not where we wanted it to be, I'm doubtless just taking stuff out on H and vice-versa. And there's something going on between Bennett and Gill, they talk all the time, plotting something.

I cave and say OK.

When Hugo and I next meet I say it's over, our future's behind us, Andy doesn't want you on the new album, he thinks you're not suited to the new material, our relationship's gone sour, we just argue about shit, it's wearing us out, etc., etc. Hugo's devastated, it's horrible, I feel like a traitor. We were *mates*.

Hugo will in the future tell me he had dinner with Glotzer soon after, who told him it was 100 per cent down to Gill whose mind was fixed on Hugo going, but he lies whenever he opens his mouth, and I believe they planned it together. Bennett wanted to remove the one person who understood our finances, and Gill wanted complete control.

Me, I'm just a rat and regret this straightaway, shaken by how it's a mirror to Pip's maltreatment of Joe Gargery in *Great Expectations*, maltreating his loyal and kind brother-in-law. It's when you realise the unreliable narrator, Pip, has become a creep and it's the nadir of his moral progress, like this is mine.

Once Hugo's gone, I've lost all juice, outvoted two to one, the last step in a Glotzer *strategy* to separate us from allies and friends, and eliminate any oversight so he can control the money.

Shortly after, Gill and Glotzer announce they want to make the new record in the US and Canada, with Gill as sole producer.

It will be an expensive mistake.

HARD TIMES

Making our fourth album, which will be called *Hard*, is a labyrinthine process.

We spend five weeks in a Montreal studio laying down backing tracks because, according to Glotzer, recording in Canada means the American Federation of Musicians won't get a percentage on sales, which is news to me, and more likely a carousel scam to avoid him having income in the US, but I can't figure out how this works.

Then it's down to New York City for five more weeks in the legendary – and legendarily costly – Hit Factory. *Everyone's* worked here – the Stones, Stevie Wonder, John Lennon – and decades from now the wonderful Beyoncé and Lady Gaga will record their masterpieces. Glotzer says, 'If someone asks, say we're not "recording" here,' although we are, 'but only "overdubbing"' – a semantic difference only Roland Barthes could deconstruct – but he doesn't say who we mustn't say this to, and no one asks.

Born in the USA was recorded here, and it's a thrill to find Bruce and the E Street Band are booked to work nights in the next-door studio and we might bump into the Boss in the kitchen! But they never show, so each morning we pillage their untouched catering table laden with luscious deli-tray delights, before the nosh is tossed into a trashcan. It's easy to get fat in the studio as unlike real life whatever you want's available all the time, and free, although it's not free at all, and the album budget tab will dig the recoupment sink-hole deeper and deeper.

My birthday falls mid-session and Bennett decides to surprise me. Our co-producers, Ron and Howard Albert, the studio engineer, Gill and I are sitting at the mixing desk when a woman dressed in an NYPD outfit bounds in, Taa- Daa!, her synthetic rack exploding from a skin-tight cop top she's fast unbuttoning over a dinky skirt as she presses her tits toward my face.

'Stop there!' I say. 'Don't do this, I don't like it.'

She says, 'I won't get paid if I don't do my job,' and I say, 'No, don't want you to, I'll sign your paperwork, it's not my thing . . .' but she restarts the routine and I say, 'Sorry, I'm off!'

I scoot out of the studio to sink birthday beers alone in a Broadway bar, the day's work sabotaged.

Bennett knows *exactly* what I think about shit like this. He *knows* I don't go to strip joints or use porn, it objectifies women, we're not the Scorpions, this is Gang of Four, etc. He's clearly decided I need a come-uppance in a saddo dick-swinging contest and booked the stripper-gram to make a point.

I've had it with the fucker, and as soon as we've nailed these *over-dubs* I fly back to the UK, glad to be an ocean away from the offensive creep, leaving Andy and the Alberts to carry on in Miami, where Sara and I'll join them in a couple of weeks for whatever. I can't wait.

MIAMI VICE

1983: Criteria Sound, 755 NE 149th Street, Miami, the famous Florida shop where hundreds of hit records from Fleetwood Mac to the Eagles have been made, where Aretha's 'Spanish Harlem' was knocked out and where Clapton laid down 'Layla' and whinged that Sally should lay down, he just wants someone to talk to – as if! Atlantic Records' production gods Jerry Wexler and Arif Mardin used the studio so often it was nicknamed Atlantic Records, which is good enough for me. The studio sits in a bland suburban district not far from the ocean bay, off the 909, and looks like a motel with its slab glass window panes and crisp white concrete walls, with leggy palm trees overlooking the parking lot which quiver in the water-saturated warm breeze. It could be an insurance building or fractional ownership holiday-homes complex.

This is where the Bee Gees produced their multi-platinum disco anthems, maximalist bangers propelled by the Gibbs' 'meaningless' – their word – lyrics, which wallow in the sensation-seeking void of capitalist life, the defining miasma of Miami. Their label boss Robert Stigwood once gifted them a platinum Cadillac for their sales; a shiny disc wasn't enough because *enough* is never enough.

A jittery Bee Gee out of rehab sometimes sits in the quiet of the lobby fiddling with his fingers as if with a rosary, twitching and muttering to himself.

Hard will be mixed here, although I doubt we'll be gifted a precious metal motor by the label. Julio Iglesias is working in the studio next door to us, showing up in the cool of the evenings for magisterial one-take recordings of Spanish-language monsters. He's a nice guy, deep-tanned the hue of his Roller's walnut dash, who *de haut en bas* small talks with us before being driven back to a glitzy uber-yacht where I'm told he spends his days catching rays and shagging babes, an MO that beats noodling songs that are circling the drain.

Other than overdubs, there's nothing for me to do. Before now, I'd shared production with Andy, but we're not aligned about what this record should be like, and I've become bored by it all. Gill will be co-producer with the Albert brothers, the so-called 'analog Kings' (*Miami Herald*) who've wallpapered their walls with over forty Gold and thirty Platinum albums. They've done it all but don't rate our early stuff – unlike Jerry Wexler – which they say is too 'jagged . . . skinny . . .' and, even worse, 'political', which I take as a compliment.

I'd wanted to make a record as we did on *Entertainment!* and *Solid Gold* – playing as a band in a room on numbers we'd rehearsed and routined until the parts were locked, with rowdy Gill guitar counterpointing my lyrics and vocal parts. But since I've surrendered co-production duties and we don't have a full band after Hugo's departure, it'll be worked out here by the producers with Sara and me sitting on the sidelines. An alternative I was up for was to do something radical inspired by new electrofunk stuff like Afrika Bambaataa's 'Planet Rock', but the old-school Albert brothers, who'd been hired to hand-hold Andy, said they wanted the parts played by *people not machines*, we'd get top session talent in, and Gill agreed.

They got the gig after Bennett had nixed Nile Rodgers working with us, which would have been sensational, a *coup de théâtre*, we'd have been Nile's first cross-over punk-funk-rock album, before Chic was chic and long before Bowie and Nile made the *Let's Dance* monster.

Glotzer claimed he canned the deal because Rodgers 'wanted an extra point', which I'd happily have agreed to, and losing Nile was tragic. Gill tells me – without any evidence – that he believed Glotzer had snagged a backdoor finder's fee for using the Criteria Sound studios, although how he knows I don't know. You can't employ the Alberts without using this place, they go together like love and marriage. Andy's not broken-hearted about Nile and I suspect they both wanted this so Andy can get his first solo production gig while being midwifed by Ron and Howard.

While I'm in London Alfa Andersen of Chic and Brenda White King have been in to record backing vocals and Joe Galdo, the world-class Cuban funk session drummer, had laid down shit-hot funk drum tracks, totally in the pocket, a one-take pro. But Andy's driven the Alberts crazy by flipping the session from being about parts played by people to him programming an 808 and replacing Joe's parts machine beat by beat, learning on the job how to do it, the sand of production time running out.

The Alberts are totally wired when I arrive in Florida and tell me Andy's 'out of control' and ask me to step up, lessen friction, and create a better vibe, a serious misreading of our now dysfunctional creative partnership.

'I'm not the guy,' I say. 'Gill won't listen to me. I may have co-written the songs but I'm just a bystander. My advice is get over it, you're the co-producers not me. What else are you paid to do?'

With little to do, most days I chill on the deck or shoot the breeze with Sara over coffee, she's always good to chat with. If the heat's *demasiado* – the humidity here's a killer – I shiver with *Anna Karenina* in the icebox reception waiting to be called in for a vocal or asked for my worthless POV, which will be disregarded. There's no point staying in the rented house an hour's drive away – everything's an hour's drive away – as it's too hot to lounge poolside, and I may as well freeze at the studio as indoors at the house.

Miami's *horrible* in the hot months for a Brit used to August highs of 70-80°F.

Andy tells Sara he wants to use bass player Jon Astrop on some of the songs, preferring his liquid-funk style to hers and she says whatever, perhaps having decided life's too short to pick a fight you can't win. I tell Gill it's bad for the band dynamic, but his mind's set on making a silky pop hit and says it's his call, flexing his first time sole producer muscles. Andy was super hyped when we played our near-hit 'I Love a Man in a Uniform' on *Dance Fever* and thought making crystal-finished sync-locked pop was the future. My love of the crash and rhythmic flex and feel of a real band was living in the past, he says, we've got to embrace the rise of the machines. I give up the debate. Astrop will later co-write Sam Fox's global smash 'Touch Me (I Want Your Body)' and buy a chateau in France, so what do I know?

To can the bad karma, the Alberts suggest we fish in the Gulf from their shiny boat, a Hemingwayesque team-bonding opportunity where we can sip Mojitos and chug Buds on the deck while waiting to murder marlin. This will be fun if fun means enjoying being an inebriated captive audience to stories about Stars We've Worked With Who Are Really Fucked Up, which is more or less everyone except Jilted John. Being a miserable bastard who doesn't want to kill animals for fun, gets terminally seasick, and finds music-biz bullshit a yawn, I'd rather stay back in the rental house watching *Hogan's Heroes*. But Gill says we need to get tighter with the Yanks, so I say all right, but this is all about *you*, mate, there's no *me* in *we*.

We chug out next day at 8 a.m., the air already oven-hot and humid under a bleaching sun in a cloud-free sky – it's *always* hot and humid under blistering skies in summertime Florida, give me Norway any day. We park up in the sixty-mile-wide lane of hot water that slices its way through grey Atlantic waters to warm the British Isles and bob about in the deep blue for hours. Nothing happens. 'Fishing's like this sometimes,' Ron says.

I spend the trip throwing up below deck, queasy until we dock in the late afternoon, the upside to spewing being not having to hear Ron, Howard and Andy bang on about fine wine and food, all they talk about when sleb gossip has played out. No fish are caught, both a relief and a mild disappointment as I'd have liked to see a marlin close up but alive not dead. Nothing's said about production logjams. Andy's lifelong negotiating technique is to do nothing and concede nothing until the other side runs out of time or will to live and it's too late to change, which almost always works.

Bennett drops by, drinks a gallon of espressos, shouts in a caffeine rage at Andy and the Alberts, and heads to a poncy restaurant on our dime, which is called *management*.

Back at the house, I go to bed early and watch *Gilligan's Island*. *That's* entertainment!

GUN CITY

After a lame day in the studio, Bennett says he, Gill and I should have dinner together to smooth things out, and takes us – on our own money, natch – to an upscale joint with ersatz Louis Quinze furniture, crystal tableware and gold leaf, and kitsch paintings of the American West on the wall, like a Trump Tower Kentucky Fried. Flush investment bankers are dining here with their nip 'n' tucked wives/mistresses/escorts, who look like they've spent a million bucks in Woolworths. Not my kind of place, as I prefer scruffier joints like Elena's L'Etoile in London's Soho, which hasn't been repainted for years, or K-Paul's Louisiana Kitchen in New Orleans, my favourite US eatery. Bennett's annoying 'personal assistant' will be with us, who I'll call *Randy*. Her appeal escapes me. She's as thick as two short planks, X-ray thin, and overshares a worldview based on crystals and star signs that can make the good times sag. Even so, personal services for *Bennett*? Yuk!

Gill and I are in Levi's, Chuck Taylor Converse shoes, and band-merch tees. Bennett is dressed in Lacoste tennis whites, and Randy's wearing denim cutoffs with a spangly boob tube squeezed tight on her scrawny chest. Although we're quiet and well behaved, with even Glotzer dialling back his stream-of-unconsciousness profanities, there's a susurration of disapproval when we sit down and the couple at the next table is seriously pissed off. Mr – probably a trader in cocaine futures – is draped in Armani, his terracotta neck colour-matched by his red tie and trophy wife's scarlet pantsuit, so tight she risks thrush. They don't like our outfits *at all*, and Ms, in stage whispers, says, 'It's *disgusting* people are allowed in here dressed like that,' I thought this was an exclusive restaurant, no one should be allowed in here without a jacket and tie, what's this place coming to, people shouldn't dine here dressed like that,' etc., etc.

Gill and I stay cool but Randy, wound up by the negging snaps, pulls out Bennett's wallet and stands up, her arm raised high in the air to unfurl a cascade of credit cards in their clear plastic pockets. ZZZZliP! She grabs a Gold Amex – a big deal now if you want to show you've got monetary juice – and waves it in the air at the couple. 'You see THIS?' she yells. 'This, this, THIS, is a Gold American Express card, THIS is a GOLD fucking AMERICAN EXPRESS CARD! A GOLD FUCKING AMERICAN EXPRESS CARD!'

The restaurant's in stunned silence. Randy's on tilt. Something needs to be done. Bennett takes the Amex from her and says, 'Sit down, honey, calm the fuck down, easy, OK, OK? I'm gonna schmooze things out, OK? ... I'm gonna schmooze everything out, OK?' He walks over to the moaners and says, 'You know, I wore clothes like yours when *I* was poor!'

It's a great gag and the restaurant explodes with laughter at the put down. The grumpy diners bail soon, humiliated, there's nothing the privileged hate more than being laughed at.

We finish our meal in silence, our *issues* parked on a mental whiteboard we'll never look at. When we've paid, the maître d' says we'd best stay until the police get here 'for your protection', as Armani man has been spotted prowling the parking lot with a handgun, doubtless to pop Bennett, which would have been a satisfying end to the evening.

The cops arrive and we split. Bennett continues to pillage our money.

ZUGZWANG

The playback party fizz in EMI's Manchester Square HQ's as flat as *Hard*, sugary and flavour-lite, the pluggers shuffling from foot to foot, staring at their hands, wondering if anyone will notice them inching out for a pint in the pub. I'm thinking the same.

'Hmm,' the new head of A & R says, '*interesting*' – the worst word in the music lexicon – his head bobbing like a nodding dog, the kiss of death. I'm thinking we'll never earn back the Everest of cash Andy and the Alberts blew making this schlock with Bennett skimming 20 per cent off the top. We're *buried* in the hole. Why didn't I Red Card them, say, 'NO! This is bollocks!'?

The seeds of this shitshow were sown in Whitechapel long before we recorded *Hard*. Gill and I weren't getting on, me pissed off he was pissed up each night, crapulenced next day, denying he's got a drink problem, me wanting a structured life. We have a summit meeting – we actually *talk* – and he says he's fed up with my *lack of commitment*, that I don't *want* it. I say, 'If *it* means wanting to be famous, I *never* wanted it. You really mean I should adapt to your drinker's hours and fit in with you. But it's not *your* band it's *our* band. I'm so bored with this shit.'

Andy says we've one more album to deliver, and wants to produce it on his own as we argue too much, and he wants to make a post-band career behind the mixing desk. I say we argued about *music* when we co-produced *Entertainment!*, not our *lifestyles*; *Solid Gold* and *Songs of the Free* likewise. He says, 'Yeah, but they sold fuck all. We need a hit.'

So Andy bowdlerised his guitar, abandoning killer riffs for layered moody washes processed through chained FX boxes, like Spandau Ballet on ludes, and says I should dial back the politics and sing more *tunefully*. Fuck's sake! I want Gill Guitar Classic in all his Wilko-meets-Jimi genius! I'm his biggest fan, don't fuck with the brand, the new Gill Lite *sucks*, give me the full fat! Whatever, I give it up. Gill for the first time writes all the lyrics to a pair of solo-writes, 'Is It Love' and 'Woman Town', which are diabolical, Andy, stay in your lane! You're as good with words as I am at guitar!

My memories curdling, back in the room with now warm Prosecco in hand, a plugger is looking at the album sleeve, a glossy photo of Sara, Andy and me in nice outfits with combed hair and slap. A PHOTO OF SARA, ANDY AND ME IN NICE OUTFITS WITH COMBED HAIR WITH SLAP! What the absolute fuck!

'Nice,' he says, meaning it's not.

The terrible *Hard* sleeve cover design ISN'T my work, I couldn't be arsed to look at the artwork beforehand, which of course Bennett said was fuckin' A. This abdication of responsibility has resulted in a shocking shot of three of us looking like Eurovision Song Contest hopefuls or a cover band's promo shot in *Spotlight* dreaming of a cruise-ship gig. This isn't a Brechtian take on disco iconography, it's a shite take on iconic disco Brechtianism! A Gang of Four record with a *band photo* on the cover, looking *nice*, it's like the *Animal Farm* pigs on their back legs, living it up with the farmers.

And the *embarrassing* video for 'Is It Love' ... For the first time, we're able to a make a video for MTV and instead of the smart arthouse film left-wing radicals like us should make, it's pretentious guff with Sara and me dressed up to the nines waddling behind Andy in some *Blade Runner* Lite street scene while he lip syncs to the track, the worst thing we've ever done ... the horror the horror. I'm sure Glotzer only blagged the bloated budget because it's all *commissionable.*

A label guy says, 'Great work,' almost as bad as 'interesting,' but says he's got to split for another *thing*, probably needing to pop into Tesco's for some Wincarnis on the way home. Looking about, I see the pluggers have bailed and the room's empty, just Andy and me and short-skirted hostility girls busy tidying up glasses, bowls of peanuts, and cold goujons. We head to the Devonshire Arms, where we find the hangdog pluggers drowning their sorrows. No one's going to make a Christmas bonus on sales of this dog.

Perhaps *Hard* is our *Let It Be.*

Andy and I are drowning not waving.

NO BLOW, NO SHOW

Sara, Steve Goulding*, Hugo's replacement, and I are being minivanned back to a motel after the penultimate show of the *Hard* US promo tour, which was OK but not transcendent. Andy's off boozing with over-excited fans who'd wheedled their way backstage and invited him to a fancy bar where he'll be comped strawberry daiquiris and Petit Chablis and will be the centre of attention. That's a no from me, I've had it with post-gig partying, it's so boring.

I'm a bit low – not unusual having got to the end of a string of dates, there's always disappointment in achievement – and feel like a fraud, the album's *beige*, the tour's no thriller, and I'm just going through the motions, a front man whose future's behind me. I don't enjoy the *Hard* set – all those *tunes* – nor being with Gill when he's off his tits, now twenty-four/seven on tour, and I'm thinking of jacking it in. I wish we'd disbanded after *Songs of the Free* and not fired Hugo, our biggest mistake in a long line of fuck-ups. At least tomorrow's Santa Monica Civic show is sold out and we can hang with friends there, and fingers crossed I'll be able to bribe my way onto first-class back home the day after.

* Steve's a fantastic musician who'd drummed with Graham Parker and the Rumour, the Associates, and the Mekons; co-wrote *I Love The Sound Of Breaking Glass* with Nick Lowe ; and played on the hit singles *Let's Go To Bed* by the Cure and *Watching the Detectives* by Elvis Costello.

In my blacked-out hotel room, I calm down as I lie down on the forgiving mattress and think to myself, it's not so bad, tomorrow is another day . . .

But when I wake up I'm told that last night Andy, off his tits, had fallen badly from a low step outside a bar and nearly broke his ankle. He'd been strapped up in a hospital and cabbed back to the hotel at dawn.

I find him in the lobby, ashen-faced and hungover, wincing as he hobbles onto the tour bus on crutches, his sprained ankle as swollen as an elephant's foot. He can hardly move, it's not good, if he can do the show at all it'll be on a stool, like Val Doonican, perhaps he could do a feedback version of Paddy McGinty's Goat. We may have to cancel. Sara and I shrug and raise eyebrows at each other, we've seen this movie before.

Bennett has a plan. He comes to the gig accompanied by Mr X, who Glotzer intros as a top sports physio with a US Olympic track squad, an expert in fixing injuries like this, a wonder worker, which is either true or it isn't. There's only a short while before show time to decide to play or pull, which will be a financial *beso de muerte*. Glotzer can't let this happen and must have banked on trousering the fee to stave off his creditors and escape being flayed, kneecapped, or hung by his ankles from a window, which would have made my day.

X unravels the medical bindings to reveal Gill's bruised and purple foot, which he manipulates before plunging it into a bucket brimfull with ice, to be left there for a half hour to reduce the swelling. The magician physio wraps the ankle again, ultra tight.

'How do you feel?' he asks Gill, who says, 'Like shit! Can't walk.'

'No problemo!' says X. 'I've just the thing!' He's got a glassine baggie of blow in one hand and the cokehead aficionado's classic McDonald's McSpoon in the other. 'The bump will do you good!' he says, clearly a fan, as he tucks the cute spoon up Gill's nostrils, 'Left!' he says, 'And . . . right!'

I'm impressed by this use of schnuff in modern medicine, old-school but effective. Andy stops whingeing, scorns his stilts, and is onstage fifteen minutes later, with no stage furniture required. Gill's brilliant, scampering about the stage like Bambi, attacking the strings, whacking the guitar into a mic stand here, bashing it on the amp there, whizzing stage left to right, frozen-facedly channelling Wilko Johnson. I need to match his pinballing, and turn it on, I'm not going to be upstaged by a gimp even if un-bumped, while Sara's totally on it, a mistress of the groove, Goulding's in the pocket, the show's a classic, the audience goes crazy.

At the end of the set, the crowd crying for more, Gill leans on my shoulder as I help him limp to the dressing room for a pick-me-up sharpener before the encore. The pain's kicking in, his ankle's ballooning, he's done a marathon on that snow, no wonder Olympic skiers favour it. We find Bennett and Mr X jabbering and declaiming, pop-eyed and sweating, utterly fried, an empty wrap under the seat where they sit.

'Where's the *gear*, Bennett?' says Gill. 'I need a line!'

Glotzer, lost in snow land, looks at Andy and says, 'Look, I *know* what's happened but can't *say* right now.'

'Yeah?' says Gill. 'Well, *I* know what's happened, too, you fuck!'

We *all* know what's happened, Bennett and the medic have snorted the lot. We've got to get back on – we're pros – so I hoist Andy back onstage where he heroically sucks up the pain, plays like a demon, and scoots about like a roadrunner on crank until we take our final bows.

'My foot will be fucked in the morning,' says Gill, on the way back to the hotel. 'Thank Christ it's the last show. Next time this happens – no blow, no show!'

As if. I don't want there to be a next time.

UNTERGANG

I've had it. I don't like what we're doing, don't like the new music, and don't like the lifestyle. Gill and I talk, he wants to carry on, he loves being in a band whatever, adores the attention, thinks we've just got to hang in, but I say things won't change if things don't change so fuck it, this is so boring, it's over.

We break the news to Glotzer.

'YOU FUCKS! The fuck you thinking? THERE. IS. NO. FUCKING. WAY. YOU. CAN. AFFORD. TO. DO. THIS! *Capiche?*'

'Uh, why not?' we say.

'Because you *cocksuckers* owe a mountain of cash to the travel agent, the booking agent, expenses, management, every motherfucker! Stop now, you'll be in the bankruptcy courts in five fucking minutes!'

'WHAAAT? You never said, we never had any accounting!'

He says, 'Paperwork's in the works, an accounting SNAFU . . . bookkeeper's got rabies . . . LA has sunk into the Hellmouth . . . tour support not enough,' etc. 'I was gonna break it to you at a better time when things improved between you guys. Look, you walk away now, you'll fuck yourself up the ass twice and then tread on your own dicks!'

Andy and I do a double take, the image escaping us.

'*Here's* the thing!' Bennett says, finger in the air. 'We announce a big ticket, big fee, farewell coast-to-coast US tour, squeeze the costs, pay off the outstanding, pocket more than chump change! Think about it! It's a win–fuckin'–win! No debts, spondoolicks for you motherfuckers.'

Late that day he tosses an A4 sheet at us with pencilled numbers that show our hole's deeper than the Mariana Trench. 'You quit now, you're fucked!' he says.

So, a farewell US tour's booked.

It's very emotional, we play our favourite songs, no dry eyes after curtain calls, all that, full circle with Andy Corrigan on front-of-house sound, just like our first ever show. Every cost is slashed, and the projected upside should clear all we owe and make us maybe a hundred grand each. But a week in, Andy says he's got bad news: one of his balls has blown up to the size of a turkey egg, it's agonising, the doc says it doesn't look good, could be cancer, he needs to go to hospital for tests and treatment asap, time is of the essence. It's terrible news and I say let's can the tour, I don't care about the money, just get fixed, we're brothers, we've been through so much together, friends for ever, none of the bullshit matters. But Gill says he doesn't want to stiff any shows, it's only a month, he wants to play, it could be his last time out, he may die. So we stick at it, Andy's a trooper and never complains. We're solid, we have fun together, the coast-to-coast tour's a blast, our final shows out West. As soon as it's over Andy flies to Mount Sinai Hospital in New York where he has major surgery for testicular cancer.

Bennett doesn't pay off the travel agent, booking agent or tour expenses, pocketing all the tour money, everyone's fucked over. Andy and I don't get a cent.

In a rammed LAX lounge clutching my cattle-class ticket back to London, I count my cash. Exactly two hundred and fifteen dollars. All I have.

We brought nothing into this world, it is certain we can carry nothing out.

This is the end.

Postscript

We won't find out for sure ('the accounts not finalised', 'LA in the Hellmouth' etc., etc.), but Andy and I were each ripped off by an estimated seven-figure sum – when a million dollars *was* a million dollars. Whatever.

A few months later, Andy and I are commissioned to write a song for a teen martial arts movie called *The Karate Kid*, one of the highest-grossing films of 1984.

Gill will make a full recovery, skips paying for his hospital treatment in the US, and banks the medical insurance payout to leave Bennett, as financial guarantor, with the bill. But Glotzer, natch, doesn't pay up. He'll be pursued by multiple creditors and bankrupted.

IN MEMORIAM

Ian Copeland
Dad
Busta Jones
Jackie
Wilko Johnson
Malcolm Owen
Ruth Polsky
Pete Shelley
Ari Up
Tony Wilson
Steve Wood

With fondest memories of Andy Gill, my great friend, music partner, and brilliant guitarist. I loved him like a brother. We had golden years together.

ACKNOWLEDGEMENTS

Thanks to:

Steve Diggle for suggesting I write a memoir.

My literary agent, Kevin Pocklington, for his enthusiasm and encouragement.

My friend Mark Haskell Smith, author and guitarist, who generously helped me with the first drafts; his notes, comments, and advice were invaluable.

Hugo Burnham, my dear friend and Gang of Four drummer, has an impeccable recall of events and put me right when my memory was off-piste.

Andrew Corrigan, Mark White, Dick O'Dell, Mike Howlett, Jim Graham-Brown, who all kindly shared their recollections.

Debbie Langdon-Davies for her proofreading and youthful memories of Andy Gill.

My Editor, Andreas Campomar, for his constructive and thoughtful insights that improved my writing, and for our stimulating conversations about books.

Holly Blood, Desk Editor at Little, Brown, for her patience and help. Simon Humphries for his feedback.

Above all I must thank my wife Debbie for her lifelong support, love, and encouragement. I couldn't have done it without her.